MICHAEL STEPHEN CLARK

Mr Buckland, Mr Walpole and Mr Young

This book was professionally typeset on Reedsy.
Find out more at reedsy.com

Contents

dedication

This book is for my wife, Bernadette.
It could not have been written without her love and support.

Acknowledgements

Louise Moyes Assistant Librarian, Advocates Library, Edinburgh

James Hamilton, Research Principal, The Signet Library, Edinburgh

Dr. Michael Pugh – Lecturer, University of the West of Scotland

Helen McGregor, Marine Scotland Library Aberdeen

Stephen Paterson, Chief Financial Officer, Peterhead Port Authority

Elaine Peakman, Vice Convener, Eyemouth Herring Queen Festival

Ailsa McLellan, Oyster Farmer

MAP

SHEWING THE PRINCIPAL PLACES MENTIONED IN THE

REPORT ON THE HERRING FISHERIES OF SCOTLAND.

1877.78.

NOTES.

1   The names of the Stations of the White Herring Fishery Board of Scotland, are printed in Capitals & underlined.

2   The names of the Places at which Sittings were held by the Commissioners are followed by figures referring to the pages in the Appendix containing the evidence taken at these places.

Scotland 1877

A Note About The Crown Brand

The curing, salting, barreling and exporting of Scottish herring into foreign markets were tightly managed and closely monitored for quality control.

In the 1878 Herring Report, there is no special explanation of domestic Crown standards, nor are there any details about the requirements specific to the large markets in Germany and Russia.

There is, however, a thorough account on pages 209-216 of the Dutch laws governing the importation of herring. The requirement to physically 'brand' herring barrels according to the size, quality, quantity and origin of the contents appears to have been adopted by the Fishery Board as a passport into European markets.

The Dutch Crown Brand came in a number of variants that show, at a glance, whether the barrel contained 'Matties', 'Spawned herrings', 'Soft herrings', or 'late Cured herrings'. The brand also designated the origin of the catch by location and the year in which the fish were caught. As if this wasn't enough, the barrels were subject to re-examination, the inspections had to be meticulously recorded, and the branding irons were required to be properly maintained.

'The branding irons to be used shall be supplied by the Fishery Board. The branding irons shall be kept by the examining officers with the greatest care in a locked-up place, and shall not be given up to anybody, on any pretence whatever, except by order of the Fishery Board.'

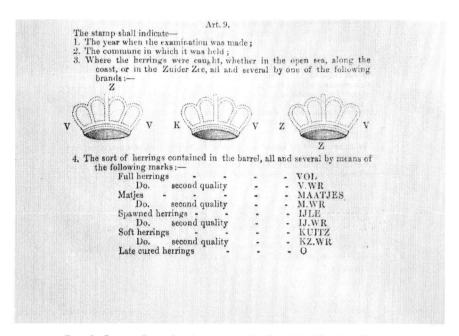

Dutch Crown Brand as it appears in the 1878 Herring Report

If officialdom ever possessed a suspicious mind then it was surely present on the quayside and in in the drafting of these Dutch regulations. Perhaps, it is here that we detect the seeds of disaffection felt among British fishermen towards European pedantry. The inference is clear, however, that the authorities were wise to all the tricks of the herring trade.

My background research hasn't revealed (yet) how diligently the Scottish curers and Fisheries officers upheld 'The Brand'. It would constitute a chapter in itself that might be an exercise in futility. What is evident from the feedback provided by the go-between Prussian agents was that the fish caught and sent to Stettin and Hamburg where buyers were not always satisfied that the product matched the description of Crown Brand herring. There was only ever one crown used to depict overall quality, but three variants are often shown in illustrations that show only the differences between them. They are not showing a system of grading from 1-3.

Introduction

There is a great deal about the collective view of Victorian Britain that is built on characterization, caricature and popularization. This highly embellished view is so prevalent in popular culture that we now casually refer to everyone who lived between 20th June 1837 and 22nd January 1901 as Victorians. The cartoonish cavalcade of toffs, tarts, and serfs in film, television and books is not *entirely* false, but it presents a fuzzy and incomplete picture.

There are a handful of Victorian archetypes that are instantly recognizable, but it seems reasonable to ask if they are truly representative of a diverse and energized society. What is often absent from the Victorian iconography (*our* popular versions of *their* complex events) are authentic voices talking about things that are important to them. These voices require context in terms of time and place, and a better understanding of status and relationships within their communities.

Fishing was very much at the sharp end of the British imperial adventure, and modern readers may be excused for feeling that its history is an open book. Maritime chronicles and fishing memoirs have been a mainstay in UK publishing for decades, and the story of the sea has been evocatively told ever since the first coracle hit the water.

The dissection of a fishing report published in 1878 might, at first glance, appear to be a dull, pedantic and pointless exercise. Nothing could be further from the truth. It was a comprehensive, scientific document and an important set of government findings that affected the lives of a great many ordinary folk. In my view, it still has important things to tell us today.

It is a serious report, but it is also full of anecdotal flavour because there is

1

so much more emphasis on qualitative data than there is on the quantitative. In short, the commissioners visited as many herring stations around the Scottish coast as they could, and asked everyone they met what they thought of the state of the fishery. It is, therefore, an important piece of social history as much as it is the outcome of an economic investigation.

I've followed Mr. Buckland, Mr. Walpole and Mr. Young in the course of their work as Her Majesty's Fisheries Inspectors all around the Scottish coastline. But, what began as a popular account of factual events involving historical figures quickly became embroiled in the very controversies it sought to merely describe.

My primary goal, however, is to offer a sense of history going forwards as well as backwards. If that sounds a little too 'New Age' for you, then consider well-worn sayings such as "History is always repeating itself", or the way we talk about "A Living History" and "Making History."

History can be also unkind to reputations, but they can be rehabilitated and restored by bringing history up to date, providing context, and disregarding subjective prejudices. Those same reputations can equally be reassessed by looking at the subject with an objective, critical eye. I am not an historian, so I don't feel the same obligation to be entirely impartial.

That brings me to what this book is not about. It is not a memoir of Frank Buckland, Spencer Walpole or Archibald Young, although it does contain a great deal about them and their lives. It is simply an attempt to bring them into the light and show them as modern people who would be recognisable to us today. They are presented here, not as historic oddities, out of time and place, but as contemporaries in a familiar debate with plenty to agree upon and much to argue about.

This is especially true of Buckland, about whom we know a great deal, yet choose to take lightly and examine slightly. Until very recently, he'd been forever described as an eccentric personality who was bizarrely preoccupied with personally testing (and tasting) the palatability of exotic animals.

It is true that he dissected his esoteric dinners at the table with surgical instruments. It is also a fact that he jumped into a fast-flowing river in order to find out for himself just what it felt like to be the king of fish scaling a salmon ladder. Yet, this is only part and parcel of his brand of interpretive showmanship, and it does Buckland great disservice to ignore his serious commitment to the public understanding of a science and natural history.

Frank Buckland had no discernable masterplan, but he did have ambitions beyond mere fame as an entertaining writer and public personality. His Museum of Economic Fish Culture, spurned at the time, foresaw the fundamental importance of fisheries in British life that could not go unstudied, unrecorded, or unvalued.

When he was finally rewarded with the position of H. M. Inspector of Her Majesty's Fisheries, it was the attainment of real status and a place in the national record of scientific investigation. His response to the honour was not to sit on his laurels, but to effectively work himself into an early grave.

I want this book to further challenge the (hopefully) residual view of Buckland as a Victorian 'character', and rebalance it with one that is much fairer and far less disparaging. If it builds on the similar argument made by Richard Girling in his 2016 biography of Frank Buckland, then it will be one more step towards understanding the relationship between creative thinking and the unmapped future.

In Girling's fine book, the caricatures of Buckland are, at first indulged, but then deconstructed, until the real Frank Buckland is revealed. It's clear that Buckland has charmed Girling, very much in the manner that he seems to have charmed everyone. It is easy to see Buckland as the kind of everyman who agelessly transcends time, but his times were as vexatious and challenging as ours, if not more so. It wasn't easy to be Frank in the nineteenth century.

In the course of my work in zoological gardens, in the field, at meetings and at conferences, I have met dozens of 'Frank Bucklands'. It might sound improbable, but I can assure you that it is true. These folk were similarly passionate, effusive and talkative on matters of zoology, conservation biology and natural history. They cared little for matters outside of that sphere and were often, in terms of modern manners and mores, oddly dressed and non-conformist.

They were also smart, funny, and always had something thing of interest to say. Only those who had not spent time in their company would describe them as eccentric. I met Ivor Cutler several times on his frequent visits to London Zoo. He loved the animals and identified strongly with the zookeepers. He was also one of the most lucid men I ever met.

These days it is quite normal, if not admirable, to appear 'unconventional', and many of the extreme personalities already disgorged by the early 21st century make Frank Buckland, who evidently attended church twice daily, look like a conservative maiden aunt.

In the pages that follow, you will not find a natural, economic or industrial history of the boom and bust herring fisheries, but it will be possible to compare notes from across the centuries. Neither is there a history of settlement and enterprise around coastal Scotland, although there is enough travelogue to provide visitors with a route map around a Scotland that is often truly hidden from the public gaze.

I must advise readers, therefore, to browse this book carefully before delving into its layered passages. There are potted biographies of the three principals, Mr.Buckland, Mr. Walpole and Mr. Young, which are offered as a guide to their respective backgrounds, personalities and motives. If you choose to join them for the duration of their tour around Scotland, then it will be in your best interest to know them better. I also provide a brief natural history of the real star of this book, the Atlantic Herring, an ubiquitous fish which, like Buckland, is something of an overlooked hero. In addition, I further include a glossary of terms that are essential to a complete understanding of the narrative.

At the time of the Report, Buckland and Walpole were already prominent citizens, although the exact currency of English celebrity in nineteenth-century Scotland is uncertain. Buckland was a writer, a publisher, and an authority on the wide-ranging, proto-science of natural history. Walpole was a senior civil servant at the Home Office who came from an extended family that included politicians, earls and a few minor baronets.

Until I came to write this book, Archibald Young had been something of a footnote in fisheries history. This is despite the fact that he was a contributing author to several H.M. Fisheries Reports and trusted enough to enjoy a status akin to permanent secondment. I am indebted to the Advocates Library in Edinburgh for essential pieces of the puzzle that, when put together with other fragments, eventually made sense of his life. Throughout these pages, I have tried to restore him to par with his colleagues. He is an interesting character in his own right, and deserves his place as a person of significance in the story of Scottish fishing.

Once you have gotten to know Buckland, Walpole and Young, you will be better equipped to join them on their investigative expedition around the country. Each chapter corresponds to a destination and they chronologically follow the route depicted on the map published with their report and findings.

We begin in Edinburgh with a familiarisation exercise designed, not as a flight of fancy, but a point of departure into another century. It is important to understand exactly where they walked if we are to follow in the footsteps of the fisheries men.

Buckland, Walpole and Young assembled at the now extinct Balmoral Hotel on Princes Street and got down to the task right away by meeting the fish curing mafia from Leith. Chapters 1-12 follow them from there, first to Eyemouth, and thence to the east coast ports of Anstruther, Montrose and Aberdeen, which appeared to be in a state of flux. They next visited the new powerbase of the herring fishery at Peterhead, and the villages on the Moray coast.

At Orkney and Shetland, they found the herring fisheries in the doldrums, and witnessed the shape of things to come. The temperature of their hearings increased noticeably as they made their way down through the Caledonian Canal towards Loch Fyne and out to the islands of Harris and Lewis. Finally, they terminated their enquiries in the Firth of Clyde and at Glasgow, where things got characteristically confrontational.

In chapter 13, I discuss their findings, which I hope will shock and confuse the reader as much as the implications disturbed me. This is not because of anything especially controversial in their analyses. In many ways, the tone is a familiar one to anyone conversant with the tidal ebb and flow of argument around the sustainable exploitation of natural resources.

The jolt comes from the expectations that build from reading the evidences sequentially, and paying close attention to inferences and meaning in the language of the fisherfolk. We are also misdirected by the commissioners who, on the surface at least, appeared to record their statements with impartiality, if not empathy.

I have tried as much as possible to allow the personalities of Buckland, Walpole and Young to percolate through the narrative by including asides and anecdotes. I am aware that this device could, if over-used, become tedious and distracting. These diversions are, however, incredibly important. They are part of the history of published writing, and a salient feature of factual nature writing in particular. The way that this book is set out, to some extent, datestamps period as much as the linguistics specific to the participants

Chapter 14 is a tribute to the anecdotal style of compendium writing that made Frank Buckland famous. I have taken all the interesting leftover tidbits of interest that are relevant to the core text and compiled them haphazardly, just as Buckland's publisher Richard Bentley might have arranged them in the nineteenth century. I hope that readers will want to dip in and out, and find them entertaining.

As the lead author of the report and an influencer in his own time, Buckland is the strongest voice you will hear. I also give him prominence because he is the inspiration for this book. I grew up in the twentieth century in an era that produced several generations of wildlife communicators, many of them ground-breaking and influential. Buckland has often been compared to some of them, but in terms of metaphor, simile, emotional punch and public appeal, Buckland, for me, remains head and shoulders above them all. Only Gerald Durrell among the moderns, had a similar ability to elicit empathy for other living things and gather around him a devoted audience. This ability is, I believe, based more on a lifelong understanding of wild animals than mere anthropomorphic identification.

I hope that this book asks more questions than it seeks to answer. I wanted to understand better what ordinary nineteenth-century Scots thought of their circumstances, how they spoke to each other, and how they related to their so-called peers. I sought to do that by examining, cross-referencing and interpreting the testaments contained in a government fisheries report, and other related biographical sources and literary references.

In the end, I confirmed a strong connection between attitudes, expressions and reactions to officialdom of that period and those of today. It was far harder, however, to divine motives, motivations, loyalties and political drivers in an authoritarian society that was, paradoxically, under-resourced to enforce the law. In the case of the 'Scotch Fishery', it struggled to impose its will on the people, especially Scottish fishermen living and working in remote communities.

If pressed to say in a single sentence what this book is about, then I would say it is about attentive communication and what can be learned from persistent, thorough and critical investigation. That is as true of the diligent writers whose work I have referenced as it is about Buckland, Walpole and Young.

Today, we tend to judge achievement in terms of flashbulb discovery rather than hard work in support of a collective effort. For me, the contribution of the individual is neither insignificant, nor definitive, but it is of singular importance. I think that motives matter more, for they must be sincere if we are ever to come to terms with the truth of our relationship with the natural world.

The commissioners were sent all around Scotland to investigate the herring fishery, and, more specifically, to confront the alarming suggestion that it was susceptible to collapse. They did a great job, but I decided to investigate *them*, examine *their* deliberations and evaluate *their* report. You could say that I commissioned myself to 'inspect the inspectors'. This book is the result of my findings, which I hope are impartial, non-judgemental and, to some degree affectionate.

M.S.C. Esq.

Edinburgh

Balmoral Hotel, Wednesday, 22nd August 1877

'I saw a little incident that would make a capital picture for an artist. In one of the jewellers' shops in Princes Street there was a magnificent tiara, with bracelets, earrings, &c., of lustrous diamond brilliants. Two little mites of children were racing to sell their halfpenny papers, when all in a moment the glitter of the diamonds struck them; they pulled up short, and stood aghast at the objects to which they were so little accustomed, gazing at them with all eyes and great wonderment. Here is a picture; Poverty and Riches.' – **Frank Buckland in Notes and Jottings from Animal Life.**

Everyone knows that time travel is impossible. Science has told us so. We cannot travel back in time to meet our ancestors, nor tunnel through the centuries to witness events from the past. Yet, here we are, with only the written word and a little imagination at our disposal, looking over Frank Buckland's shoulder on Princes Street, sometime in the eighteen hundreds.

Now that we have the hang of it, why don't we time-hop to another location; say, the entrance to Waverley Station at five p.m. on the afternoon of Tuesday 21st August 1877? Stand still, and let time do the travelling, backwards in a blurry confluence of memory, history and invention. Touch something solid and real, and feel its connections: old stone, weathered timber, iron railings, and rough brick.

A sensational smell, such as smoking coal or burning oil on steel wheels may be all that it takes to transport you into another time and another place. If you apply a little imagination to circumstantial evidence then it is easy to reconstruct a credible scene in which the reader is both actor and director. In this particular case, we are in nineteenth-century Edinburgh waiting for a train to arrive. It departed from London early that same morning, and it's due anytime now. This is where our story begins - in the past.

It was busy that afternoon. It's always been busy at Waverley, even in the dead of night. That's because train travel is a kind of time travel itself, particularly so in the 1800s when it was still new and exciting to be in London in the morning and Edinburgh in the afternoon.

There was a great urgency that came with the railways and Edina felt it keenly. Half of the Old Town was demolished so that the rail line could gouge a trench straight through Princes Street Gardens right into the heart of the Scottish capital. People were constantly arriving while others were departing. Some were just hanging around, perhaps seeing someone off or anticipating an imminent arrival.

On this particular day, one of those waiting was perhaps a little more relaxed and a lot less energized by the commotion of station life. He had an air of authority about him. After all, he was there on government business. He doubtless paced up and down, as anyone would when waiting for the impending arrival of a train, and checked his pocket watch against the time on the station clock, just as you and I do today. Time is everything.

While we're waiting with him, let's take the opportunity to look him up and down. He is a real, live, mature Scots gentleman of the Victorian era. He was born in 1820 and he is now in his 57th year. He will live on until 1900, sharing his personal timeline with the sovereign's entire reign. He is, I venture to suggest, tall and lean, and very fit for his age. This is the result of an active life as a keen sportsman and a lover of outdoor pursuits. He is a professional man and dresses accordingly for his status as a prominent advocate in the city.

This gentleman has come by hackney cab straight from his chambers behind St Giles Cathedral on the High Street, and his frock coat, pinstriped trousers, crisp wing collar and polished footwear are topped off, naturally, with a brushed-silk, top hat. It is more than just appropriate headgear. It is a symbol of aspirant officialdom. He checks his pocket watch again and looks upwards in the direction of Castle Rock. A distant whistle would indicate that the train appears to be on time.

His neat, white hair peeks discreetly from beneath a brim that shadows a tanned, angular, inscrutable face with a tight-lipped mouth, narrowed further by tumbledown, mutton-chop sideburns. He looks a canny sort with wise eyes that miss nothing and a gaze that gathers everything for future reference. His name is Archibald Young Esq, and he is a prosperous solicitor from a family of successful lawyers with a home address in the conspicuously desirable environs of Edinburgh's opulent New Town.

When the train finally arrived, Young not only had his hackney standing by, he also had his hired man, with cart and draught mare on hand. Archibald was an organised man in mind, body and spirit, and he stepped forward with his platform ticket held politely between thumb and forefinger for the guard to inspect.

The two gentlemen whom Mr. Young had arranged to meet were easy to discern, even though they'd disembarked some way down the platform. One was tall, neat and fair of complexion, while the other was short, stocky, thickly-bearded, and a little bit unbuttoned. The taller one had a slightly diffident, patrician air about him, while the other engaged himself in jovial conversation with a baggage porter. They had all met before in their respective capacities as servants of H.M. Government, and they greeted one another now as friends and colleagues.

And so it was that a reunion took place between Francis Trevelyan Buckland, a small man with a large personality; Spencer Walpole, the career civil servant; and Archibald Young, the erudite advocate who was the man who got things done in Scotland.

Together, they were commissioned to investigate the herring fishery in Scotland and their enquiries would take them to every significant coastal community on the mainland, and out to the far-flung islands of the north and west. Their immediate destination, however, was the Balmoral Hotel on Princes Street, a short carriage drive from Waverley Station.

In 1877, the old Balmoral Hotel ('which commands the finest views of the Modern Athens') stood opposite the gardens, almost on the corner of Princes Street and Frederick Street; barely a ten-minute walk from the Young residence at 22 Royal Circus. Frank Buckland, Spencer Walpole and Archibald Young, as we shall see, valued forward planning, economy of effort, and satisfying ergonomics in almost all of their endeavours.

Once settled in their hotel, with bags and trunks discharged from the cart, the porters tipped and the drivers paid, there was time for a light supper and a brief discussion of the next day's orders. The first of their many hearings would be convened at the Balmoral in the morning, with submissions to be received in person and in writing from fishermen, fish curers and fishing bureaucrats. In the meantime, there is Empire tea in fine china, Empire biscuits on silver salvers and, no doubt, some very fine imperial port, with perhaps a cigar or two for added creature comfort.

The welcome mildness of an August evening in Scotland's capital might also have invited an undemanding stroll along the capital's Athenian thoroughfare. Frank Buckland was a man who liked to be out and about and in the thick of things. We should join him as he steps out onto Princes Street, and follow him, for his gimlet eye is bound to notice something of interest.

The castle broods severely against the fading light, and looks oddly threatening, for it is still an active, if somewhat ineffective fortification. The streets are alive with activity and the lights in the windows of *Hamilton and Inches* illuminate a dazzling window display of valuable jewellery. We know it's valuable because the owners take turns sleeping in their newly acquired premises overnight as a deterrent against break-ins. Buckland lights a cigar, takes a deep draw, and expels a cathartic cough. This is not at all speculative, for it's a matter of fact that Frank was a heavy smoker and his health was already a matter of concern.

If anyone lived life in the moment then it was Frank Buckland. This chapter began with a quote from his pen that testifies to his affection for observational documentary and snapshots from life. It may be embellished rather obviously with the journalist's penchant for the emotive, but he was too full of humanity to be insincere.

A little farther along, Buckland stops at John Moffat's, one of the many photographers' studios to be found along Princes Street. The example images in the window are usually the formal portraits of recently engaged couples, or portrayals of the benign paterfamilias with his dutiful wife and their enormous brood. Relatively few surviving snaps of Buckland are in the public domain, but they do communicate a great deal of his character.

In one particular picture, set against a countryside diorama, he is presented as an outdoorsman complete with fishing pole, notebook and satchel. In his left hand, he holds what looks like a set of binoculars. He looks like a man who dresses for comfort and not for status. It is a convincing picture because it is an authentic depiction of these known facets of his personality.

Buckland on Princes Street puffs on his cigar and reminds himself to stock up with pipe tobacco for the next few days. In those days, the tobacconists were warm, oak-lined sanctuaries where men shared their intimate knowledge of blends and brands from the Indies, Africa and the Americas. The concept of the smoker as a discerning connoisseur and a man of taste and style was a masterstroke of Victorian marketing, and it persisted long into the twentieth century.

The shops remain open until eight-thirty or perhaps even nine in the evening, so there is time yet to idly peruse the businesses tucked beneath the swanky hotels on either side of the Balmoral.

Heading westwards towards Haymarket we'll pass: Sanderson's Jeweller, Lapidary and Engraver, since 1795; Wheeler and Wilson's Sewing Machine showroom beneath the Windsor Hotel; Edmonston's English and Foreign Library; Taylor's Umbrella Emporium; Pottage's Homeopathic Pharmacy; and McLaren and McNiven's Book Store.

We have time enough before the lighting of the gas lamps at one hour past sunset to walk back and admire the Scott Monument. If we are observant we will notice, opposite, a rather unremarkable department store. It was established in 1838 and occupied the corner of Princes Street and St. David Street. The 1877 incarnation isn't much to look at, but many an iconic retailer has deceived everyone with an unprepossessing start.

The original Jenners building burnt to the ground in 1892, but in 1895 the department store rose phoenix-like from its ashes to become 'The Harrods of the North', a temple to the high-end spend. It just goes to show that you can't judge a shop by its original frontage, any more than you can tell a book by its finely bound cover.

Anyway, it's late now and time to make our way back to the Balmoral for a nightcap, but first we pass The Royal Institution and the Scottish National Gallery. The former is now more familiar as the Royal Scottish Academy, but in 1877 it was, conveniently enough, the HQ of the Board of Trustees for Fisheries, Manufacturers and Improvements in Scotland.

The Board was established in 1727, mainly to oversee the growth of the fishing and manufacturing industries until its ultimate dissolution in 1906. Other tenants of the property at the time included the Royal Society of Edinburgh and the Society of Antiquaries of Scotland. Frank Buckland was in his element in that *milieu*, but he was no aesthete, and perhaps less excited about the new national art gallery, barely ten years old in 1877.

It is quite possible that Spencer Walpole, watching Frank return from his evening constitutional, was looking out across horse-dunged Princes Street, still populated with late evening hackneys, diligences, carts and the occasional horse-bus. His satisfied eye could follow the ascending curve of The Mound and settle on the red sky behind the silhouetted castle.

Everything about Edinburgh, from the architecture to the ambience served as a vindication of Empire and a testament to Victorian supremacy. Yet the 'Scotch', for all their enthusiastic subscription to enterprise, were different, and had to be handled differently. Walpole was enough of a politician to understand that, and fortunate to have Archibald Young on hand to smooth raised hackles and bring his lawyer's rationale to bear upon the strongly held beliefs and opinions of Scotland's fisherfolk.

The next morning, our commissioners, Mr. Buckland, Mr. Walpole and Mr. Young, no doubt having slept well and eaten a good breakfast, began gathering evidence for their report, and their first witness, the Secretary to the White Fisheries Board, had a great deal to say in his submission.

The Edinburgh Evidences

There is ample evidence to suggest that Frank Buckland wasn't especially attached to formality, yet he seemed sufficiently able to move up and down the social strata with relative ease. Spencer Walpole, in his rather backhanded obituary of Buckland in *The Spectator* later described him as a 'subordinate civil servant', yet Frank seemed to be entirely accepted into aristocratic, scientific and highly learned company.

Similarly, there is something about the fisheries business that transcends class. Those who are closely involved in it are more likely to be passionate about points of discussion than they are about the social and economic of the belligerents. It seems clear that ceremony was largely set aside in the course of these investigations, and in Edinburgh they got off to an encouragingly democratic start.

The Secretary, Bouverie Francis Primrose (1813-1898), was the uncle of Archibald Primrose the 5th Earl of Rosebery, also known as Lord Dalmeny. Bouverie, widely known as BFP, lived to see his nephew's short tenure as Prime Minister for a year between March 1894 and June 1895.

Archibald Primrose, by all accounts, had trouble condescending to democratic processes, leading Churchill to witheringly observe, *"He would not stoop; he did not conquer."* It's a critique that was hardly likely to bother the owner of twelve very large houses, including Dalmeny House, Mentmore Towers, and The Durdans in Epsom.

Bouverie Primrose was a much more accomplished diplomat and administrator than his entitled near relative. He was an extremely diligent, conscientious and industrious senior civil servant *par excellence*. BFP put himself about and travelled Scotland visiting the fishing stations. He regularly worked punishing hours at the office, gathering endless data and collating it in detailed reportage that bordered on pedantry.

In his evidence, he presented a concise account of the main challenges facing the herring fishery, namely the disruption caused by heavy-handed legislation and the woeful absence of investment in harbour development. As if to underline his first point in blood-red ink, he stated to the commissioners that, " *..it is impossible to repress any mode of fishery without great risk of life, especially after that mode of fishing has been free for years".* In this sense, he is paraphrasing Thomas Henry Huxley's libertarian observation that, *'every new law, creates a new offence'.*

Primrose went on to re-iterate that east coast fishermen, beginning in Montrose in the mid-century, had begun to fish much further out into the North Sea. The catches were bigger, the fish were bigger and the return more lucrative, but this expansion demanded construction of larger, decked boats. They, in turn, required larger harbours, and more of them.

In a piece of gunboat diplomacy of his own, Bouverie Primrose tartly presented the awkward fact that the total grant aid set aside for harbour construction of £3000 per annum was dwarfed by the development costs of £40,000 for Anstruther harbour alone. It suggested a lamentable lack of arithmetical application to the question of investment in the herring fishery.

The irrefutable, logical and economically rational testimony of this most exasperated administrator contrasted sharply with the opportunistic grievances of the Leith curing company of James Methuen.

In the rather shrill account given by Methuen's manager, Alexander Mc-Creachan, great claims were made regarding the *"injurious"* May fishery in The Minch, the large expanse of water that lies between the Outer Hebrides and the west coast of Scotland. This fishing, he warned, commenced *"too early"* and employed nets that were *"too small"* to catch *"sub-standard"* and *"immature"* product. The continental markets were *"thus glutted, the consumers offended and the prices brought down by the capture of immature fish".*

This is all well and good, until you consider that Methuen's was one of the single largest fish curing companies in the herring fishery. The business was aggressively expansive with its headquarters at Leith and ownership of several other stations around the coast.

Methuen's was also a conspicuous presence in Leith. There were fish 'spilling out across the street' wherever their sheds and outdoor gutting benches, or 'farlings' were set up for processing fish throughout the season. The firm employed over a thousand men and women annually, including fishermen, coopers, curers, gutters, packers and overseers.

All of this is preserved in commonplace images from the east coast that depict fishing boats cheek by jowl in the harbours and young women, shoulder to shoulder at the farlings. It will come as no surprise to learn that Methuen's expert witness recommended a *'close season from 1ˢᵗ - 23ʳᵈ April from Ardnamurchan to Cape Wrath.'*

This, of course, would mean the killing off the Minch fishery, consolidating the Methuen power base on the east coast, manipulating demand, and driving up prices. Conveniently enough, there were also supportive words from 'local fishermen', Messrs' Bisset, Linton, and MacArthur, who each piped up their agreement that a close season in the Minch was a matter of urgent need.

Similarly, another local merchant, A. W. Beda, had much to say about the continental market for Scottish herring, but he seemed to be primarily interested in pushing the lucrative, government branded, 'Full Crown' product rather than the general health of the fishery. It's probably worth mentioning that Beda was also a Prussian honorary consul based in Leith. It was a cushy posting across the bohemian diaspora, and such individuals were well placed to further their personal business interests.

The Leith merchant, Mr. Wilson, showed off his understanding of niche marketing when he averred that the immature 'mattie' herrings from the west coast of Scotland were supplied to meet the demand in eastern Russia, stating with great insight (and we assume first-hand experience) that, *"wherever there is a Russian noble he has a barrel of herrings"*.

Neither the fisheries officers, nor the commissioners, were much swayed by the argument for a close season in the Minch. They were too long in the tooth and too wise to sharp practice to be confused about the purpose of their enquiries.

Laurence Lamb, a fishery inspector of thirteen years standing, came straight to the point. *"There is no decrease in the (herring) fishery, quite the reverse"*, and he went on to *"reject entirely"* the notion of a close season for 'matties' in the Minch. James Wares, a fishery officer, felt compelled to big up the quality of the Scottish product (perhaps even jumping to his feet, his chest bursting with pride) by declaring that, *"the Peterhead and Stornoway herrings are the largest in Scotland".*

Perhaps the last word from Edinburgh should fittingly go to B. F. Primrose. He clearly saw that, *"an improvement to the harbours on the east coast of Scotland would do more to develop fisheries than any other thing. The area of harbour accommodation is insufficient. The herrings must be delivered (landed) within twenty-four hours of their capture."*

These remarks are an affirmation of purpose over and above recording the concerns, interests, prejudices and imperatives of the different actors in the enterprise. Then, as now, growth and prosperity make a handsome couple, but they cannot properly flourish without infrastructure, organisation and strategic direction. The fishing industry, perhaps more than most, is well placed to understand the need for firm hands and a clear head in the wheelhouse.

In the following chapters, we will see how our commissioners fared, and what they found as they travelled around the coast and into the otherworldly experiences in Shetland, The Orkneys Isles and the Hebrides.

Reekie Re-Invented

In 1877, the population of Edinburgh was around 185,000 compared to the 500,000 souls that inhabit the city and its suburbs today. Add in the denizens of twenty-first-century commuterville and you have close to 1.3 million folk living and working in the wider cachement.

In order to comprehend the alterations in the geography, it has to be remembered that in the mid to late nineteenth-century Leith sat some distance away, linked like a conjoined twin by the thread of Leith Walk. The city limits barely extended beyond Stockbridge to the northwest, Roseburn to the west, and the Royal Edinburgh Asylum at the leading edge of Morningside in the south.

Corstorphine was a Victorian commuter village, and the hilltop zoo, carved from solid rock, would not exist to welcome peripatetic penguins and loafing lions until 1913. The relatively static nature of the populace also meant that Edinburgh definitely had the feel of a busy, bustling metropolis.

What was markedly different at that time was the tale of two cities that split Edinburgh into profoundly different social, economic and architectural hemispheres. The migration of the professional classes from the closes, stairs and cuts that characterize the 'Old Town' began in the previous century when they forsook its dubious charms for leafy Georgian suburbia. This precipitated the year-on-year decline of the 'Old Town', and sealed its reputation as a den of iniquity.

The New Town remains an affluent area, suitably adorned by glitzy restaurants and chic bars, but seductive lighting and upholstered luxury, however discerning, cannot outshine its status as a World Heritage Site. If it underscores the persistence of social inequality, then it as well to remember that showpiece architecture is an essential element of Edinburgh's tourism honeytrap. If the New Town had never been built, then something else perhaps less mollifying would surely exist to fill the vacuum.

It is somehow ironic too that the utilitarian castle, once seen as little more than a redundant hangover from the Napoleonic Wars and surplus to requirements, should become Scotland's number one tourist destination. The whole area around it is the same 'Old Town' abandoned by the gentry, but now it is droves of visitors, and not dragoons, that daily march the route up the Royal Mile, and down the narrow Canongate.

The latter is arguably one of the most interesting quarters of the 'Old Town', for it is rammed with history, which is shared freely in a cluster of public museums near the Canongate Kirk. Everything that you ever wanted to know about Edinburgh, but were afraid to ask, can be found in the Museum of Edinburgh, The Museum of Childhood and The People's Story Museum.

In 1877, your motives for visiting the 'Old Town' might have been considered questionable. R.L Stevenson, an author who never seemed to outgrow his bohemian phase was a frequent visitor throughout an extended rite of passage on the wild side of life. He is known to have visited the many brothels, drinking houses and opium dens, developing an almost fatal fascination for them.

Life on and off the Royal Mile is just as colourful today, if not legal and (for the most part) quite above board. However, it is a street life that demands a significant reduction in social distance expectations and a heightened tolerance of human body odour.

At the height of the Festival Fringe in late August, the sardine crowds will routinely shoal in front of clowning acrobat and marvel at every street magician. They dawdle everywhere and gawp gauchely at every, single living statue. A slow, steady, tortoise pace rewards the observant eye, for the tourists are quite unaware that they too are part of the passing parade.

First date lovers can be seen tentatively holding hands, old friends link arms, staying together like birds of a feather. A small child squints up into the sky, more fascinated by an escaping balloon than any juggler's skills. Summertime in Edinburgh at Festival time is only a challenge if you are in a rush to 'see everything', and is best experienced at walking pace and at street level.

If you are minded to escape the throng then it's simply a matter of perambulating down The Mound towards the National Gallery of Scotland, or toodling down Milne's Court steps to the Assembly Hall. It looms famously at the top of The Mound, very much like a grave minister glowering over an imposing pulpit. The Church of Scotland built it in the 1850s and still uses its halls for its annual National Assembly. Fringe fans will know it better as one of the pivotal venues during the six-week programme of impossibly diverse events.

Frank Buckland would have loved to loiter on the streets of Edinburgh at this time of year. He was an inveterate people-watcher, with a particular interest in sideshows, extraordinary performers, and curious-looking persons. In his journals, he records how he frequently rode around London on the top deck of the horse bus, simply for the sake of being outside and watching the world at work and play.If he was at our side as we made our way onto Princes Street, there is much that he would naturally recognize, and be reassured by its persistence. It's possible too that several differences would give him pause, but a forward-thinking Victorian gentleman is nothing if not cognisant of inevitable change.

The Royal Institution is now the Royal Scottish Academy, and it's been the physical and spiritual home of contemporary art in Scotland since 1911. It exists to promote the visual arts with scholarships, residencies, and funding, and is noted for the annual RSA Open Exhibition of Art, which runs throughout the festival period. It is, as it suggests, a showcase for contemporary artists, and it is seldom anything less than stunning in its scope and ambition.

In many ways, the works on display are a compendium of modern thought that reveals how we see ourselves. Yet, if there is one thing that is as perennial as any examination of the human condition, then it is the artists' regard for nature. Like me, Buckland would, I am sure, pick out those works that celebrate the intrinsic worth of the natural world.

In one example from the 2017 open exhibition, a rare bird, possibly a migrant, sits atop a dorico'd building in the midst of a botanic collage. The piece is called 'Pale Visitor' and it's by Ann Ross. It limpidly pools the design values of nature with patterns we've conceived by approximating nature. It is for others to say whether it is outstanding art, but it certainly works as a visceral picture.

The most curious creatures on Princes Street are, however, more mechanical than cultural. The re-introduction of trams into the heart of the city in 2014 have altered first impressions and completed the liberation of Auld Reekie from its cocooned past into a modern, metropolitan peacock.

The trams, which everyone acknowledges, had a long and troubled birth, have quickly established themselves in Edinburgh's contemporary iconography. They are not a retro-chic indulgence, but the spine of an integrated, centre-city transport hub. If anything, they retain the shock of the new and an uncompromising approach to determined change. It's also joyride and a rare hurl from Haymarket to Leith on the tram, although much more can be seen from a standing position than when seated.

On the whole, changes to the face of Princes Street appear to have been relatively benign, unless you have an idea of what has been altered or replaced. Perhaps the most significant difference is that the pre-eminence of the large hotels in the nineteenth century has been replaced by the dominance of the retail marque.

The 1877 National Library of Scotland (NLS) map shows more than a dozen hotels between the General Register House in the East End and Shandwick Place. Of those, all of them except for The North British/Balmoral, The Royal British and the Old Waverley Hotel have either been destroyed by fire, demolished, altered or subjected to a radical change of use.

The original Balmoral Hotel is long gone, demolished and replaced by a department store that today seems to be as deserving of equal prominence on Google Maps as a landmark like the National Portrait Gallery. Ironically, the old North British Hotel at Waverley, has been thoroughly re-furbished, upscaled and re-invented as The Balmoral Hotel, but that would only be confusing if you retained fond, extremely faded memories of the original at 91 Princes Street.

A short distance away in George Street, Buckland would still be able to observe jaws dropping at the sight of tastefully decorous displays dripping with diamonds in the windows of Hamilton and Inches. It is safe to say that the owners no longer sleep under the counter at night as a security measure. Today, it is video technology, face recognition software, and DNA analysis that offers a deterrent to all but the most determined and highly organized heist specialists.

In the New Town itself, Archibald Young would recognize his own front door and find the exterior of 22 Royal Circus pretty much as he left it when he died in 1900. In his day, there was a butcher, a baker, a candlestick maker and, naturally, a couple of taxidermists providing Circus Lane with a bit of Dickensian 'Olde Worlde' charm.

Today, we are terrified of walking a hundred yards without the option of a frothy *Americano* or a chocolatey *cappuccino*. George Street, Queen Street, Hanover Street and Frederick Street are simply overflowing with *lattes,* topped with double cream and served with quadruple choc-chip cookies, or exotically fruity muffins. It's bright, brilliant and beautiful, brimming with disposable income and pretty people who lunch lightly.

I rather imagine Archibald Young as a man who much preferred his own library and tea in his study while keeping up his correspondence with *The Scotsman.* If your imagination alone doesn't do it for you, then there are numerous opportunities to grasp the experience of living the privileged life, most readily in The Georgian House, a National Trust for Scotland property located at 7 Charlotte Square.

Although restored to its eighteenth-century pomp, it is nevertheless revealing for its proportions, its scale and the way that ambient light fills the rooms. It's yet another challenge to the received wisdom that life before electricity was full of half-tones, dark corners, and dim shadows. It's also an enduring example of the design values demanded by those who will not settle for anything less than the best.

At the opposite end of George Street, a little out of the way I grant you, is Dundas House, a Category A listed building that has since 1825 been occupied by the Royal Bank of Scotland. It was originally a statement of mere personal wealth by its first owner Laurence Dundas, but now you can check your balance like a boss in surroundings that make an architectural point about cash.

The original house dates from 1772 and, set like a country manor in its own grounds, it was once the grandest house in the New Town. The Royal Bank of Scotland bought it in 1825, and made several lasting changes perhaps designed to strike such awe into depositors' hearts that they did not dare make a withdrawal without written permission from the manager.

The immense foyer features a huge, star-stippled dome supported by four enormous arches that lead into a voluminous banking hall. It is unlikely that Frank Buckland, much less Walpole or Young, would have been intimidated by its grandness, but rest assured, even the likes of you and I may enter freely.

The difference today is that our Victorian friends will have been reassured by the power of money, whereas we have developed a grudging acquiescence to its omnipotence. Edinburgh, whether you see it as a money wheel, a cultural megastar or an awayday destination for concerts and rugby tournaments, needs to generate wealth over and above general levels of economic activity. This is because Scotland has expectations of it, not least since the Scottish Parliament sits at the bottom of the Canongate, but also because nothing succeeds like success.

Edinburgh has been in danger of being defined by the Festival and its associated Fringe, and gigantic though they both are, there is something else that is perhaps more significant. The Scottish capital was once the epicentre of The Enlightenment, and reams of praise have been written about that, much of it hype and bunk. Nevertheless, there is a persistent appetite for enquiry, discourse and proposal that manifests itself in events at places like The Scots Story Centre, the National Library of Scotland, The Poetry Library and Edinburgh's many museums and art galleries.

This discourse is carried on today, much as it always was, except that it does not take place in church halls, assembly rooms and Quaker Houses as they did in Buckland's time. The debates continue in the workshops and seminars of book festivals; in the music that is made in home recording studios; in the bars, coffee shops and cafes in the Grassmarket and Cockburn Street; and in expositions where every exhibit offers up a dozen talking points. The questions are perennial and subject matter is similar, if not the same, as those that took place around the feeding of the nation two centuries ago: 'Who are we, what do we want, and where are we going?'

To my mind, it costs very little except your time and a bit of daydreaming to re-visit the past and make useful connections with the present. Simply looking at the things that are immediately around us, and altogether self-evident, is a form of time travel that rewards the observant explorer. Soon, you begin to realize that the past is more recent than you realized, and that the conversations begun by Buckland, Walpole and Young continue, appropriately enough, in cyberspace.

The core subject matter at the heart of this book is an investigation into the condition of the herring fishery in Scotland in 1877, and readers could be forgiven for feeling that we have digressed. Not so. This book is essentially about conversations, connections, and shared values, and, as we shall see in the next chapter, there is a lot more to fishing than just catching fish.

Eyemouth

Home Arms Hotel, Thursday, 23rd August 1877

"I was fortunate enough to be at the railway station when the train arrived with a number of fishwives from Newhaven. They were all dressed in serviceable blue serge; some were young, some old. They all had their creels or baskets of fish with them. I observed that it took two, and sometimes three porters to lift these heavy creels on to the women's backs. The creels are so made that the weight rests along the length of the spine, and are balanced, as it were, by a band that cross the forehead." – **Frank Buckland in Notes and Jottings from Animal Life.**

The best time of day to catch a train is early in the morning, just as the city stirs to life, but a little before the first commuters and day-trippers start arriving. On the morning of the 23rd, Frank Buckland took a hackney cab to the station just as the butchers, fishwives and fresh produce sellers were setting out their stalls in the surrounding markets. We know that he ought to have started early because he was on his way to hear evidences at Eyemouth more than fifty miles to the south on the Berwickshire coast.

The sights and sounds of Victorian Edinburgh are relatively easy to imagine but the smells of the city are another matter. It may require more effort among we deodourized moderns to conjure the stench of meat, fish and poultry, not quite on the turn, mixed with the stink of livestock and the pervasive, pungent whiff of horse dung.

If you have ever been to a mixed market where blood and flesh putrefy

24

in the absence of refrigeration, for example on the Comoros Islands or Madagascar, then you may perhaps have less trouble recognizing the olfactory potency of salted herring, live chickens, cow pats, lemons, pig meat, oysters and sweating cabbages. But let's be realistic here. The people stank too, especially the fishwives who sat with baskets at their feet and up to their elbows in eyeballs, guts and scales.

Buckland records an inter-action with such women, who were in all likelihood examples of the plain-speaking Newhaven fishwife, who did not suffer fools, nor foolishness gladly. His suggestion that 'I would like very much to put you in my museum' went down, as might be expected, like a ton of hake, and it is certainly more likely than not that he received a suitably frank rebuff. His description of being chased down the street and having a basket flung at his head, however, sounds like journalistic embroidery, although the necessity of a tactical retreat is easy to accept, English gent or not.

In any event, these Newhaven women, who came from the Forth fishing village adjacent to the busy port of Leith, did indeed become museum specimens of a sort. If Buckland found their traditional and highly individual costume fascinating, then so did the pioneering photographer David Octavius Hill. His famous study of Newhaven fishwives is held at the National Portrait Gallery in London where their lost identity is captured and preserved for posterity. The women, who wore striking, pyjama stripe pinafores and bonnets, over thick, woollen day dress appear suspiciously clean in well-starched aprons and hats. Hill invariably posed them with their baskets, which were often empty save for a few fish laid out for artistic effect.

Fishing may make good art, but it is an unsentimental occupation and a serious business for those who undertake it as an occupation. Regardless of the romanticism attached to the seafaring life depicted in etchings, songs, stories and legends, the industry has plenty of home truths in narratives of its own making. The 1800s saw numerous mortalities amongst Scottish fishermen that were swollen by two notorious disasters in each half of the century. The first was at Wick in 1846, and we will hear more of that later.

The second tragedy took place less than five years after the commissioners made their report. It involved the fisherfolk of Eyemouth, and it was the kind of catastrophe from which communities rarely, if ever, fully recover.

Buckland, however, was all about the business in hand when he caught the east coast train on the North British Railway line from Edinburgh to Burnmouth station. From there, a coach or cab would take him a couple of miles into Eyemouth where he would meet with local fisheries officer, Peter Wilson to hear evidence at The Home Arms Hotel. The hotel is still present as a going concern, and it's been a prominent feature of the quayside overlooking the foreshore with breath-taking sea views from its large light-friendly windows for more than one hundred and fifty years.

Now, I am sure that attentive readers will be curious as to the whereabouts of Spencer Walpole and Archibald Young, for they are not only credited as co-authors of the 1878 report, but they are also clearly identified as being present with Buckland at every single one of the evidence gathering sessions. In the course of this book, I will present circumstantial yet compelling evidence that the trio worked both together and separately on the demanding task of circumscribing Scotland in the space of six weeks.

In the meantime, let's relax for a moment with Buckland, who no doubt took the opportunity to kick off his boots and enjoy the stunning views from his carriage window. We know that he liked to write up his notes and jottings on train journeys, scribbled in a hurry with a stubby pencil held firmly between his oddly slender fingers. It wouldn't be fair though to describe Frank Buckland as an oddity, a loner, or physically compromised. He was a reasonably fit, fifty-year-old man with an independent outlook, and the kind of boundless enthusiasm and energy that might exhaust a lesser mortal.

I have no doubt that sharing a carriage to Burnmouth with him would be a memorable experience, since he never missed an opportunity to engage in diverting, if not, tangential conversation. You would, however, have to put up with the reek from his pipe tobacco for an hour or so, but he would oblige you by leaving the carriage window open. Frank liked the fresh air. Neither is his habit of going barefoot wherever possible at all fanciful. It is a matter of record by Spencer Walpole, who seems more astonished than impressed by Frank Buckland.

It is widely noted that Buckland wrote almost ceaselessly, travelled constantly, and investigated something natural or unnatural every day of his life. He was a most curious man, that's for sure, but he hardly deserves to be dismissed, as many have done, as a fallible eccentric undone by his own single-mindedness. It's fair to say too, that Buckland liked to dress sensibly for the outdoors.

There are one or two faithful images of him, both of which show that he readily adopted the increasing informality of mid to late nineteenth-century menswear. He clearly favoured the loose-fitting trousers, with ample room for a generous walking man's thigh, and the even more liberal sack jacket for the well-built gentleman.

One of the most iconic photographs of Buckland is indicative of his unconventional disregard for propriety and presentation. In it, he stands as if stopped in the middle of an important task while the photographer snaps him wearing only loose breeks, braces, worn slippers, a collarless cotton shirt and, not at all incongruously, his bowler hat. He holds a piece of roof slate in one hand, a scallop shell in the other, and a billhook dangles inexplicably, like a mildly provocative fashion statement.

I cannot imagine why he needed an arboricultural tool indoors, but Buckland always had his reasons, even if they remained obscure to others. More importantly, the famous notebook is wedged tightly in underneath his trouser brace, and it is perhaps the only real clue that the picture is posed rather than candid.

Aside from his overnight bag, we could fascinate ourselves by imagining what kind of professional man he might be from the accessories bulging from every pocket, including measuring tools, several notebooks, pencils, pipes, tobacco and perhaps even something only he would have considered edible. He may even have had rod and tackle with him, for he was an early riser who liked to fill every day with some kind of productive activity.

Buckland recorded much of his travels in Scotland in some detail, but little of it seems to be about Eyemouth. Perhaps, he didn't manage to revisit the nearby River Tweed, which he'd inspected with Archibald Young during their investigation of Scottish salmon rivers in 1870.

In 1877, Eyemouth was already known as a fishing community with a fiercely independent streak. Less than twenty years earlier, a heated protest by fishermen, led the indomitable Willie Spears, successfully forced the Church of Scotland to give up its arcane and spurious levy on the Eyemouth catch. The church's claim was based on outdated practices and shaky legal precedent, but mainly it was the result of blind determination to maintain influence where, in reality, it had none.

Much has been written about the truculence of the fishing community in Eyemouth at that time, but regrettably less emphasis is placed upon the persistent provocation by remote authorities with misplaced ideas about ownership of lives and livelihoods. In many ways, those old enmities, repeated over the decades in countless situations inform the attitudes and have contributed to the social cohesion that is emblematic of fishing towns and villages everywhere.

Nevertheless, no amount of determination or willpower can make fish jump into your nets. When Frank Buckland and Peter Wilson opened the hearings in Eyemouth, the herring fishery had, in less than a decade, become a shadow of its former self.

Eyemouth in 1877 was a thriving fishing community, bigger than a mere village but perhaps not yet as substantial as a regional town. Its 2,667 inhabitants lived, worked and learned in a close-knit society where families inter-married and surnames became synonymous with the location. Eyemouth was set like a twinkling jewel in a sheltered, picturesque inlet between the azure northern ocean and the emerald hinterland of rich Berwickshire farmland. A former haven for sixteenth-century smugglers and an anchor point for seventeenth-century traders, its harbour was initially quite small, but it offered excellent access from Scotland to rich fishing grounds and, further afield, the continental market places of Europe.

The town prospered and the nascent fishery of the early 18th century grew quickly in tandem with the establishment of boat-building in the Tweedmouth area, and the continuing coastal trade in livestock, grain, and agrarian produce. Although Eyemouth's principal strength lay in the diversity of its economy, fishing grew hand in glove with an endemic spirit of enterprise.

The Eyemouth district became significant as Scotland fourth most productive herring fishery. In 1867 alone, it is recorded that 689 boats from Dunbar, North Berwick, Coldingham, Holy Island, North Sunderland, Craster and Amble, landed enough herring to produce 47,749 barrels of cured fish and 31,237 crans of fresh fish. The 1878 report, however, indicates a slow but steady subsequent decline in the headline take. Year on year, fewer boats put to sea and less fish is landed until, in 1876 there were only 270 boats leaving from the fishery area, returning with half the produce.

In Eyemouth itself, more recent analysis of the export data for herring suggests that the true picture is one of fluctuation following a bonanza year in 1857, when more than 19,000 barrels were exported from the town itself, crashing to 333 in 1870.

When Buckland visited Eyemouth in 1877, the herring fishery there was actually emerging from a protracted downturn, and entering a period of recovery and growth that he would not see in its full ascendency in his lifetime. Production increased from 1878 onwards and, despite slippage in intervening years, there were bumper harvests in 1884 (29,135.5 barrels), 1895 (41,004.5 barrels) and twelve years later in 1907 with 42,977 barrels, peaking in 1909 at a staggering 119,231.5 barrels.

The fisherfolk of nineteenth-century Eyemouth can be forgiven their dismay and pessimism in the absence of data that allowed for projection far into the future. In a subsistence economy skewed in favour of landowners, property owners, boat owners, fish curers and merchants, their needs were immediate. Fishermen who caught no fish had no other means of support, and to suggest that history shows their anxieties were misplaced is to wilfully misread the past. In their experience, they were in the midst of a crisis that would culminate in 1881 in tragedy, loss, guilt, and everlasting grief.

The Eyemouth Evidences

Buckland's immediate concern, however, was to hear evidences that had already begun to sound suspiciously like petty grievances. First up was someone who really ought to have known better, David Gillis, a fisheries officer with twenty-two years service under his belt and formerly stationed at Wick, Fraserburgh, Campbeltown and Orkney. In common with his fellow fisheries officers, he'd been responsible at Eyemouth for inspecting the quality of the fish and assigning the crown brand to cured barrels for export.

His diligence was beyond question but he doesn't come across as an especially impartial and objective officer. He is careful to report that, *"The fishermen here attribute the decline to the sprat fishery in the Firth of Forth"*, but ventures no further into what is already clearly a controversy. More illuminating is his observation that the fishing between Eyemouth and Dunbar had all but evaporated, whilst south of the border at Berwick-on-Tweed the Sunderland coast had pretty much held its own.

It's interesting too that Gillis alludes to dips and rises in sea temperature and, almost in the same breath, suggests that even minor changes can prompt the fish to move away from the shore into colder, deeper waters elsewhere. Herring are temperature sensitive, but that is not sufficient as an explanation for periodic desertion of otherwise suitable habitat.

The contention that too many small, immature herring were routinely caught up in the act of trawling sprats in the Firth of Forth was a common complaint among fishermen attached to locations where the fishing was in steep decline.

Sprats, or 'garvies' as they are traditionally called in Scotland, were certainly important as part of a diversified fishing economy in the 19th century. Dozens of boats plied their trade in the Forth, but it was, perhaps, the status of King Herring as the dominant export product that gave herring fishermen a sense of entitlement, which clouded sound reason and fair judgement.

William Wilson, a herring fisherman of thirty years experience, gave rather contradictory evidence by first complaining bitterly that the *"trawl fishing for garvies accounts for the loss of the fishery here."* Yet, he is under the impression that garvies are young herring. Moreover, he has *"never fished for sprats himself...(but)...has seen sprats caught at Newhaven, and they are always mixed up with the young herring."*

Wilson went on to advocate regulations to impose larger gauge fishing nets in a proposal unlikely to find favour with sprat fishermen. More importantly, his thinking, like many of his contemporaries, is based largely on supposition and hearsay. There isn't a shred of arithmetic in it, much less direct observation and evaluation. It may be true that young herring were often caught in the nets of sprat fishermen, perhaps even in large numbers, but as a piece of speculative population dynamics, it is full of holes.

There then follows, apparently inserted into Wilson's call for net mesh size to be "36 meshes to the yard", an odd little passage.

It reads, *"Lots of nets are now 40 (meshes) to the yard, and catch too small herrings. This would enable only the largest herrings to be caught. The herrings are used for bait for cod; ling; etc, and are the best bait that can be got. It would not do to interfere with this. If the mesh were 36 to the yard, it would be impossible to get bait."*

The paragraph quoted above is, for my money, written in the hand of Frank Buckland and no one else. It is also inserted as an observational response to Wilson's suggestion that that net meshes should count 36 to the yard. It is typical of Buckland, throughout his published natural history writing, to insert his own thoughts and reactions unexplained and without qualification into the middle of a report.

The writing also features his colloquial tone (he writes like someone giving an informed talk), and grammatical mannerisms, especially *"too small herrings"* and the arbitrary use of 'etc'. He often resorted to this writing tactic when required to produce a tedious list, or he'd pop it at the end of an incomplete sentence that he couldn't be bothered to complete. It is Frank Buckland at his most infuriating, and endearingly vague.

It seems that only two other souls were on hand to offer evidences. John Dickson, a fish curer, and Andrew Glen a fisherman, both of Eyemouth gave brief but apposite testimony to the waning of the local herring fishery. Glen's views are jotted down in short, sharp sentences, as if the writer were tiring of hearing scattergun remarks such as *"The early (spring) fishing in May frightens the shoals out to sea and prevents them from coming in"*, or long-established, self-evident facts like *"The small herrings won't stand carriage per railway. They must be used at once".*

Dickson, on the other hand, confirmed a much more serious and pressing issue for local fisherman. *"..the harbour here should be enlarged and deepened. There are very few undecked boats here. The fishermen are sensible of the comfort and safety of the decked boats, but these larger boats require decked accommodation. Last year, the Burnmouth boats had to come in here, and they had to lie at the back of the harbour (seaward side) for lack of room. The harbour accommodation is only a question of money."*

It's not clear at all why there are so few fishermen, or even others with a vested interest, in attendance at the Eyemouth evidences. Perhaps there was a prevailing mood of scepticism, or maybe even a dismissive disregard for authority. Some important things did come to light, however, and they were not lost on the inspectors, even if those in the corridors of power failed to react with any kind of urgency.

The herring were already being pursued further out to sea, a method that demands bigger, better and sturdier boats. The harbour at Eyemouth, like so many others around the coast, was not only too small, it was not fit for purpose. It is almost a modern cliché that the cost of rectifying anything 'not fit for purpose' is of course 'prohibitive'. That was the case in 1877, when the cost of improvements at Eyemouth was set at £10,000, making it a nailed-on certainty that they would never be undertaken. As we shall presently see, the ultimate cost in terms of human life was much, much higher.

The Herring Queens of Eyemouth

There are many pretty places on the east coast of Scotland, and Eyemouth is one of the prettiest. There is also more than one coastal village or town that has suffered heartache and loss in a long and sometimes torturous relationship with the sea. Eyemouth, and the fishing hamlets that snuggle alongside one another on the Berwickshire coast, are unhappily prominent among them.

The 1878 herring report called loudly for improvements to harbour accommodation where it had been neglected, overlooked, or disregarded. It also argued with surprising candour and force for funds to be allocated and responsibilities to be taken accordingly. Their words fell on deaf ears and the men, women and children of Eyemouth paid the price.

Anyone visiting Eyemouth today cannot leave without a deeper and better understanding of collective loss. In 1881, less than a year after Buckland's own untimely death aged fifty-three, no less than one hundred and twenty-nine Berwickshire and East Lothian men and boys were lost in a storm as they vainly attempted to run for safe harbour. In such circumstances, no one in the community is left untouched and all were affected. Eighty-nine of them came from Eyemouth alone with the remainder leaving grieving families behind in Newhaven, Coldingham, Burnmouth, St. Abbs and Newhaven.

Events such as these leave an indelible mark and are never, ever forgotten. In one of those great cosmic coincidences that God and Fate are fond of putting together, you can stand in front of the Home Arms Hotel and imagine the scene of Buckland's rather underwhelming hearing in 1877.

If you look immediately to your right, you will be quite unable to miss a small memorial set upon a postage stamp square of mossy, green grass. The names of the Eyemouth dead are etched into the marble and, should you visit on one particular week in July, you may be lucky enough to witness one of the most remarkable and life-affirming customs anywhere in Scotland.

Each summer, a local lass is picked to personify the healing process of renewal and restore faith in the future as the Herring Queen of Eyemouth. She arrives by boat, and leads a procession up the short esplanade where it comes to a halt at the Eyemouth memorial where a wreath is laid. The dead are duly remembered, honoured and cherished.

Certainly, there is a tear here and there for those who had no business dying so unfairly, or in remembrance of other griefs and other kinds of loss.

Eyemouth chose to commemorate the end of the 1914-1918 war with a 'peace picnic' or 'fishermen's picnic', and the event became firmly established in the town's summer calendar. It was held each year on the grassy expanse known as Gunsgreen which gives its name to the rather fine house designed by John Adam and built for local 'smuggler and merchant' John Nisbet.

Gunsgreen House is owned and operated by an independent trust and is an interesting diversion in its own right. It's home to a small, but deceptively diverting local museum that tells the tall-ish tales of Eyemouth's past as a hotbed of smuggling and intrigue. If you feel you've heard it all before, then a guided walk from Eyemouth to Burnmouth might offer an authentically vicarious experience. You will truly be following in the footsteps of the fisheries men.

Tradition has it that a small army of similarly peripatetic bairns marched around the town on the day of the picnic, finally arriving at Gunsgreen in time for tea and sticky buns. Whole families attended, and they boiled their own kettles, filling the tea urns in an act of communal catering. Even the kids took along their own tin cups.

It was a fun day for Eyemouth families, rather than the tepid, usually deflating, 'Kid's Fun Day' that we perpetually foist on our youngsters. The egg and spoon races and sack sprints of yesteryear still persist here and there, but the three-legged race is more often revisited at the National Library of Scotland's online film archive than it is resuscitated for the summer gala.

The crowning of the Herring Queen was a later addition, derived from similar festivals that were still extant in coastal villages around northeast Scotland. The committee that organised the picnic, unlike most committees, agreed unanimously that a Herring Queen was just what the town needed to reflect its values and its identity.

Mary Craig became first Herring Queen in July 1939 and she reigned throughout the hiatus of the war years. The young monarch passed on her crown to Ann Rosie in 1946 and set in motion an uninterrupted tradition that continues today.

Through the years, The Herring Queen has acquired quite an entourage. She has also become an official civic representative. Formerly selected on the basis of academic proficiency, the Herring Queen has, since 2001, been chosen by a panel of local townsfolk.

I have to say that Herring Queen Day and the gala Procession of times past sounds pretty exciting. The Queen has always arrived by boat at Eyemouth Harbour, which is a good device for building anticipation. At one time, she arrived mob-handed with a Queen's Court full of lads, lasses and office bearers, many of which were nominated by the skippers of the Eyemouth fleet.

The procession used to be a highly choreographed affair with three boys in traditional navy blue 'gansies' and bell-bottomed breeks', who carried before them a model of a lifeboat. Behind them, came up to twelve girls and six boys carrying a model of an Eyemouth fishing boat that symbolized the Scottish Fishing Fleet.

Next, the Queen's Flower Girls trooped along, brightly dressed and bearing garlands. They were followed by members of the court including, The Bearers of the Queen's Pennant, her Cipher, her Sceptre and her Crown. The 'Cipher' is simply the Queen's initials beautifully wrought in flowers carried on a sea blue cushion placed inside a scale model of a "scull", the tiny craft used by fishermen to carry fishing lines to and from their boats.

The Maids of Honour walked behind the Queen in a formation representing the points of the compass. But we're not done yet. The Queen's procession was followed by the *retiring* Queen's procession, accompanied by the skipper of the boat that had brought her into port the previous year.

The present-day procession has been developed from the original and will no doubt evolve and adapt further. These days, there are Lifeboat Boys, Heralds, Retiring Queens, Court-Sailors, The Queen, her Trainbearers, her Maids of Honour, The Gift Bearers, and the Office Bearers.

The ceremony used to be held at Gunsgreen up until 1996 when the construction of the present deep-water basin forced the moved to the harbourside and the adjacent harbour car park. In past times, the Queen's procession would tour the streets of the town. Wreaths were laid on the War Memorial and the Memorial to the Fishermen of Eyemouth who were lost at sea during the Disaster of 1881.

Wreaths are still laid, with just as much reverence and passing sorrow as ever. Yet, the way that The Eyemouth Herring Queen has made herself part of this story as a relatively recent tradition is fascinating. She personifies many visceral responses such as loss and renewal and the gut reaction to time gone by and times still to come. It's also remarkable as an authentic folk festival steeped in its own short history, and perhaps more meaningful than many specious revivals of the ancient and obscure.

Today, there is room only for the Queen, her immediate coterie, and a few minor dignitaries on board the RNLI lifeboat that now brings her to shore, but the sense of occasion is undiminished. This is still a big day in Eyemouth and everyone is there to greet The Queen's boat as it sails straight into the heart of the town. The skipper of the boat escorts her to the Ceremony, followed in a dignified manner by The Court Procession.

The parade now seems to include pipes and drums for added value and extra Scottishness, but they are a good fit and contribute to an ambience that is generally happy and mainly celebratory. Mostly, the Herring Queen celebrations are about resilience, strength of character and community identity in a place where ancestors, histories and surnames are shared, many of the latter etched upon Eyemouth's resonant memorial.

The fortunes of the town, like so many others of similar size, scope and situation have waxed and waned. There are initiatives, investments, projects and, all too often, false promises of inward investment and revival. The population of Eyemouth has grown modestly since 1877, and has remained steady at about 4,500 for some considerable time. A small, inshore fishery survives, dealing mainly in crabs, lobsters, mussels and shrimps. It is very much part of the local colour, but it's also an extremely important component of the town's macro-economic matrix, landing fresh-off-the-boat, premium produce on a daily basis.

Eyemouth is also too far from the nearest metropolitan conurbation to ever truly become a dormitory town, but it is hardly a sleepy backwater. It retains too much of its original, bred-in-the-bone character to be anything other than a genuine descendant of a couthy, straight-talking, plain-dealing coastal settlement. The town has not expanded like a helium balloon and taken flight, nor has it withered like a flower at the end of summer. It's a small resort now, with plenty for sightseers, caravanners, windsurfers and even naturalists to discover and enjoy.

In 1877, there were millers, bakers, coachbuilders, grocers, boat builders, several tailors, a chemist, a saddler, a stonemason and a watchmaker in Eyemouth. Fairs were held on the first Thursday of each June and October, and a magistrate held court once a month in nearby Ayton. Today there is, perhaps reassuringly for campers and daytrippers, a couple of hypermarkets, a leisure centre, a swimming pool, a holiday park, a museum, and a modest retail park.

Yet, the modern shift to everything under one roof hasn't yet killed off diversity and variety in the heart of town. On a short walk the length of the High Street, from the bank on the corner of Market Place towards Beachcomber Amusements opposite the Home Arms Hotel, you will pass a number of pleasant diversions. They include a Turkish barber, an ice cream parlour, a couple of cafes, a bijou jewellery shop, a newsagent, a solicitor (if you like window shopping house prices), a general store, a Chinese takeaway, a bakery, a post office and an ergonomic supermarket with its own car park.

The most significant addition to the townscape, however, is Jill Watson's evocative sculpture *Widows and Bairns*. Commissioned in 2014 and unveiled in 2016, it depicts a line of bronze figures looking out to sea, clearly in a state of mounting anxiety. These are the 178 women who were made widows, and the 182 children who were made orphans by the 1881 disaster. Although it is relatively small in terms of civic sculpture, its impact is immediate and raw.

The distress of those represented is obvious and awful, and it's made a little worse when you understand that each figure corresponds to a named person and their respective age at the time of the disaster. There are also smaller, but no less visceral sculptures, conceived as a series and installed along the coast at the other affected villages of Burnmouth, St. Abbs, and Cove. On one level, it is a lasting tribute and a salutary reminder that although the dead have suffered, the living suffer more.

On another level, it is part of a growing culture of grief tourism peculiar to the 21st century. Collective mourning isn't quite the respectfully observed, introspective ritual it once was, and it's difficult to visit these memorials without feeling like a voyeur.

The only memorial that pays tribute to the life of Frank Buckland is similarly public, even if it is tucked away in a corner of the Scottish Fisheries Museum in Anstruther. As we'll discover in the next chapter, it's a little easier to have a quiet moment with Frank and leave a personal tribute in the shape of a kind thought.

Anstruther

Commercial Hotel, Friday, 24th August 1877

"Mr. Young has the most extraordinary memory for localities and figures. He has apparently the whole of Scotland mapped out in his mind, and he astonished us mightily during our journeyings by telling us off-hand and with the greatest accuracy the height of almost every mountain we saw, the depths and fishing capabilities of every loch, the lengths and peculiarities of every salmon river, and the names and proprietors of most of the shooting lodges and gentlemen's properties that are to be met with so plentifully in Scotland." – **Frank Buckland in Notes and Jottings from Animal Life.**

Archibald Young's house at 22 Royal Circus in Edinburgh's fashionable New Town was a spacious, three-storey, mid-terrace villa with attic rooms and a service entrance in the basement. Archibald's father William bought the property from an Admiral Duff sometime between 1855 and 1865 as a family home for himself, his wife Agnes, and their four all-but-adult children, Archibald, James, John and Agnes.

As a conservation area, the New Town is a window into the past etched with the iconography of affluence. A large house in Royal Circus was a status symbol then and, for many, it remains a dream home today. The present residents of number 22 may be a mix of leasees and private owners, but their identities are neither moot nor relevant to this book. The incumbents might be aware of the history of the house and the special nature of New

Town life in the late nineteenth-century, but this is unlikely since it has been remodelled into separate flats, and is thus an inexact example of Playfair's vision.

William was a Writer to the Signet and a law agent to the Church of Scotland. As a high-ranking legal adviser to the Crown, the Church, and Commerce, he was very much at or near the heart of the Scottish establishment. His sons pursued successful careers in the church and in the law, while his wife and daughter ran the household and undertook charitable work.

James Gerard Young became a Church of Scotland minister and was a strong and influential figure in his parish at Monifeith. John, like his father, was a successful lawyer and a Writer to the Signet. Archibald Young, also an advocate, could perhaps claim an even more elevated position in society when he was appointed first as a Commissioner, and then as a full Inspector of H.M. Scottish Salmon Fisheries.

In 1877, it seems clear that Archibald shared the house with his brother, sister and mother until first his mother died in 1889, followed by his sister in January 1900. John William Young did not marry, but he too lived continuously in the family home until his death in 1897. Valuation Rolls from 1865-1885 for 22 Royal Circus record the mother, Mrs. Agnes Gerard Young, as the occupier/proprietor, after which time, ownership passed to John William Young. After his death, the control and peculiar fate of the estate becomes shrouded in uncertainty and litigation.

Archibald lived a bachelor's existence for most of his seventy-nine years, and did not marry until very late in life in 1895. The marriage was short-lived, for his wife Alice, who was twenty years his junior, and is not interred in the family crypt, pre-deceased him by five years, and after only ten months of wedlock. They clearly had no children and, although a 'Trust' was formed the final beneficiaries of the Young family's property, money, personal belongings and private papers are the stuff of a mystery that begs to be investigated.

Although Archibald left a detailed will, it would be a hard task to unravel the family's affairs, for even James Gerard Young in Monifeith, despite a long history as a prolific correspondent, left no documents to posterity. Upon his death in 1899, someone (unknown and unnamed) burned all of James's letters, essays, and articles, undoubtedly including a great deal of family correspondence.

Archibald Young, as a Victorian professional with no family to support, was in a position to employ sufficient staff to maintain the upkeep of the house and provide all the domestic services necessary for someone of his status. Or at least, his mother and sister could.

We can reasonably assume then that on the morning of the 24th August, a generous breakfast was already laid out for him. Given the day's work ahead of him, he'd benefit from a hearty bowl of porage, a bit of bacon with devilled kidneys and poached eggs, doorstep slices of fresh, white bread, all washed down with sweet tea or bitter coffee according to his taste.

He'd be travelling from Leith to Anstruther, most likely by packet steamer from Customs House Quay, or perhaps even on a chartered boat. On his arrival, he would meet Peter Wilson, the fisheries officer charged with responsibility for inspecting and branding herring exports from the East Neuk of Fife. To my mind its more likely than not that Young undertook this evidence alone, unaccompanied by the diffident Spencer Walpole, or the fatigued, and perhaps even indisposed, Frank Buckland.

Let us leave Archibald to enjoy his breakfast in peace, while I explain why I am persisting with the speculation that the trio, at times, worked together and separately in order to gather their evidences as efficiently as possible. It was feasible, but rather unnecessary for Buckland, Walpole and Young to travel together in a cumbersome entourage, even if the inference is always there that Young is present primarily as an emissary and go-between.

It is just about believable that during these early inspections over the course of two days, the three men (and their luggage) could travel between Edinburgh and the Berwickshire coast, back to Edinburgh and onwards to Anstruther. They might then have returned to Edinburgh for the weekend before travelling on to Montrose on Monday 27th August, or more sensibly stopped in Anstruther at the Commercial Hotel, where the evidences were to be held.

Their report published in 1878 lists all three men as present at every single hearing in August and September 1877 in every single location and suggests that they were accommodated locally. It also describes a return visit to Ballantrae in November that year, and evidence gathering in Sunderland in February 1878. The report describes a circular journey even though that convenient narrative is subverted by common sense.

At this early stage of the commission, our three heroes would have had to catch the Edinburgh train on the North British Line to the terminus at Burnmouth, where a carriage would meet and transport them to Eyemouth, three miles away. Once the rather scant evidences had been heard, they could either stay the night at the Home Arms Hotel, or return the same laborious route back to the Balmoral Hotel in Edinburgh.

If the official version is to be believed, they all returned to Edinburgh, and travelled by carriage to Leith on the morning of Friday 23rd. where they took the boat to Anstruther. It's a lot of effort in order to hear very little that the fisheries officer could not supply either in person or via correspondence. It all seems like a lot of needless travel for so little return, so why would they bother with all the doubling back and forth?

As I've already indicated, the Eyemouth evidences bear the hallmarks of Buckland's easy way with reportage. The Anstruther evidences are, by contrast, more properly ordered into meaningful sentences that flow coherently from one topic into another, and there is more use of facts and figures to flesh out a discussion. It has the touch of the lawyer's pen about it, and at times strays into legalese in its treatment of relatively minor points and details.

Young is nevertheless able to write engagingly for a lay audience, as seen in his memoir 'Summer Sailings'; his *Scotsman* obituary of Frank Buckland; his 'award-winning' essay on harbour accommodation; and his correspondence to the newspapers.

Archibald's prose is conversational and his style is economical and informative. Indeed, his writing is largely indistinguishable from the contemporary language that we regard as modern. It has little of Buckland's pedantic, arcane and slightly fanciful flourishes, and only adds to my suspicion that Victorian verbosity is an affectation repeated *ad nauseam* that has little to do with everyday speech, communication and vocational writing in the late nineteenth century.

Spencer Walpole was a Whitehall mandarin attached to the War Office, a noted historian, and an exemplary administrator. His own writing supports the view that he favoured clear and concise language, devoid of extravagant turns of phrase and loquacious erudition over purple prose. Walpole, in quoted speech and in writing, was routinely direct, detailed, informed and assertive. We will see some more evidence of that when we come to the Montrose evidences.

At the time of the commission, Montrose had supplanted Berwickshire and Firth of Forth fisheries in both volume and importance. Buckland may have been the notional lead author of the report, but the attention paid to Montrose indicates that Walpole, the government man, had to be present in a location where the commission was required to investigate matters much more closely and in much greater depth. It is neither necessary, nor practical for all three, much less Walpole, to understand what was going on in Eyemouth and Anstruther, where the issues were already understood.

The Crab and Lobster Reports, which document the tasks and travels they undertook together as fisheries inspectors in the summer of 1876, offers an even more persuasive clue. The route they took around Scotland back then was almost identical to the map and itinerary described in the herring report and, in several cases, one or other of them is credited as the sole author at evidence gathering in specific locations. If they split up in 1876 for reasons of efficiency, then it doesn't seem credible that they'd be any less sensible in 1877.

I therefore think it more credible that Archibald Young finished his breakfast and packed an overnight bag. He made his way by carriage to Leith docks where the regular Leith to Anstruther steam packet left from Custom House slipway on Commercial Street. I originally wondered if the quickest route to the point of departure might not take Young down Leith Walk, but Archie was a town gent who liked the country life, and he wasted no opportunity to go fishing, walking, climbing and sailing around Scotland.

It seems more likely to me, looking at the 1877 map, that he directed his driver along Henderson Row, past Canonmills, and down Inverleith Row. At that time it was a pleasant carriage ride past the natural panorama provided by the newly completed Botanical Gardens. There were also lovely open, green spaces on either side of the avenue all the way to the tollbooth junction at Ferry Road.

Turning right into this long, straight boulevard offered a relatively stress-busting alternative to joining the processional traffic on Elm Row and Leith Walk. The streetscape there had already become chokingly industrial, although we time-travellers might be fascinated to view, from the safe distance of social history, the goods station, the coal yards, the gas works, and the nascent chemical plant.

This route took Young all the way to Coburg Street, which fed directly into Commercial Street. If his pocket watch was accurate, then all he need do now was alight from his carriage, and step directly on board the scheduled boat to Anstruther. In any event, Archibald would, I fancy, have taken the opportunity to dress down and opt for the maritime look.

Young spent many of his extended summer holidays under sail, often travelling far afield by steam yacht. He wrote about his experiences extensively in 'Summer Sailings' and corresponded frequently with the *Scotsman* newspaper on the sights and secret landscapes to be discovered around Scotland's coastline.

He also made journeys further afield to London (from Leith in fifty-two hours), continental Europe and Norway. It's well known that the nineteenth-century middle classes were in the grip of a sailing mania, driven by the speed, efficiency and relative comfort of steam-powered travel. Archibald Young, for one, certainly had the means to indulge in such an expensive pastime.

I feel certain he would have had the togs to suit the occasion; a jaunty cap instead of a topper perhaps; a blazer or double-breasted reefer instead of a formal frock coat; and carefully neglected cotton twill breeks over his well-made, but unpolished, comfortable, workaday boots.

In his writings, and in 'Summer Sailings' particularly, Young writes fondly about the characters he encountered on these expeditions. I see Young as a city sophisticate who liked nothing better than to escape the pretensions of his professional existence and mix with working people who lived closer to the elements and very much according to their wits.

His writing in the following extract is showy for comic effect, but the *mise-en-scène* has trickled down through decades of re-invention in popular culture.

" *We returned to the yacht about six o'clock...and found that our worthy sailing master had met with an old acquaintance at Fort William and had returned on board in a state of perfect happiness and inebriation which produced a curious effect upon his saturnine temperament. He was overpoweringly kind and attentive, smiling at everything and everybody, to the intense delight of the crew...*

....we turned in at an early hour; but we were not destined to enjoy unbroken slumbers, for, a little after midnight, we were all aroused by a tremendous row proceeding from the cabin where our worthy skipper was enjoying the sweets of repose and sleeping off his debauch at Fort William. We found the ancient mariner yelling like a maniac, and twisting about as if in the last agony. In fact, he was struggling with a nightmare, and appeared to have decidedly the worst of the contest."

The Anstruther Evidences

If we assume a journey time across the Firth of Forth, depending on the weather, the currents and the tides, of no more than two hours, then we can safely place Archibald Young in Anstruther just in time for lunch with Peter Wilson, the local fisheries officer.

If you feel this is too much conjecture already, then I can say in my defence that the Edinburgh Post Office Directory of 1877 thought the service even more capricious and arbitrary.

'*In consequence of the repeated changes that occur in the times of sailing of Steamers, parties are advised to consult those services of information now so easily available, or apply at the office to avoid disappointment.*'

What I can say for certain is that the Leith to Anstruther steam packet service sailed on Mondays, Wednesdays and Fridays from Custom House Slip. It may not be anything other than circumstantial evidence in support of my arguments, but it is a bit of a smoking gun.

The evidences from Anstruther were to be heard on Friday 17th August 1877 in the Commercial Hotel, which sat on the quayside close to the outlet of the Dreel Burn separating Anstruther East from Anstruther West. In antiquity, and well into the twentieth century, these communities were quite separate administrative entities, even though we know that by 1877 they were firmly conjoined as Anstruther in the public mind. Between, 1930 and 1975 *Kilrenny, Anstruther Easter and Anstruther Wester* each enjoyed burgh status before they were absorbed into the present-day unitary council area of Fife.

Young found at Anstruther a herring fishery in sharp decline, despite the recent completion of works to enlarge the already substantial harbour. The pattern of the herring 'take' from Anstruther and its associated district had experienced considerable fluctuations between 1857 and 1871, when the downturn became precipitous. From a peak in 1860 of 105,000 barrels of cured and fresh herring combined, the yield had, by 1876, fallen to an all-time low of 5,928.

This was doubly alarming when it is understood that the fishing ground extended from Buckhaven further west along the Firth of Forth, all the way around the East Neuk to Tayport in the Firth of Tay. The fishing stations, including Largo, Pittenweem, Cellardyke, Crail, Kingsbarns and St. Andrews suffered accordingly and never really recovered their status as important landing sites.

But was it the harbinger of a more general decline in the Scottish herring fishery? It was enough to set bells ringing at the Fisheries Board and in the Home Office, and the need to know became paramount. Herring was simply too valuable a commodity to ignore, or place at risk.

Local fishermen pointed the finger of blame squarely, and predictably, at the prevalence of beam trawlers and the disruption caused by the sprat fishery in the Forth. However, the imposition of an experimental moratorium on trawling over three consecutive years between 1862, 1863 and 1864 did not result in an increase in the herring catch.

Perhaps more significantly, the 1877 evidence from Anstruther is largely historical and presented as much by spectators as the fishermen themselves. Among the many subjective observations made, the lengthiest remarks recorded are those from a net manufacturer, a solicitor, a merchant, and a surveyor. Five fishermen, three of whom were very elderly, gave evidence, but they merely echoed each other's sentiments and few, if any, new facts emerged from these witnesses.

For his part, Young elects to flesh out his report with a preponderance of facts, figures and tables. He happily informs us that, *"...the length of a herring net averages sixty yards. Each boat carries forty to sixty nets. Two hundred and fifty boats would have nearly five hundred miles of netting."*

Elsewhere, summarising the evidence of David Gillis (net maker), we learn that *"his nets are all made of cotton. His twine comes from Manchester. There are a good many makers of herring net cotton. The cotton is finer, more durable, and fishes better than (traditional) hemp. A cotton net weighs 13lbs,* a hemp net 25 lbs. *The nets are 360 and 400 meshes deep. Netting is sold by the yard."*

In these passages, Young almost tests the patience with his lawyer-like exposition. It's full of filibustering detail that seems designed mainly to disguise how threadbare the evidences were. Even William Gillis, the fisheries officer, seems to distance himself from evidences informed by prejudice. He simply reported what the local fishermen felt, but conspicuously took no side in the arguments. We're none the wiser about the true reasons for the catastrophic decline in the herring fisheries of Anstruther and district, nor any more convinced that beam trawlers or sprat fishermen are the main culprits.

There is little doubt, in principle, that dragging a heavy wooden beam along the sea bottom is more destructive and invasive that leaving a drift net to hang in the middle depths. The circumstantial evidence for its negative impact is superficially compelling, but lacking in sufficient specific examples and experiments to be scientifically compelling.

Similarly, there is little argument that small mesh nets targeting sprats will routinely ensnare a significant by-catch of immature specimens of larger species such as herring. Yet, it remains a prodigious leap to prove unequivocally that these two evils accounted for the disappearance of hundreds of thousands of fish from inshore waters. The true picture was likely to be more complex, and the commissioners were far from blind to other possibilities.

As we travel around Scotland with Buckland, Walpole and Young, we can sense their empathy with hard-pressed fishing communities, but equally we can admire their commitment to hard-nosed and dispassionate evaluation of the facts at hand.

None of this helped to ameliorate the impact of a collapsed industry and a severely dented local economy in the East Neuk. in the decade that followed, Anstruther and District drifted like a loose net in the North Sea, but Fife folk are a determined breed (some might even say thrawn) in the face of adversity. They don't put up with misfortune for long.

Although the herring fishers migrated to other ports, Anstruther reaped the benefits in other ways. Boat building persisted at Anstruther, as did commerce in the town and agriculture in the hinterland. The luxurious proportions of the state-of-the-art harbour supported smaller-scale, but more diverse fishing activities, and attracted more trippers and sightseers as one industrious century passed into another.

It's true that the harbour remained too shallow, and its muddy bottom needed to be dug out if it was to accommodate much larger vessels. The proposition to excavate was made many times but the expense was always deemed prohibitive.

Yet Anstruther thrived, and the area has since become a commuters' paradise for affluent city professionals. It offers a cutesy-cottage lifestyle among the picture- postcard, dormitory villages that sweetly dot the East Neuk shore from Crail to St. Monan's. It's also a convenient weekend getaway for fatigued academics from the university towns of St. Andrews and Dundee, who come to slum it with the locals in one of Anstruther's many fish and chip shops.

Anstruther has, more by historical accident than grand design, successfully balanced backwater charm with a mixed, modern economy. It is a place that pursues an industrious living, but it also offers the interested, casual, or first-time visitor an open window into its working life. In many ways, it offers a more satisfying and fulfilling experience than more famous destinations that are, by comparison, merely exhibits set into the landscape.

Some Curious Things About Anstruther

Anstruther, and its supporting cast of sparkling, whitewashed, olde-worlde villages in the East Neuk, is one of Scottish tourism's biggest and most unassuming stars. It is an almost perfect mix of the contemporary, the traditional and the authentic. The town is best approached somewhat circuitously along the A917 coast road from Lundin Links in the west, through Upper Largo, Elie, St. Monans, Pittenweem, Anstruther Wester and across the Dreel Burn into the main *body-o'-the-kirk* in Anstruther Easter.

The western part of Anstruther looks, on the map, like a vestigial appendage attached to the more substantial rump of its former cousin. It has, nevertheless, refused to settle into a state of permanent marginalisation. The recently re-opened Dreel Hall is the centrepiece in a compendium of places of interest, primarily as a community resource, a leisure hub and a cultural venue. It's perhaps a little under-exposed as a feature of the area's tourism portfolio, but it's an important feature in the civic landscape.

Outwardly, the preservation of the Dreel Hall's architectural integrity assures continuity of local character, style and identity, which is reflected on the inside of the building by mixed use and varied activities. It is through such rolling programmes of community events, meetings, exhibitions and gatherings that the character of a place is, I think, revealed.

The charm of a flower show, an exhibition by local artists, a model railway display, or a charity coffee morning are all pleasantly commonplace. They are the nice surprises that separate genuine hospitality from the nasty shock of opportunistic exploitation. These things aren't as garish as the cash-cow attractions that despoil so many coastal resorts, but I suspect that they are much more enduring and certainly more endearing.

Nothing in Anstruther is prohibitively expensive, and the best things, such as the early morning light of spring on the boat-bobbing, sun-dappled water, or the view across the Forth towards the Isle of May are free.

Fast, fresh food is readily available from one of the several fish and chip shops, some of which are attractions in their own right. Connoisseurs of fine cuisine may find this upsetting but people come in droves just for the cod and fried onion rings, served on a paper plate, and eaten with the fingers. It's so good, so hearty and so 'more-ish' that even the gulls are denied all but the most meagre scraps and leftovers.

Anstruther couldn't resemble a model maritime village more if had been laid out for that very purpose. The harbour is capacious in proportion to the size of the town, but it's a busy mix of private boats, fishing vessels, small motor-boats, motor cruisers and visiting pleasure craft.

The round trip from Anstruther to the bird sanctuary on the Isle of May is a bit pricey, but it guarantees experiences and perspectives that live long in the memory and provoke reflective thought. The world looks quite different from a boat, and wild places, small and isolated though they may be, teach us that a world populated solely by guillemots, razorbills, eider ducks and puffins is not at all unthinkable. It's food for thought, just as much as freshly caught haddock is sustenance for the body.

Walk with me then along the Anstruther quayside from the Dreel Hall, where we can enjoy flat-white coffee and lemon drizzle cake, and buy some embroidered handkerchiefs with our initials stitched into the fine linen weave.

We could catch the boat to puffin-land on the Isle of May National Nature Reserve, and return in time for a fish-cake supper and a shared piece of beer-battered cod. Sit with me on the bench outside the lifeboat station where colourful, nautical souvenirs are on display in the window and a sobering exhibition upstairs tells its stories of unthinking heroism and unswerving commitment.

The Anstruther lifeboat has been operational since 1865, and the service has answered countless distress calls and saved many lives. The statistics from the seven vessels that have launched from the station in its long history show that the need for the service today is as great as its ever been. The sea is no less dangerous and we are seemingly no more sensible of it either. Certainly, The Kingdom of Fife all-weather rescue boat has been launched so many times it would suggest that life, leisure and work at sea present as many hazards today as they did when the nation was largely under sail.

The station also uses a Class D inflatable boat for inshore rescues. It's designed to be 'self-righted manually' by the crew in the event of capsize, and this piece of foresight concentrates the mind as much as raw data. It's a reminder that, even for experts, any relationship with the sea must be based on respect for its unpredictable temperament.

Directly across from the lifeboat station is one of the finest small museums in Scotland, which on closer inspection isn't small at all, and contains one of the most curious exhibitions in the land. It is even more curious given the subject matter explored in this book. The National Fisheries Museum at Anstruther would be interesting enough on its own merits, but it is doubly of interest to us for its sequential history of the herring boom in the nineteenth century, and as the spiritual home of Frank Buckland Esquire.

I first visited the museum, the only one of its kind in the UK, in the summer of 2007. It contains just about every conceivable maritime artefact including life-size recreations of a wheelhouse, seaman's quarters and a fish shop. There are too many model ships and boats to count. They sit in clear glass cases underneath dozens of eye-catching paintings, flanked by lethal-looking implements that would still be dangerous in the wrong hands.

Once you have absorbed an incredibly concise and compact history of fishing from earliest times to the present day, you can cast your eye over the seductive lines and surprisingly large proportions of real boats that have been rescued from the scrapheap. The whole experience is profoundly affecting, tremendously informative and almost criminally inexpensive. I was on my way to take advantage of the keenly priced tea and buttered scones when I noticed something that stopped me in my tracks.

It was a marble bust; unmistakably the head of Frank Buckland, with his ungovernable hair, his thick beard and his quiet, self-assured, well-fed features. It stopped me in my tracks like a chance meeting with a major rock star. Frank, to explain, is something of an adopted hero of zoo keepers, not unlike myself, who have come to know and love his revealing vignettes of life at London Zoo in its early years.

Better still, Buckland was good friends with Abraham Bartlett who furnished Frank not just with inside information, but with exotic specimens both dead and alive, and sometimes even in a state of comatose *bardo*. Frank Buckland's close ties to London Zoo as an erstwhile taxidermist, pathologist and proto-veterinarian provided a rich vein of material for his collected essays. They, in turn, contributed to his legend as an 'all-round animal man', and an iconic communicator of broad-spectrum natural history.

One of Buckland's great passions was his obsessive mission to establish a Museum of Fish Culture and Economics. Its purpose was never quite as clear and organised as the Fisheries Museum, but Buckland was looking into the future rather than recording the past. He had acquired a great many aquatic specimens of all shapes and sizes and made casts of them in order to populate his museum with exhibits. It was an impressive, if somewhat disjointed collection of fish and fish-related paraphernalia, which was undoubtedly huge, but never properly counted or catalogued.

Neither could he find a permanent home for the hundreds, if not thousands of items he had in his possession, even though he left them all in his will to the Natural History Museum at South Kensington.

The NHM allowed only a much-reduced temporary exhibition within its hallowed halls and, in an astonishing act of curatorial elitism, it broke up Buckland's collection and dispersed it without recording its fate. Perhaps, it was deemed to gimmicky for the inclusion of his 'fish hatching apparatus', or too unscientific for the haphazard nature of the acquisitions.

Certainly, it seems that it was of limited interest or relevance to the upper echelons of nineteenth-century natural science. As a result, Buckland's vision was unfairly disparaged as the misdirected passion of an unfocused personality. His commendable initiative continued to be met with scepticism for years afterwards, in spite of the best efforts of Archibald Young who continued to carry the torch for Buckland's ideas.

The paramount importance of scientific fisheries management, marine conservation and stewardship of the seas has proved most of Buckland's severest critics quite wrong. This trident approach continues to vindicate his lifelong held view that humanity cannot live off the land alone, and that the sea could be the primary source of food for the people. His mantra is repeated on a daily basis by modern stakeholders in the fishing industry; the fish uneaten and unfished far outnumber those that few species that are the basis of a boom and bust enterprise. It is a circumstance that provokes endless controversy, heated argument and, all too often, sterile debate.

Buckland averred in 1878 that there were far more herring in the sea than we could ever remove for our own sustenance and/or economic wellbeing. He lived in the midst of accelerated industrialisation and rapid economic expansion, but he could not have predicted the coming of voracious klondykers, the factory ships that are still in use today in many fisheries, and the cynical, gluttonous practices that led to a complete and utter collapse of the North Sea herring stocks in the 1970s. None of that recent history has made a liar out of Frank Buckland.

The Fisheries Museum, which today accommodates the registered office of The Buckland Foundation and a small collection dedicated to his memory, impresses upon the visitor the need for good sense to prevail in the responsible management of our seas. Calm heads and informed discussion need to take precedence over unsubstantiated hearsay and opinionated commentary.

If there's one thing we can learn from the 1878 Herring Report, it's that the bigger picture offers a general impression of the facts, but that the truth of the matter is to be found buried in the detail. It takes strong personalities to dig that out, just as it does today.

We can expect future debates and conflicts around fishing to be as hot under the collar as ever they were; but once the red mist has cleared, then reason surely must prevail. Only due diligence and fairness of mind can guarantee an honourable living and deliver the full bounty of the sea to the people.

Montrose

Queen's Hotel, Saturday, 25th August 1877

"I noted several other matters during my journey of enquiry in Scotland which I should like to record. The first thing that struck me was that everybody in Scotland appears to be educated. At about nine in the morning, at every place, both town and village, the children may be seen 'away to school', and they seem to enjoy the prospect of learning lessons – quite a contrast to the state of things in England sixty years ago" – **Frank Buckland in 'Notes and Jottings'.**

There is every reason to believe that Buckland, Walpole and Young would find Montrose diverting enough to compensate for any inconvenience involved in getting there. It is set on the edge of a tidal basin in one of the most picturesque counties in all of Scotland. Angus is also the seat of the earliest Scottish kings and Montrose, as a significant port, has enjoyed periodic prosperity as a centre of commerce.

In Buckland's time, and for some time after, the spirit of enterprise embraced most of northeast Scotland from Dundee to Stonehaven. The commercial directory of 1907, for example, demarcates the area to include the coastal towns and villages from Broughty Ferry to Stonehaven, and, further inland, the farming parishes around Forfar and Brechin. Strictly speaking, Montrose fell within the boundaries of Forfarshire, but the 1878 Herring Report squarely places the town at the centre a string of pearly settlements perforating the coastline from what is now Tayside, through

Angus and up to Kincardineshire.

The commissioners' route north was a little circuitous because the ill-fated Tay Rail Bridge, almost completed, was still officially under construction. Trials took place on 22nd September when the first, solitary engine tentatively tested the structure on the same day that the commissioners were hearing evidences in Inverary. Until the bridge opened to passengers on 1st June 1878, travellers to Montrose and the northeast had to take a detour.

In order to get there, our party of Victorian gentlemen would have judiciously taken the Edinburgh to Aberdeen train (via Dundee and Perth), alighting at Dubton Junction Station to take the branch line from there to Montrose. It would, for them, be a simple matter to have the bulk of their luggage forwarded to Aberdeen, where the next set of evidences would be heard. They would then be required to carry only what they needed for an overnight stay at the Queen's Temperance Hotel on Montrose High Street.

Travelling light makes sense given that the hearing at Montrose would be taking place on the afternoon of the day of travel, and the testimonies to be recorded involved only a few influential individuals. Nevertheless, the activities of the herring fishers based in Montrose were central to a better understanding of recent developments and significant changes in the herring industry. These circumstances, along with the rather genteel aspect and cultivated image of the town, lend weight to the suggestion that all three inspectors made the trip to Montrose.

A turn about the streets of Montrose in 1877 would be extremely illuminating, if not eye-opening for a curious London gent. It was, at that time, a small, ergonomic and elegantly appointed little town. Its street map shows deliberate efforts to lay down a New Town grid of terraces and avenues between the High Street and the grassy links that led to the wide sandy beach. Montrose also boasted several elementary schools, an academy, a museum, half a dozen substantial churches, a linen works, a stone-built railway station and, of course, a busy harbour.

The main thoroughfare, Montrose High Street, was lined with shops and businesses catering for every need. The town also supported several commodious hotels, a number of ale-houses, and at least one large eating house. A long circular walk to the Queens Hotel would take the casual visitor (or time-traveller) on a gentle perambulation along the High Street, down John Street where the Montrose Review and the Montrose Standard had their offices.

As a devout churchgoer, you might raise an eyebrow at the presumptuous size and assertive architecture of one of the three 'Free Churches' in the town. Certainly, Buckland and his colleagues may have been somewhat ruffled by the ostentation of an upstart denomination, thought to be little more than a disruptive breakaway element in the Church of Scotland.

A stroll across the mid-links and down to the beach (dodging golf balls on the way) would offer immediate respite from the clattering cartwheels on the High Street. The noise of the town centre will fade but the smells from the linen works and tannery might linger, and follow at a distance, depending upon the prevailing direction of the wind. The gardens and tennis courts were new and excited the eye; further inferring cultivated thinking in the minds of the town fathers.

Returning via the harbour, up George Street and back towards the High Street, it might be possible to appreciate a reticent kind of affluence. Observant explorers, perhaps even those with a little local knowledge, might begin to notice the way that many a deceptively large property makes a large footprint behind the po-faced facades of the main streets. Narrow lanes, closes and snickets lead, at length, down alleys and through gated entrances into huge townhouses, and spacious tenements. In the case of the Queen's Hotel, an intimate close led to a very well-appointed hostelry on three floors with its own large restaurant and space for billiard tables.

On the other side of the High Street, the passageways led away to much humbler properties that hugged the shoreline of Montrose Basin, an inland tidal estuary that surely foreshortened the lifespan of any building located along its sandy edge. In August, the birds of interest at the Basin had already flown, which is a pity. Buckland in particular would have found enormous winter aggregations of wildfowl and wading birds worthy of a paragraph or two among his 'Curiosities of Natural History'.

As it happens, it appears that Buckland, despite enjoying an all expenses paid jaunt around Scotland (and undertaken in relative comfort), found time to complain that he was being fed 'finan haddies everywhere he went in Scotland'. Given the immediate proximity to bountiful farmland only a few miles out of the town, it seems reasonable to assume that Buckland protests too much. His objections surely could not apply to Montrose, much less the sophisticated cities of Scotland.

Victorian hotel menus can be readily found on the internet, and they seem to offer pretty wholesome fare. Certainly, it's hard to believe that the Queens Temperance Hotel would skimp on meals for these distinguished officers of H.M. Government; especially when the proprietor, John Heckford Esq., was also the treasurer of the local Unionist Association.

Dishes like Scotch broth, Irish stew, poached salmon, fresh oatmeal herring, broiled mutton chops and fried kidneys feature prominently in Mrs. Beeton's 1859 book of household management. It therefore follows that a provincial hotel, even a 'Scotch' one, would be able to aspire to such modest heights of culinary expertise.

Personally, I would feed Frank a nice piece of cold salmon fillet as a starter, followed by a roast beef dinner. That way, I feel sure that a positive, word-of-mouth review might be the outcome for me and my temperance hotel. Certainly, the last thing I'd want is a bad report from a popular writer like Frank Buckland.

The Montrose Evidences

It is more likely than not, that Buckland, Walpole and Young, following a hearty lunch, sat down sleepily to hear the news from Montrose on full stomachs. Perhaps that is why this part of the report seems curious for being incurious. The witnesses were few in number, and fewer still were fishermen with first-hand experiences to relate. This is usefully explained away by James Johnson, a fishcurer who declared that Montrose was, "*always a curing station and never a fishing station.*" It's a sensible enough observation when you understand the nature of fishing in nineteenth-century Scotland.

In 1877, the Montrose herring station was considered equidistant between the fishing hamlet of Broughty Ferry in the south and busy Stonehaven in the north. Previously, boats from Aberdeen had been included in the inshore fishery administered from Montrose. The Granite City, however, famously grew in importance as a major fishing port, and from 1875, it had been regarded separately.

In contrast, the Dundee herring fishery was deemed to have *'dwindled to a small winter fishery'*, and was also notionally excluded from the official Montrose station figures. This seems incongruous to the modern mind, since catches from Broughty Ferry, a community less than five miles from Dundee city centre and now considered a posh suburb, inexplicably remained in the total reckoning for Montrose.

Coastal villages such as Ferryden, Gourdon and Johnshaven are steeped in fishing history, while towns like Arbroath and Stonehaven are synonymous with freshly caught seafood. They were historically productive because of heir reservoir of traditional fishing expertise as much as economic necessity. Then, as now, their relationship with fish and fishing was inescapable, so it perhaps comes as no surprise to learn that north-east fishermen were among the first to venture further out to sea in pursuit of the silver darlings.

The absence of fishermen from the Montrose hearing rather suggests that most, if not all of them, were either away at sea, or landing fish elsewhere. The inspectors instead rely heavily on the largely unedited report written for them by local fisheries officer, David Gillis. In it, he declares encouragingly that, *"the fishing is in a prosperous state"*, and it is his voice that emerges authoritatively from the pages of this section.

His testimony would also appear to be free of Buckland's editorial interventions, save for one short passage speculating on the movement of herring further away from the shore. *"Thinks that fish are being driven further away from the land"*, and, *"...is not sure whether fish are intercepted sooner, or whether they are driven further off"*. Both of these interjections sound like Gillis' responses to some rather idle questioning, especially when the conclusion reached is that, *"both opinions are held here"*.

For the most part, Gillis is allowed to state his findings, the most significant of which is, *"the boats now go further out to sea than they used to do...60 to 80 miles out"*, and *"12 or 14 years ago they used only to go from 6-20 miles out"*. Moreover, his observation about the relative failure of the catch in 1876, which was effectively halved, was *"due to exceptional storms"* is helpful, and is further qualified by his remark that *"1874 and 1875 were exceptionally fine seasons"*. He is, however, quick to add that *"There is great want of harbours at the east coast...the larger boats require deeper harbours...Peterhead is the only harbour to which they can run"*.

It is a good point, succinctly made. It also sounds like an unsubtle dig at a complacent, foot-dragging, London bureaucracy. Indeed, it's just as well that Gillis' report is so complete; the only other evidences were presented by two prominent fishcurers, namely James Johnson and Alexander Mearns.

Johnson had a lot to say for himself. He was a significant merchant in the town who had contracts with *"50 or 60 boats for their catch"*. It is he who makes the distinction between curing ports and catching ports, yet it is, presumably, his 50 or 60 boats that he claims have been *"sailing from Montrose for herrings"*. It also seems to have escaped his notice that Montrose boats, since the mid-1860s, had averaged one-fifth of the east coast fleet. Many of them will have sailed from bustling Ferryden, situated only a mile or two away from the town on the opposite bank of the River South Esk.

Date	Summer		Winter	
	Boats (Av)	Total Catch (crans)	Boats (Av)	Total Catch (crans)
1864	250	24,417	77	1,293
1865	250	19,600	80	368
1866	300	28,842	24	292
1867	300	29,384	34	570
1868	280	28,423	30	104
1869	327	34,270	24	60
1870	325	30,809	20	80
1871	411	39,120	42	776
1872	324	32,005	56	925
1873	255	37,945	34	301
1874	257	38,135	110	4,939
1875	194	30,017	60	893
1876	198	25,327	57	1,562
1877	225	39,883	20	324

Table 1. Total Number of Boats Sailing from Montrose and Distict[1]

Johnson goes on to corroborate Gillis by agreeing that *"the failure of the herring fishery in 1876 was entirely due to weather"*, and concurred with the view that harbour facilities had become woefully inadequate. *"In Ireland, there are harbours but no fishermen. Here there are fishermen, but no harbours. Stonehaven, if the government would spend the money, could be made available for the fishermen of this coast."*

Alexander Mearns, thirty years a fishcurer at Montrose, was the only other witness recorded as present. It's not clear whether he was economical in his speech, or whether his testimony was edited down for brevity's sake. It reads like a heavily summarized paragraph included as a courtesy, for Mearns adds very little to the discussion. He simply repeats much of the testimony already given by Gillis and Johnson without contributing much in the way of quantitative evidence. He does, caution, however, that, *'There is a good entrance to the harbour at Montrose, but there is a very rapid tide that*

---

[1] *Prior to 1869 The 'Montrose District' included Aberdeen, before the latter became more important as a whitefish fishery. The Broughty Ferry catch, although tiny, is also included, even though it is not 'officially within the Montrose station cachement.*

prevents the boats getting up.'

The inspectors may have had a fairly simple and pleasant task at Montrose, but they still managed to commit a small but diverting sin of omission. Throughout the 1878 Report, there is a degree of uncertainty about the exact location of herring spawning grounds in Scotland's inshore waters.

Many of the references to the topic are rather vague and clouded by contrariness and scepticism. James Johnson tentatively named, *"The Bank of the White Spot"* and *"Bank of the Shallow Water"* as spawning grounds, although they sound too Tolkien-esque to be credible as modern geographical locators. David Gillis seemed confident enough to report encouragingly that, *"they do spawn at Berrie Hettle, near here."*

Quite what or where *'Berrie Hettle'* might be is left to readers to guess for themselves. I suspect that even the oldest citizen alive today in Montrose would struggle to explain what is inferred in this strange place name. I can reveal with the help of a rather ancient Scots-English dictionary that a *"hettle"* is a range of subterranean rocks of indeterminate length is associated with shallow, calm waters between the *"shoreline and the roadstead"*.

It is easy to imagine herring spawn, containing millions of eggs, clinging to the uneven, rugged, irregular and sheltering features of such an underwater rockery. When hatched, the fry at least have a fighting chance of survival among gaps and crevices inaccessible to predators; but what exactly is a *"roadstead"*?

Maritime types will tell you that it is a natural or man-made body of water that is not a harbour, but is a place sheltered from rip currents, spring tides or ocean swell. It's a location where ships can lie reasonably safely at anchor, and in maritime law it is described as a *"known general station for ships"*.

If 'Berrie Hettle' was a talking point between Buckland, Walpole and Young, then no record of the conversation survives. It is anyone's guess what they talked about around the billiard table at the Queens Hotel. I expect they talked about all the fine folk that they knew, the places they had visited, and the facts they had learned. Perhaps, one of them even remarked what a fine little town Montrose had become. The church, education and morality may have been among the topics discussed, and Buckland seemed especially enthused about Scotland's commitment to schooling its young.

Buckland, Walpole and Young were three educated men who, in the subtlest of ways, personified macro-stratification in Victorian Society. We're used to thinking in terms of a notional myth that still persists of a people sorted into lower, middle and upper class 'types'. This has given rise to the lie that is 'social mobility' achieved on merit.

In Buckland's time, social standing was much more nuanced, complex and uncertain; and the evidence is to be found in the margins of biography. Walpole, in 1877, represented a comparatively impoverished branch of a famous political dynasty. Archibald Young was a respected Edinburgh advocate from a family of advocates and clergy, with strong links to the establishment in Scotland. Buckland was the son of William Buckland, Dean of Westminster and a part-time palaeontologist who was something of a celebrity himself.

Walpole began a long career in Whitehall humbly enough as a nineteen-year-old clerk in the War Office, entering the civil service straight from Eton. His father, twice a Foreign Secretary under Lord Derby, could not afford to send either of his sons to University so they both had to settle for a life of plodding political service, rather than the rapid advancement and personal fame enjoyed by those with more money or better contacts.

Spencer Walpole had to win his spurs as a person of note among the upper echelons through diligence, deference and duty. He became a respected historian and a popular governor of the Isle of Man, and his reward was to round off a successful professional life as Postmaster General.

Buckland, on the other hand, seems to have landed on his feet for much of his early life. His father, as one of the leading churchmen in England, inevitably brought his family into contact not just with the great and the good, but with the high and mighty too.

The Bucklands enjoyed a kind of fame long before Frank's widespread popularity as a writer and communicator. William Buckland, whom Frank adored, was an enthusiastic, if provocative, would-be polymath whose interests outside his pastoral responsibilities included fossil hunting, philosophy and natural history. He also understood the importance of strong friendships and lasting connections with people of greater influence.

These relationships were crucial whenever Frank's brilliant career looked like faltering; firstly with an assisted passage through Oxford University where he passed his final exam in human anatomy at the second time of asking, and then only by the skin of his teeth. Frank was clubbable too, thanks to his father's friendship with an influential co-sponsor, and his acceptance into the Athenaeum in London helped Frank to widen his social network considerably.

It meant a great deal to have one's name dropped in such elevated circles. It goes some way to explaining how an underachiever at school managed to eventually produce a *curriculum vitae* that included three years as surgeon at St. Georges Hospital, eight years as an assistant surgeon with Queens Own Life Guards, ten years as a writer, editor and lecturer, and fourteen years as a senior Inspector of Her Majesty's Fisheries. Frank Buckland may have been a commoner in courtier's clothes, but he was completely aware of, and sensitive about, his status as an English gentleman of some consequence.

Archibald Young was a very well educated, informed and articulate Scot and, until I came to write this book, his role in the Herring Report has been acknowledged almost as an afterthought. There is commentary from Buckland and, to a much lesser extent from Walpole, which implies that Young was little more than a guide and emissary, blessed with local knowledge and a persuasive tongue. The inference throughout, although their roles are nowhere defined, is that Buckland is the lead author, Walpole is the government presence and authority figure, and Young, cast as the go-between, is almost caricatured as 'Our Man in Scotland'.

It is clear that at the time of the Herring Report in 1877, the three of them knew each other very well. Young's obituaries of Buckland and Walpole are warm, while Walpole's recollection of Buckland still enjoys some fame as a great example of a concise 19th Century memoir of a friend and colleague. Little, if any, correspondence between them seems to have survived. If it has, then it is not in the public domain.

The probable reason for an almost complete absence of materials to source is a little sad and painfully bittersweet. Neither Buckland nor Young left any direct descendants and the bulk of their private papers seem to have been either lost or dispersed. Walpole's only daughter died without issue and much of his unpublished writing and communications would seem to be held anonymously in private hands.

Buckland, Walpole and Young were almost compulsive writers and committed communicators who wrote for a living. It is astonishing therefore that virtually no correspondence between them, or with their relations seems to have survived. Worse still, we also know that Archibald's younger brother, James Gerard, was a similarly prolific writer of letters, articles, opinions and proposals whose entire archive was evidently destroyed after his death. It is also one of the most disconcerting footnotes to the Buckland-Walpole-Young narrative, because any communication between the two brothers would almost certainly yield a great deal of biographical detail about Archibald Young.

James Gerard Young, only a year younger than Archibald, was a career clergyman and Church of Scotland minister about whom we actually know a great deal more. He was an imposing man and clearly a parish priest with vision, energy and willpower. James' parish was at Monifieth, twenty-four miles south of Montrose, and less than three miles from Broughty Ferry.

James was responsible for the building of the village hall, a community school and a cottage hospital in this unassuming little Angus village. He was also a keen historian with an active interest in Angus folklore and legend in a county strongly associated with early Scottish kingship and Celtic cultural artefacts. James' fascinating story awaits the attentions of another biographer, but it is frustrating to think that so much revealing information about Archibald, and the Young family in general, was lost with the destruction of James' letters and papers.

One saving grace, perhaps the only one, is that a photograph of James Gerard Young is currently held in the archives of Angus Council. It is a tantalizing clue to the appearance (and perhaps demeanour) of his sibling, and supports the suggestion that Archibald, as a long-lived, lifelong outdoorsman was every bit as fit healthy and strong looking as James appears in this image. If any family resemblance is true, then it waits to be confirmed by the discovery of a photographic likeness of Archibald Young.

Montrose - Scotland in Microcosm

Montrose, like Scotland as a whole, sits in the middle of the ebb and flow of good fortune. It is subject to the natural cycles of life and the consequences of economic change. It is a place where town, country, coast and culture meet in a happy confluence of geography and opportunity. Sometimes those opportunities are seized to great effect, whilst others seem to slip through the fingers like the brackish waters of Montrose Basin on the outgoing tide.

Once upon a time, linen was king in Montrose with several large works stretched out along the length of the backstreets running parallel behind the High Street. Brewing, shipbuilding, coopering, fresh produce and, later, food processing all contributed to mercantile history of the enterprising wee town. On many occasions, Montrose has threatened to grow from a town that consistently punched above its weight into a cruiser-class city, prosperous into perpetuity.

More recently, a service sector that grew from the explosive growth of the North Sea Oil brought supply boats into the harbour and helped to populate nearby Rossie Island industrial estate as a base for supporting industries. Often referred to simply as 'the base', it created high-value jobs on par with the town's top employer Glaxochem. The overspill from the oil bonanza that began in the 1970s trickled down to Montrose and brought with it good-for-business, disposable income, but it all evaporated with an economic downturn that began in 2008, and shows no sign of receding at the present time.

The town is, quite rightly, popular as a minor resort and long may it remain small and beautiful. It is Scotland in microcosm, and a place of simple pleasures where time passes slowly. In winter, spring and autumn, Oystercatchers prise open mussels nestling in the shipwrecked bladderwrack. Sawbilled mergansers, duck and dip for sprats beneath the rail bridge. Fat Eiders doze on the foreshore while redshanked waders probe for annelids in the rich, tidal mud. In summer, kids and dogs are at summer games on the beach, and local events pepper the calendar all year round.

Visitor attractions at Montrose are relatively few, but they are proportionately to scale, like the Air Museum, which is full of informative charm and thought-provoking narratives. It has a replica Spitfire, a couple of training aircraft, dozens of models and a couple of immersive dioramas. Perhaps more importantly, it devotes considerable space to the sobering story of Polish pilots who flew from Montrose during the Second World War. It's an important chapter that is also a timely reproach to those who have actively promoted an especially nasty and sneering brand of toxic xenophobia in contemporary Britain.

The town museum that overlooks the Mid-Links is an excellent example of civic iconography, constructed simply and elegantly, like a small temple to aspirational learning, according to the modest means of the town fathers. It is neither imposing nor underwhelming. It knows its place and it's just the right size in relation to the almost-but-not-quite-affordable cottages, villas and townhouses that surround it.

Inside, it is comfortingly familiar; a time capsule containing the tale of the town and its surroundings. What made Montrose, what it became, and the DNA of its character is preserved her in gouged-out canoes, Neolithic maps that light up and a specimen-stuffed natural history room that mirrors the living world just a little way beyond its large, light-box windows.

Farther along from there, the tennis courts and bowling green, familiar features from Buckland's time, are still there; and, peeping through a series of tree-lined, rose-gardened lawns, a Congregational Church stands at the opposite end of the broad avenue.

My own daughter was baptized in this church by Canon Idris Jones, who later went on to become Primate of the Episcopalian Church of Scotland, and has since retired. Idris remains a forward-thinking, Welsh churchman who was extremely socially aware and he remains active in a pastoral capacity in Southampton having found retirement, *"much more unsettling than I'd imagined"*.

Montrose is also one of the few places where something resembling night life bears more than a passing similarity to authentic socializing in the early 21st Century. There is a long-established folk club, a circuit for bands playing hard-boiled, seventies pub-rock and the town has hosted, rather extravagantly, a gigantic outdoor music festival. Mofest ran from 2008 to 2017, but late cancellations in 2018 in 2019 have made the event's long-term future less certain.

Nevertheless, its promoters brought the likes of the Beach Boys, Madness and Bryan Adams to the beach links where thousands party'd like it was 1969, 1989 and 1999, respectively. If Mofest truly is no more and destined to be a future feature in the local museum, then there is always the Highland Games. It's one of the few gatherings that takes place by the sea, and the beachfront location makes for an almost-the-end-of-summer experience that embeds itself in the memory like a mussel in its shell.

In addition to piping competitions, tossed cabers and a red rosette for the best-groomed Clydesdale horse, there is any amount of gleeful Highland dancing and mercifully short and indistinct speeches from the organiser's stage. There is also another colourful example of a re-established tradition made modern in the crowning of the Rose Queen.

This particular royal flower has been chosen by the youngsters at Montrose Academy every year for more than fifty years, and she is accompanied at the heart of the pre-Games parade by her beaded, embroidered and pink-petaled Rose Maids. A very large pipe band is also in attendance to lead her down to the Links where she is duly crowned in the kind of enduring ceremony that defies cynical makeover. In another tiny wrinkle in the time-space continuum, music trivia fans will be fascinated to learn that the Rose Queen made her debut in August 1968; the same month that those (much younger) Beach Boys were bothering the UK singles chart with *Do It Again*.

I am sure that Buckland, born too soon for rock 'n' roll, found every nook and corner of Montrose interesting purely on its own merits. He'd be pleased to see the Academy, the churches, the museum and the gardens exactly where he found them in 1877.

The rail bridge across the estuary would be a welcome change, for its absence in his time necessitated the circuitous approach via Dubton. Similarly, the natural history of the basin can be enjoyed in relative comfort at the nearby Scottish Wildlife Trust's Visitor Centre. There is always something to see all year round, and examined more closely from one of several hides placed around this highly accessible tidal lagoon.

In the crisp and colder months of autumn and winter, the Montrose basin becomes internationally significant for the influx of migrating wildfowl. It is worth placing a bookmark in your diary for mid-September when migrating pink-footed geese arrive from the north in their tens of thousands to gather at Montrose.

They aggregate on the basin before they disperse to roost at feeding sites up and down the eastern seaboard. The geese are readily seen at various locations up and down the coast moving back and forth from daytime feeding sites inland to their nightly sandbank roosts. From Forth country in the south, up to Aberdeenshire in the North, their presence is one of the great unchanging, natural spectacles of Scotland, and a conspicuous feature of the winter landscape.

Big changes come slowly, and in manageable quantities to places like Montrose. Much more of its persona has endured rather than has been erased by unscrupulous and thoughtless developers. This is perhaps because those areas of the town, made redundant and flattened to make way for new housing stock, lie out of sight and out of mind. They sprawl incognito behind Murray Street, which leads through traffic out of town on the A92 trunk road.

These post-industrial developments began in the late 1950s and their footprint is large. These are the former sites of factories, workshops, sheds and yards, ancillary to a harbour trade that brought raw, bulk materials like flax for the long-extinct linen business. The linen works are not much missed and the focus today is on the optimistic re-invention of the 1980s swimming pool as a cinema complex.

At the opposite end of the High Street, the former Queens Temperance Hotel is today a mute witness to our contrary, if not eccentric relationship with civic character and heritage. We receive our sense of place not least from our surroundings, yet we so often treat them with contempt.

We like to delude ourselves with meaningless epigrams such as *'the more things change, the more they stay the same'.* The truth is that far-reaching change is irrevocable, and that must be a worry for Scotland where heritage and history are linked umbilically to economic wellbeing.

We will never get Buckland's time back, but we can still glimpse it in the architecture of the 'B'-listed 'Queens Close Group', which includes the original hotel and eating house. It was, for a time, a hostel for homeless men, and the upper floors are now crudely converted flats. On the ground floor, there are shop units with businesses that have been there for decades, providing another small piece of civic continuity. One of those fixtures is none other than the *New Hong Kong Chinese Takeaway*, an affordable eating house with an extensive menu and good food at very reasonable prices.

Aberdeen

Imperial Hotel, Monday, 27th August 1877

"Torry (is) a fishing town on the right bank of the Dee, opposite Aberdeen. It has a post office, with a money order department...a battery with fortification and barracks, a pier, a Free Church, and a public school with about 115 scholars. Pop. 1281." – **Rev. John Wilson in 'The Gazetteer of Scotland 1882'.**

Aberdeen has been called many things in its time and won fame in many areas of innovation, education and enterprise. To many, it's the shining Silver City, but to others it's a place of grim, grey granite. More significantly, it's been the Houston of the North and the oil capital of Europe. Speaking personally, it's my hometown and it will always be a special place for me, even though I have not lived there for many, many years.

The city for a long time had a great sense of community and couthy fellowship. Roughhouse harbour life nudged cozily (and boozily) alongside liberal academia and the 'small-c' conservatism of a minority middle class. It's a big city that has long been out of short trousers, but it lost some of the sweeter side of its nature relatively recently.

The twentieth century, for those who lived through a great deal of it, was largely preoccupied with the destruction of old orders. Everything, from civic architecture to the redrawing of land borders and the appropriation of outer space, was informed by an appetite for change and a craving for modernity.

Those chaotic years now sprawl behind us like the scattered debris from an explosive experiment in self-harm. It's true that progress and change deliver benefits, but nature tells us (and keeps telling us) that there can be no benefits without cost. Aberdeen is a case in point, but it has preserved most of its good looks and warm personality relatively intact.

Cities like Aberdeen, once a great fishing port and then a major centre for oil exploration know only too well what it means to prosper from the rich rewards of economic opportunism. It means living with the constant, nagging worry that one day, some day, it will all come to an end. It's worth asking here what Aberdeen *did* before the fish poured onto the harbour quayside and oil money began to flow into the town.

In Frank Buckland's time, the fishing from Aberdeen was growing in importance and making a significant contribution towards economic growth and diversification. But nineteenth-century Aberdeen was no humble village. It is too easy to forget that substantial industries such as textile production, papermaking and shipbuilding had long underpinned the city's progressive and continuous development. Those industries have since been massively downsized or consigned to history, but they had staying power that the average tech start-up can only dream of.

The last vessel built in Aberdeen was the mailship RMS St. Helena, which was launched in 1989 and enjoyed active service as a mailboat until her retirement from duty in 2018. Nevertheless, the ship, re-named MV St. Helena still works for a living carrying paying passengers and cargo in the Southern Atlantic between St. Helena, Ascension Island and Cape Town. Small scale papermaking continues in Aberdeen, and textile production persisted until 2004.

Aberdeen was also a specialist manufacturing centre for the production of hosiery garments that we might more usefully describe as stockings. In 1877, not everyone could afford stockings, socks and shoes, but that didn't mean they were happy about it. Hosiery manufacture in Aberdeen, first established in the late 1700s, grew, and continued to grow alongside personal income. What was once out of reach for a disturbingly large number of poor bairns soon became an integral part of the most basic wardrobe.

People of a certain age may yet remember the hosiery department as a stand-alone feature within large, city centre stores, usually sandwiched between ladies lingerie and bed linen. It was there that you could discover the nuances of seamed denier, the luxury of silk and the sheer homeliness of the 'wool and cotton mix'. Kilt socks, football socks, climbing socks, knee socks, tights, stockings, slip-ons and slipper socks still make for lucrative lines of essential clothing, but they're not made in Aberdeen anymore.

Another industry that is long ceased in Aberdeen is quarrying, but it gave the city its most defining characteristic and a lasting civic identity. The stone, sourced from Rubislaw to the west of town, was silver-grey granite, rich in glittering, reflective mica that changed the face of Aberdeen. It is a face that it wears today and one that Buckland, Walpole and Young would find as instantly recognizable as the Craigleith sandstone mansions of Edinburgh's Royal Circus, or the Portland Stone façade of the British Museum.

When they arrived in Aberdeen, Buckland and his colleagues needed only to leave the railway station, stroll across nearby Guild Street, and meander behind the Tivoli Theatre to find their lodgings. They stayed at the Imperial Hotel, a large building at the apex of a generously proportioned triangle marked out by Stirling Street, Trinity Street and Carmelite Lane. You can walk in their footsteps today if you like, and you will see the place much the same as they saw it. It is now called the Carmelite Hotel, and it is still quite upmarket, but arguably less exclusive than the Imperial in Buckland's time.

The Imperial was less than ten years old at the time of commissioner's stay and it probably struck them as something of an architectural anomaly. It follows the triangular footprint of its setting and its three, sharply angled corners, although rounded off, are burdened with lumpy detail and edgy crenellations. The peculiar mix of scotch baronial and classical lines, laced with lashings of gothic affections might well have offended innate conservatives like Buckland, Walpole and Young. I suspect, however, that the prospect of a 'bon-accord' welcome and a right good dinner would have been enough to allay any lingering doubts or fears about their accommodation.

Aberdeen in 1877 was a fine-looking city and Buckland may well have seen it at its Victorian best. It can still look clean and pristine on a bright, early Sunday morning before the boorish, animal traffic stirs awake. The silver city positively gleams in the low light of late summer, anticipating perhaps the bright, but contrasting coolness of soon-to-come September. Fine mornings make for uplifting feelings in the heart. All is well in the world as long as there is light in the North.

The Post Office directory for that particular year isn't crammed with advertisements as it is in the Edinburgh or Glasgow editions, but the listings provide evidence of substantial commercial and retail activity in Aberdeen.

Victorian philanthropy and condescending largesse are also conspicuous with the inclusion of comprehensive entries for dozens of churches and their associated good works in the city. There is a society or charity for virtually every destitute or morally compromised element in the community. It's a pity that the compassion did not extend to a dignified description of the recipients perceived defects.

The Institution for Deaf and Dumb at 13 Belmont Street no doubt meant well, but the employment of a Superintendent and a Matron in the form of Mr. and Mrs. Franklin Bill is quintessentially Dickensian. Elsewhere, we find the *Aberdeen Female Orphan Asylum* in Albyn Place, an *Industrial Asylum and Reformatory for Girls in Mount Street*, and a *House of the Aged and Infirm of Both Sexes* at Nazareth House.

It is hard to tell whether a stern-faced or deeply compassionate kind of charity prevailed, but Aberdeen was nothing if not schooled in religion. The directory nevertheless illustrates, rather pointedly, the deep and serious schism in the Church of Scotland at the time. I've already pointed out in the previous chapter that it might be fun to poke fun at the prescriptive, medieval philosophies of 'wee frees', but the Presbyterian-minded Free Church of Scotland enjoyed serious momentum.

In Aberdeen, Scotland's third-largest city, the 'wee free' places of deeply devout worship outnumbered those of the established church by two to one. If you add in Catholics, Episcopalians, Baptists and Adventists along with various sundry sects, then you have a city steeped in holiness and pious virtue.

Buckland, taking his post-dinner constitutional needed only to walk around the block to get the flavour of Aberdeen, a city on the up, not least because of its established proximity to Balmoral and Royal Deeside. A stroll along Guild Street would take him past Bannerman's *Steam and Household Coal* at 2 Trinity Quay overlooking a harbour rammed with fishing boats. A left turn into Market Street, the prime location for eating houses, leads up and on to bustling Union Street; a central boulevard of world-renown, famous not so much for its impressive width and extent, but for the biting, winter gales that blast along its length like a polar twister trapped in a wind tunnel.

The directory throws up some interesting localizations that denote the idiosyncrasies of life in the Silver City. We're clearly not in Edinburgh anymore. Advertisements for Roe and Red Deer Hides catch the eye, as does the name George Jamieson, the jeweller by appointment in the northern region of Empire. His premises were situated in a prime location at 107 Union Street, conveniently located for a monarch in need of priceless trinkets for the servants at Christmas.

Services that were more specific to the locale were the granite polishing services offered by Alex Petrie in Constitution Street and the brass foundry operated by John Blaikie and Sons, again on Union Street, who supplied 'gas meters and fittings of every kind.' Blaikie was also a 'Royal Appointee', but evidently just an 'ordinary' one.

Buckland's quick circuit would take him westwards along Union Street where he might, with care, cross the road and visit St. Nicholas Churchyard. Further on, he'd certainly pause on the Union Bridge that spanned the Den Burn and look down upon the remains of a stream through a small, wooded valley. The place had been used historically as bleaching green, and subsequently as a recreational area for the swell occupants of Union Terrace. Two years after his visit, the Union Terrace Gardens opened as formal public space and it remains so to this day.

Crossing back over Union Street would lead him intuitively into Bridge Street, which squares the circle by descending into Guild Street. Any Sunday morning, quite early, you can walk this route, and turning a blind eye to the banalities of modernity, see the city much as he did. You may not be as reassured by the strong establishment ties as he surely was, but you will begin to see the sheer audacity in the Victorian upscaling of the provincial landscape.

I wonder too if he was impressed by the marked formality of the advertising spiel in Aberdeen. Victorian retailers elsewhere were positively funky in their use of the Queen's 'own brand' of English compared to the 'Austen-esque' elaborations of vendors in Aberdeen.

One I especially like is by Archibald McKenzie who *"begs to intimate that he has now commenced business on his own account....and respectfully solicits the public support, which it will be his endeavour to merit by strict attention to Business, and the supplying such quality of Coals as will give satisfaction to Consumers."*

Bannerman's former manager was apparently striking out on his own, and understood very well the need to establish his credentials.

At the opposite end of the Victorian marketing and communications scale we find this perfunctory and strangely insensitive entry from Alex Innes and Sons, a funeral undertaker at 4 & 6 Barnett's Close, whose premises, not at all encouragingly, included his 'House Above (the) Shop'. Profit margins must have been so tight that Alex couldn't afford superfluous grammar. His advertisement makes for blunt reading, *'Adult Coffins in Cloth....20 shillings and upwards....Juveniles from 3 shillings and upwards'*. That's all he wrote, but it speaks volumes about attitudes, of some at least, to death a commonplace thing.

You have to wonder if Buckland, an aficionado of idle pursuits, was tempted up the opposite end of Union Street by the recreation grounds at Queens Cross, where skating, lawn tennis and 'American Bowling' were on offer for a shilling a head.

Perhaps, that is a digression too far for us all. We are here to evaluate serious work, and the ergonomy of the inspectors' itinerary at Aberdeen starts to hint at considerable forward planning and administration necessary to accommodate the three principals in their labours.

The Aberdeen Evidences

The herring report evidences from Aberdeen are disappointing for their lack of serious engagement with the questions to which the inspectors sought serious answers. Even Buckland, a credulous soul at the best of times, must have been dismayed by some of the obdurate, contrarian and entrenched views laid before him.

The opening statement by fisheries officer William Cowper spoke bewilderingly, and almost exclusively, about the failure of the fishing in Moray and Beauly Firth ten years previously. His only other contribution was to state the obvious by explaining that the boats, plainly visible in Aberdeen Harbour, were larger, completely decked, and sturdily built in order to fish for herring beyond inshore waters.

The inspectors had leading questions about mesh sizes, harbour provisions, correct identification of species in the juvenile condition and information about herring spawning grounds. Mostly what they heard at Aberdeen were prejudices, received wisdoms and strange interpretations of known natural phenomena. James Scott's testimony seems a little more clearly thought through, and it's intriguing less for its content than the way it is recorded.

Scott was a fisherman of twenty years standing and he hailed from Lossiemouth. He talks sensibly enough, but his evidence looks like two distinct sets of notes conjoined to make one account. I'm going to stick my neck out here, and say that I think that most of it, like the arpeggio passage below, was written by Buckland, perhaps supplemented with numbers from Walpole.

'The herrings have fallen off in number. They have fallen off, on the whole, in every place by one fourth since he began. Thinks this is due to catching all the young fish. Has seen them from the size of a pinhead upwards. The young fish are generally caught in the autumn. Has seen roes and milts in them when they were only three inches long. The young fish are used for bait and also sold as food. Does not think them good enough for food.'

In the foregoing extract that I attribute to Buckland, he jumps around from one topic to another in consecutive sentences like a butterfly floating from one interesting flower to another, very much in the manner of his own 'notes and jottings'.

Here's another sample, *"(he) fishes from half a mile to seventy miles out to sea. Would allow no net to leave the factory without a statutory mesh. Thinks that Dutch and French nets are no narrower than thirty-three (meshes) to the yard. Plenty of herrings fall out of the nets which are now used."*

The words in parentheses are ones omitted by the writer and, while it's all relational, it's hardly easy reading. Similarly, Some of Scott's quotes are barely comprehensible. Quite what *"a garvie is to herring what a man is to a boy"* might mean escapes me.

Compare that to the inserted passage that picks up the narrative with *"There is a falling off of one fourth in the fishery. Each boat now gets more fish than it did twenty years ago. This is entirely due to the increase of the nets and the improvement of the boats. Twenty years ago each boat carried twenty-four nets, made of hemp, each net forty yards long, with 28 or 29 rows to the yard, and 10 to 12 score deep, and weighing 25 pounds. Each boat now carries 45 to 60 nets, made of cotton with 35 rows to the yard and 18 to 20 score deep, weighing from 12 to 14 pounds. The substitution of cotton for hemp has enabled the fishermen to double the netting without increasing the weight"*

One hand is inconsistent and erratic, while the other is much more formal, numerate, sequential and direct. Both inspectors, though, understood that they actually had something they could work with, and sought to translate the vernacular and give it meaning and relevance. If nothing else, it would be an interesting enough diversion from the hypothetical.

Alexander Slater, a fisherman from Hopeman in the Moray Firth, contributed his understanding of predator/prey relationships in terms that muddled first-hand observations with folklorish interpretation. He speculated that (for some unspecified reason) there was *"a failure of dog-fish in the North Sea"* and (as a consequence) the herring were not *"driven to the shore by their natural enemies."* This was his explanation for the 'falling off' of the herring fishery in Moray over the previous ten years, which he codified with the inexplicable, *"The amount of herrings that men catch is nothing to do with the failure (of the fishery). There are as many fish in the North Sea as ever, but they want power (i.e. dog-fish) to drive them into land."*

Buckland, Walpole and Young must have been ready to throw themselves into the North Sea following the quarrelsome testimony of David Murray, a dislikeable and confrontational representative of Sharp and Murray, fish curers and net manufacturers of Cellardyke.

Unsurprisingly, he advocated larger net sizes, saw no problem with trawling up *'hundredweights of herring spawn'*, and then discarding it. He considered the garvie fisheries to be irrelevant and thought that *'nothing whatsoever is necessary'* to manage the herring fisheries, and that trade should be *'left free'.* He then went on to stick the boot into the Town Council for favouring golfers and threatening to deprive fishermen of access to drying grounds on the links. The Harbour Commissioners *"give herring fishermen insufficient accommodation for landing",* he complained bitterly.

Murray appears to be one of those people, recognizable today, as one who cannot see further than the end of their own nose, one that is, in any case, firmly lodged in the trough. It was left to Henry Best (R.N.) to slap him down by pointing out that the fishermen were to be prohibited from using a portion of the links, which was, in any case, *"given to the public for the purposes of recreation and not for the purposes of trade."*

A more useful, merchant's eye-view was offered by Theodore Jahns, an agent from Hamburg and Stettins who obtained herrings primarily from Norway and Great Britain for sale into the Russian and German markets. His words should have been music to everyone's ears when he said, *"Lewis Herrings are considered the best, and pay the best".*

It's possible that this sentence would be enough to quash any reservations and misinformation about the herring fishery in the Minch. A cynical person might conjecture that complaints about early season fishing around the Isles amounted to little more than professional jealousy. It got better too when he declared, *"The Norwegian fat herrings are not well cured and do not carry so well"* and *"the Scotch herring is better than the Flemish".*

Jahns comes across as a well-travelled European with an encyclopaedic grasp of his industry, offering insights into the distribution of herring *"as far as the Turkish frontier"*, pithy remarks about quality control *"the (crown) brand ought to be more discreetly given"*, and describing the use of draft nets by the Norwegian fishery that can *"keep fish alive for days"*. Even his anecdotal evidences are compelling when he describes the super-abundance and subsequent desertion of herring along the coast between Stavanger and Bergen, adding archly perhaps, that *"this is a great (i.e., considerable) length of coast"*.

Buckland, Walpole and Young didn't tarry in Aberdeen. Its name may still be synonymous with a fishing industry of old, but in 1877 it merited only six pages of coverage in the 1878 Herring Report. The great fishing years would come with the introduction of steam trawlers in the following decades and the post-1918 diesel vessels of the new century.

The next port of call for Buckland Walpole and Young was Peterhead, a much smaller place that generated ten pages of densely packed, fact-led evidences, indicative perhaps of the shifting fortunes of fishing communities up and down the eastern seaboard. We will join them there in the next chapter.

Aberdeen Again

One hundred years after Buckland's visit, fortune favoured Aberdeen in a wholly, totally different manner. Oil was discovered in the North Sea and Aberdeen, as the nearest principal port, became the petroleum capital of Europe, pretty much overnight. The history of oil extraction in the region is well documented elsewhere, but probably most comprehensively in Aberdeen's Maritime Museum. In fact, the museum's emphasis is skewed more towards the more recent past than the preceding centuries, and you leave it with a sense of disconnection.

Perhaps, there's something about being 'stuck on an oil platform' in the middle of the North Sea that is a fundamentally different experience from 'going to sea' in a fishing boat. Such musings may be completely idle, given the finite nature of fossil fuels. It isn't really a matter of debate whether 'the oil' is running out or not, so much as how long Scotland will remain in denial about it. New discoveries further afield may extend its lifespan a little, but Houston will decide when to pull the plug, and it will be done with little ceremony and few parting gifts.

Aberdeen has left it late, but not too late, to start planning a new life without oil. The divorce papers were served with the redundancy notices, and enough time has elapsed to start thinking creatively. The city was and will always be a place of enterprise for enterprising people. The universities and colleges are perhaps even more reliable and durable engine rooms for innovation and invention. They understand how to build relationships with industry and share expertise across related sectors. Robert Gordon's, once a mere institute of technology, is now one of the big go-to hubs for engineering research.

King's College in Old Aberdeen was established in 1495, but merged in 1860 with Marischal College to become the Aberdeen University we know today. It is a large university with umbilical links to Forresterhill teaching hospital and the Rowett Institute for Animal Health and Nutrition. Aside from that, its prospectus is broad and its standards are high, making it one of the top educational institutions in the country.

My point is that 'where there's brains, there's brass'. It is the mantra of a twenty-first century that seeks to take the sum of human knowledge to the next level. The perceived reward is the usual crazy dream of world domination in one field or another, whether it is in robotics or patents for life eternal. It is to be hoped that investors will remember a little thing called ethics, and that researchers in Aberdeen continue to promote the appliance of science for the benefit of all.

All that notwithstanding, Aberdeen's economy could still stand a little more diversification. It's been tone deaf to the cultural klaxons sounding off in Edinburgh, Glasgow, Perth and, more recently, the Cinderella city of Dundee. It was a message received loud and clear, however, when Aberdeen failed to make the cut in its bid for City of Culture 2017. The ballot left derided Dundee waving the saltire for Scotland, before suffering defeat with dignity at the hands of equally deserving Hull.

The result gave Aberdeen, which had perhaps confused wealth with worth, a cultural wake-up call to which it responded immediately. The tired, neglected and under-used Music Hall has recently undergone a seven million pound 'transformation', as distinct from a mere makeover. It is now restored as the flagship venue of Aberdeen Performing Arts (APA), which had been upgraded from a glorified booking office to a hands-on, not-for-profit management group in 2004. APA also operates His Majesty's Theatre, refurbished with a glitzy frontage in 1999, and the funky but fine Lemon Tree venue on the disorientatingly monikered West North Street.

One conspicuous response has come from Aberdeen's Art Gallery and Museums Department, which has assumed a more pro-active role than it has enjoyed in the past. It manages several sites comprising the Art Gallery, the small, but perfectly formed Cowdray Hall, Provost Skene's historic residence, the Treasure Hub, The Tolbooth Museum and the Maritime Museum. Venues like these don't thrive on neglect, and there is a growing awareness of the need to make them fit for purpose of attracting and growing audiences.

The main focus is on the Art Gallery and the Cowdray Hall involving another transformation, this time to the tune of thirty million pounds. It is encouraging to note, if that's not a pun too far, that music is mentioned in the same breath in the promotional blurb for this project. It suggests that Aberdeen, after four decades of chicken-in-a-basket mediocrity, has finally woken up to the twenty-first-century version of modernity.

Culture, art, music, engagement and public participation (if not immersion) are must-haves in the contemporary metropolis, otherwise you're not even at the races when it comes to outbidding your rivals for public attention.

Yet, the little jewel near Crown Street is the restored Victorian theatre that sits on Guild Street, barely a minute's walk from the Imperial Hotel. Frank Buckland, Spencer Walpole and Archibald Young might easily have stopped for a moment as they passed by, perhaps to read the playbill or tut-tut at the down-market innuendo twice brightly and three times at the weekend.

The Tivoli is now a Grade A listed building, but it began its long life in 1872 as Her Majesty's Opera House. Improvements and redevelopments were carried out in 1897 and 1909, and in 1910 it was re-christened the Tivoli of Varieties. In addition to the Aberdeen Scout Gang Show of 1961, which I attended with my granny from Torry, the theatre has previously hosted some of the world's best-known performers, including Charlie Chaplin, Stan Laurel and W.C Fields.

The building continued to entertain theatregoers until 1966, when the main auditorium became a bingo hall. In 1997, the Tivoli closed its doors, seemingly for good, and a famous Aberdeen landmark was allowed to fall into complete and utter disrepair.

In 2009, the Tivoli Theatre Company bought the site and embarked on a programme of restoration, regeneration and re-invention. I suspect the place exceeds its former glory, for I can't imagine modern punters tolerating a gale force, upper circle draught in quite the same way as their predecessors.

The programming mix on offer today is just that – mixed -but probably no more incongruously so than at any other time in its history. It's often said that the days of variety theatre are long dead, but maybe it's in the nature of variety to transform itself in ways that are not necessarily comprehensible to those who knew and loved it in another guise.

The Tivoli, of course, puts on the usual plethora of tribute acts, some more convincing than others, which are interspersed with television faces, pantomime dames, up-and-coming singers, evergreen crooners, smart-mouthed comedians, and franchise shows such as High School Musical. Like I said, it's variety; there's something for everyone.

Who knows, perhaps Aberdeen will learn again how to live life to the full like they did when there was a cinema on every corner, when the Beach Ballroom bounced to the sound of Dankworth's bopping jazz orchestra, or even when the Tivoli Theatre rang to the sound of full-on, diva-driven opera.

I began this chapter with a quote about the humble parish of Torry from The Gazetteer of Scotland edited by Reverend John Marius Wilson. It's essentially a dictionary of 'everywhere in Scotland' emulated and updated by Robin Smith in his wonderful compendium *The Making of Scotland: A Comprehensive Guide To The Growth Of Its Cities, Towns and Villages* (2001).

It's a place that I know very well from my childhood and young adulthood, and for many years, it was a home from home for me.

I often spent much of the summer holidays with my grandparents at Balnagask, which is a mixed bag of two up, two down maisonettes, pensioner's houses and, where the land levels out behind Nigg Bay, blocks of uninviting flats. It's a housing estate that doesn't feel like one, probably because the streets undulate rather than spread, and there is a constant sense of the sea nearby.

A maze of footpaths ran like rat-runs behind the low-rise flats opposite Pop and Mary's very modest terraced house, but they were a short cut to the tennis courts on Victoria Road all of five minute's walking distance away. A little further up, on the same side of the road there stood a building that always fascinated me.

The Torry Marine Laboratory was, for locals like my relatives and Torry pals, *"the place where they keep a' the fish"*, and even though I later came to know someone who worked there, I never got the chance to take a look inside.

It's 1968 again. I am twelve years old and the 'Marine Lab' is utterly mysterious to a young person weaned on sci-fi Saturday morning movies and Quatermass conspiracy theories. Inside, there is a security guard, a reception desk and corridors leading into disinfected stairwells and watery rooms where men and women study sleep in fishes. I always wondered if they studied sharks in there, swimming around in large tanks, glaring open-eyed with mouths half-open, exposing their bloodstained teeth.

The reality is well documented. An embryonic Torry Marine Research Station was built at the Bay of Nigg in 1899 and it couldn't have been closer to the north-east fishery if it had been placed in the sea. The lab eventually outgrew itself and relocated to Wood Street in Torry. The subsequent South Block was added in 1954 and presented a new front door facing onto Victoria Road. Back then it was already a very large site with a library block, a conference room and laboratories.

It was, for a time, prosaically rebranded as The Fisheries Research Services (FRS) Marine Laboratory, but was always simply the 'Marine Lab' to me, even though it progressively became a much-expanded, highly sophisticated facility. The original Torry lab building is no more, replaced by a new complex on the same site with a stylish atrium entrance. It is a contemporary look much favoured by the modern, forward-looking agency, tech startups, and religious organisations who want churches that don't look like churches.

This Marine Laboratory, now under the auspices of the government directorate Marine Scotland, undertakes three-pronged research in the fields of Aquaculture, the Aquatic Environment and Fisheries Management. Much of this work is carried out at sea from the research vessels *FRV Scotia* and *FRV Clupea*.

The building houses research aquaria, engineering facilities, a fish house, and a 'taste panel' department. It's all about fish but nothing 'fishy' goes on there. The staff aren't mega-minds breeding mega-sized sharks at all. They are, in fact, merely scientists doing science, most of it of necessity and for our direct benefit.

The purpose of the taste panels concentrates the mind acutely, for they are concerned with the detection of contaminants in the food chain. It is an indictment of the cumulative disregard for the environment that we now rely on science to tell us whether the fish in the sea still tastes like fish and not something more sinister.

There is something strangely circular and satisfying about a passage of writing that begins with a personal experience and ends with an affirmation of Buckland's vision. It is pleasing to think that Buckland, on a visit to the Marine Laboratory today, would be vindicated in his belief that fisheries science is important and that environmental pollution represents an existential threat.

The Torry connection somehow completes a personal circle too. In 1975, I was taken on as a keeper at The Aberdeen Zoo in Hazelhead Park, in an age when such things were still advertised in the local Job Centre. I immediately found that friends and relatives, including Pop and Mary Clark, weren't as impressed with me as I was with myself. *"It'll probably do until you get a proper job",* they said bemusedly.

These are words I imagine Buckland heard more than once in his lifetime. It perhaps goes some way towards explaining why the thoughts and writings of nineteenth-century natural historian have been such a source of encouragement to me.

Peterhead

North Eastern Hotel, Tuesday, 28th August 1877

"When at Peterhead on the crab and lobster enquiry, my friend Captain David Gray, of the whaling ship 'Eclipse', informed me that every year in the months of July and August, when the herrings appear off Peterhead they are invariably followed by large Finner whales....I understand that these whales generally worry the herrings, not by rushing into the shoal, but by swimming around the edge and driving them together, just as a colley dog folds sheep." – **Frank Buckland in Notes and Jottings.**

Peterhead is a town on the northeast coast of Scotland whose name has been synonymous with fishing ever since a harbour was first established there in 1593 by George Keith, the Earl Marischal. It has also earned fame, in its time, for distilling whisky and manufacturing linen. 'The Blue Toon' has similarly enjoyed an element of infamy for its prison and dubious renown as Britain's 'top whaling port'.

Today, it is home to the largest fishmarket in Europe, landing over 3,000 tonnes of fish each day. The population there has never risen much above 20,000 souls, yet it wields power and influence disproportionate to its size.

This is principally because the Admiralty decided in 1884 to enclose Peterhead Bay as a National Harbour of Refuge there. It is a place of safety protected by a 900-metre breakwater, which was constructed by convict labour in two phases between 1892 and 1956. The structure has, since then, shaped Peterhead's fortunes and ameliorated the negative effects of industries made redundant, and the butchering of railway communication at the hands of Beeching.

In the course of Buckland's short lifetime, Peterhead was a diversified fishing town, whaling town and whiskytown; and it was inordinately productive in all those spheres of work. Herring and white fish were landed in abundance and canned *in situ*. A success no doubt toasted regularly with a dram or two from the 400,000 litres of Glenugie Malt that was produced each year.

In 1821, the harbour would see a peak of sixteen domestic whaling boats leave to hunt down Greenland Right, Minke and Sperm Whales. By 1857, the Peterhead fleet of whalers and sealers exceeded thirty vessels, followed by a precipitous decline. The last whaler to work out of Peterhead was the steam and sail ship *Eclipse*, which was finally sold off in 1892, and later became a survey ship registered in the USSR.

Buckland had a strong connection to Peterhead through his association with David Gray, the owner of the *Eclipse*. He was one of Frank Buckland's many correspondents, and the two men had met previously to exchange information and views about the sustainability (or otherwise) of sealing in Arctic Europe. In 1876, they had proposed a close season for seal hunting to give stocks a chance to recover. Their proposals were accepted but proved impossible at the time to enforce.

It may seem an anomalous thing for us to celebrate, given contemporary attitudes towards the hunting and killing of sentient wild mammals in the wild. Buckland and others, however, sought to influence the way that natural resources were perceived by ignorant administrations and disinterested lawmakers.

Buckland and Gray were not promoting the idea of species conservation for its own sake, much less the preservation of biodiversity. They were interested in good management of a resource and fully understood the catastrophic consequences of gratuitous destruction. Species extinctions at the hands of surplus-killing humans was, after all, nothing new.

In America, the passenger pigeon, perhaps the most notorious victim of gratuitous slaughter in the nineteenth century was well on the way to extinction by the time Buckland arrived in Peterhead. Twenty years previously a spectacularly myopic Senate Select Committee had declared that such a 'wonderfully prolific' bird, could never be destroyed.

By 1880, the species was effectively extinct with a handful of records vying for status as 'the last of kind' persisting into the early years of the twentieth century. That honour went to a captive bird called Martha, the last known passenger pigeon, which expired at the Cincinnati Zoo in 1912.

The question of sustainability was at the front of Buckland's mind in the course of all his investigations, surveys, writings and reports. Nature *appeared* to be limitless in its bounty, yet humanity clearly had a voracious appetite for consuming its reserves, not always effectively, and all too often, gratuitously.

Sustainability is at the heart of the 1878 Herring Report, one of several important documents that are increasingly seen as pivotal to grasping the nettle of sustainable harvest. This is because it underscores the value of early warnings and the cost of ignoring them. The report also shows, early on, that harvesting other living things is informed by a matrix of complex issues. It is not, as many would still have it, a matter of mere cause and effect.

Frank Buckland is often characterized as an eccentric but tirelessly enthusiastic naturalist, whose passions and energies were sometimes misdirected. This does him an injustice for it underestimates his skill as an ambitious explainer who was able to move freely and communicate effectively with all levels of society. Nevertheless, the competing interests within the sea fisheries presented him with contradictions that were difficult to resolve satisfactorily.

Buckland, Walpole and Young could easily travel by rail from Aberdeen to Peterhead and they wasted no time getting there. The leg of their journey from here onwards is something of a whistle-stop affair. They covered a lot of ground, and there may not have been much time to stop and stare on the journey from Peterhead Railway Station to the North Eastern Hotel.

Advertised as a *"new and commodious establishment nearest to the railway station"*, the North Eastern's proprietor, one Alexander Mac Donald, went out of his way to *"confidently assure those who may honour him with their patronage that nothing shall be wanting on his part to render their stay agreeable."*

The North Eastern Hotel was centrally located in Chapel Street, very near the harbour, in an area that stands today as it did then, perhaps even improved as a semi-pedestrianized zone with restricted access for traffic.

But Mr. MacDonald was, quite frankly, fibbing about the station, which is now the site of Peterhead Leisure and Community centre. It's a good fifteen-minute walk to Chapel Street from there, although the inspectors, with petty cash in hand, could easily cover the cost of a shuttle cab. Passengers travelling on a budget, or the financially embarrassed, may well have been dismayed that the station lay so far out of town.

An extension from the main station was added in 1865 and it looped around the outskirts, terminating at the North Pier. It's not clear, though whether this add-on was built to accommodate passengers. It seems unlikely since the 1868 map shows no minor station on or near the harbourside, which was, in any case, thickly populated by fishcuring works.

Study of this particular map, with its trains, ships, factories and concomitant human resources, tells the story of a scaled-up approach to commercial fishing, designed to respond to exponential demand. It tells of the marriage between the private enterprise of fishers, fishcurers and shipbuilders on Peterhead's Seagate, and strategic support, albeit remote in London and Edinburgh, but still able to think creatively from time to time.

It's possible that those at the centre of fishing activity in Scotland during the late 1800s did not fully foresee the long-term effect of this synergy. The whalers, and then the railway companies, were among the first to experience the boom-and-bust consequences of hyper-expansion. Fishing was changing too, and the significance of an economically important species such as herring being used for bait, although reported in their findings, seems to have escaped our inspectors.

In many ways, line fishing for cod, ling and hake in 1877 may still have been viewed as a bit of a specialist branch of the fishing industry. Herring were caught near the surface, and so are easier to locate and capture with nets, much improved by the use of cotton.

Mid-zone and deep-sea species caught by the long line method of baited hooks strung out at intervals were more work for an uncertain return. But cod is a big, valuable, meaty fish. It's definitely worth pursuing if you know where to look and good bait is on hand to lure them onto your lines. The uptake of new technologies at the end of the nineteenth century was typically rapid, and the advantages of steam over sail were already obvious.

It's true that there were many reservations, if not hostility, surrounding the destructive nature of trawling; that much emerges from the pages of the inspectors' report. But this was an age that valued and encouraged innovation with the sole aim of putting it to use as quickly as possible. A new century and a new world were beckoning, and no one wanted to be left behind. Yet, few of the major players in the herring fleet feared the rise of the powered trawler half as much as we fear artificial intelligence today.

Fast reliable boats, lighter nets, improved communications and even refinements in preservation and refrigeration were all known quantities. Yet, there was no shallow gradient shift from one target species to another. In the space of just a few years, Aberdeen had switched its focus from herring to white fish and proceeded to annihilate those stocks until they inevitably crashed.

Peterhead similarly enjoyed relatively brief fame and won short-term benefits as a herring port, but fishing as an occupation often comes hard-wired. The herring fishers simply kept on after the silver darlings until fate and circumstances forced them into a jolting, far-reaching stop. In the end, it was black gold that rescued the entire north-east from obscurity and backwater provincialism.

The Peterhead Evidences

On the night of the 18th August 1848, disaster struck at Peterhead. A massive storm got up along the entire length of the east coast. Huge waves and driving rain, carried along on the shoulder of a hurricane force gale, placed the north-eastern herring fleet, up to 1,000 boats from Wick, Peterhead,

Fraserburgh, Aberdeen and Stonehaven, in immediate peril. There was nothing else to do but run for home.

In the ensuing scramble, many boats from Peterhead did not make safe harbour. Those that did still had to negotiate their entry through a barricade of wrecked boats, which partially blocked the entrance to the harbour. Hulls were gored to the gunnels by rocks lurking in the shallows and fifty-one lives were lost, many within sight of the quayside.

Twenty-one bodies alone were recovered from the Peterhead shoreline before nine a.m. the following morning in a *'scene of the most appalling description'*. In all, ninety-four men and boys from the coastal communities of Buchan, Moray and Caithness were lost.

Almost thirty years later, the enquiries of Buckland, Walpole and Young presented the harbour trustees with a long-awaited opportunity to press home to government the case for expanding deepening the harbour. The need had always been there, but they must have sensed there was a rare chance to get their message deep inside the corridors of power. They left nothing to chance. William Boyd spoke at length and his appeal for funds is recorded over six pages, but the words were not his alone.

Sir John Coode, perhaps the most renowned harbour builder and engineer of his day, had previously written a compassionate, comprehensive and compelling statement of support for their case. In his missive, he utilizes every conceivable argument in favour of extensive harbour works, pointing out every advantage from the pragmatic to the patriotic.

"The north-eastern portion of the coast of Scotland, from the Firth of Forth to the Cromarty Firth, a seaboard of 160 miles is of a bold and dangerous character. It is exposed to frequent easterly gales of great violence, but although much frequented by shipping and comprehends within its limits the most important stations for the prosecution of the fisheries in Scotland, it offers no place of safety to which vessels can run for refuge when overtaken by storms."

In fact, Peterhead had been earmarked in 1857 as a potential harbour of refuge by a parliamentary select committee. Coode, an internationally known luminary in his day, should have been pushing at an open door, especially when he pointed out that naval vessels in defence of the realm were just as vulnerable to the elements as fishing boats from Peterhead. Coode also flew a couple of attractive kites by dangling the prospect of increased tax revenues from a bigger, busier port, and an enlarged pool of potential recruits for Royal Naval Reserve. In the end, it smacks of exasperation, if not desperation, in its attempts to make the authorities see sense.

David Gray Jr., the second-generation whaling magnate of Buckland's acquaintance, felt that hard-headed business sense made an incontrovertible case for a bigger, deeper harbour stating flatly, *"an improvement of the harbours would double the Peterhead fishery"*. His evidence also suggests he was a man used to getting his own way, and willing to bend half-truths to fit his argument. In 1876, the herring catch had failed miserably. Gray blamed innate caution amongst the workforce and, by inference, foot-dragging by government

"In doubtful weather, the boats do not go to sea at all... the boats can only get in at half tide and the area is too small to shelter the boats that frequent the harbour."

Mishaps, with the potential for serious damage, often occurred, and Gray, as a ship owner, took a dim view of that too.

"This very morning the harbour was blocked up. The boats were coming in on top of one another. Harbour accommodation has not kept pace with the size and increase in the number of the boats."

John Brown, rather cynically backed these views with the somewhat semi-detached observation that *"deepening the harbour will increase the revenue of the trustees, as vessels will run for shelter"*. Run for your life, by all means, but don't forget your mooring fees, now will you lads?

The commissioners' report bends over backwards to be impartial, but the inspectors can't help what people say. Their job primarily was to record testimony and summarize their findings. It is close reading that reveals the subtext, which becomes more visible through the telescope of historical perspective.

When the commissioners visited Fraserburgh the following day, they dutifully jotted down that Alexander Bruce, a fish curer, was *"in favour of the Mutual Assurance Company for boats that has been started here."*

Flipping back one page of the report, we find fisherman John Noble's related contribution, recorded almost as if it were a throwaway remark. *"There is a Mutual Assurance Company for boats, but he is not insured himself."* In an age when ordinary householders are terrorized by the BBC over a mere television licence, we have to be boggle-eyed at the notion of going to sea uninsured.

In the end, it is more likely than not, that a combination of business imperatives and national interest that eventually commanded the involvement of the Admiralty, rather than the well-being of fishermen.

Larger, bulkier, decked boats represented a considerable investment on the part of those who owned them. It's not at all clear how widespread the uptake of insurance for boats, much less nets or men's lives, was at that time. It certainly wasn't compulsory and it may have been a margin-cutting expense too far for many.

The herring report is, because of its nature, repetitive. It records time and again the empirical and anecdotal, with little in the way of physical evidence or data from the witnesses. It is largely word of mouth, but it remains a valuable example of conflicting evidences that have little scientific basis beyond direct observation, reportage, and simple arithmetic provided by fisheries officers.

The conflict arises, not from a lack of consensus or accurate evidence gathering, but from an absence of established interviewing methodologies and the quantitative evaluation of results. These are modern ideas that apply equations to things like age, gender, experience, bias, prejudice and personal history. There was little need of that in the 1878 Herring Report. Mostly, it was all about the numbers.

In 1876, the 78,171 crans landed at Peterhead were around half the take from each of the previous six seasons (See **Table 2**). The cause for such failures elsewhere is variously described by several respondents, and often in quite contradictory ways.

Years	Boats	Crans
1867	477	107
1868	540	136
1869	590	120
1870	650	161
1871	630	171
1872	705	180
1873	776	215
1874	746	226
1875	740	190
1876	700	111.5
1877	712	73

Table 2. Number of Boats at Peterhead and Average Take Per Boat

The herring failed, because of the *'early fishing in the Minch'*. Alternatively, the herring failed because *'the foreigners (Dutch, Flemish and French fishers) are shooting their nets over the banks (at night) and leaving them there all day while they are curing the fish'*. Less convincingly, the herring failed because of the depredations of dog-fish. The herring failed because there were no dog-fish to *'drive them into the land'*.

In Peterhead, there was similar speculation about the failure of the inshore herring fishery in the Moray Firth, and general agreement about the fall-off in the increasingly pelagic herring fishery at Peterhead in 1876. It was consistently reported that the weather had been especially bad that season, a situation no doubt exacerbated by the lack of safe harbour facilities, limited access during half and low tides, and the relatively short, but intense, duration of the summer herring season.

It's worth looking forward here a little into the future to look at data from Peterhead that places the 1877 findings in their proper context. An exhaustive table, published in J. T. Findlay's 1933 *'History of Peterhead'*, showed that the fleet almost immediately went on to consistently land large catches totalling well in excess of 150,00 crans (*See* **Table 3**).

There are periodic declines in the comprehensive dataset (1840 - 1932) that could be construed as 'crashes', but the most alarming dips in productivity occur between 1914 and 1918, and the years of the Great Depression, particularly 1925. Those figures tell their own bleak story of a catastrophic war and economic misadventure, but so too do those that vindicate David Gray's earlier assertions.

In 1907, the catch peaked a whopping 291,173 crans from only 430 boats, twenty-three years after the Admiralty instigated work on the harbour, and fifteen years after the first phase of expansion was completed. The take was indeed doubled from the early 1870s, employing far fewer boats compared to the 700 or so that previously departed Peterhead to hunt the silver darlings.

Year	Boats	Crans	Av Crans per Boat	Barrels Exported
1907	420	291,713	695	315,017
1908	450	209,054	464	207,530
1909	470	201,685	429	200,922
1910	430	228,855	532	230,061
1911	420	191,463	456	194,067
1912	352	196,475	558	210,982
1913	430	221,545	515	240,924
1914	466	170,566	366	152,134
1915	-	-	-	27,124
1916	143	80,047	559	40,694
1917	109	47,550	436	-
1918	120	55,051	459	25,858
1919	227	148,464	654	95,533
1920	262	104,080	397	39,498
1921	137	55,314	404	82,120
1922	124	53,178	429	30,366
1923	197	94,613	480	72,034
1924	178	127,020	714	126,225
1925	145	48,504	335	29,581
1926	192	123,508	643	121,215
1927	226	148,941	659	159,239

Table 3. Statistics of the Herring and White Fishing Industries of Peterhead between 1907 and 1927 from J. T. Findlay's, 'History of Peterhead' (1933).

The herring fishery in Scotland grew organically from small beginnings into a lucrative commercial concern of national importance. It was at first, practiced locally from a daisy chain of fishing villages that lay between the larger ports. It was a sit and wait strategy, with inshore fishers on different coastlines watching out for the vast armies of herring to arrive off the coast.

Later, as their boats became bigger, the fishers on the east coast ventured much further out into the North Sea. Although they met with competition from others, notably the Dutch and Norwegian fisheries, there seemed always to be more and more fish waiting to be found.

This is the central plank of the inspectors' final summary, placed strangely, but handily for us, at the beginning of the report. They introduce an element of common sense thinking when they apply crude quantification to the self-evident natural predation of herring stocks. Here they are on page *xi* of the summary:

"2,400,000,000 herrings must be taken by the four nations, the British, The French, the Dutch and Norwegian..but prodigious though this capture is, there are grounds for believing that the destruction of herrings by man sinks into significance if compared with the total destruction effected by agencies over which man has no control whatsoever."

They seem to have been distracted by examples like this one,

"The destruction of herrings by gannets is also enormous. It is estimated that on Ailsa Craig alone there are 10,000 gannets. Assuming that each bird only takes six herrings a day, the herrings on Ailsa Craig alone must consume more than 60,000 herrings a day, 1,800,000 herrings a month, or 21,600,000 herrings a year. On the assumption that there are 50 gannets in the rest of Scotland for every one on Ailsa Craig, the Scotch gannets must consume more than 1,110,000,000 a year, or 37 percent more than all the Scotch fishermen catch in their nets."

Adding...

"Whales, porpoises, seals, coalfish, dog-fish are constantly feeding on them from the moment of their birth. The shoals of herrings in the ocean are always accompanied by flocks of herrings and other sea birds, which are constantly preying upon them....it seems no exaggeration to conclude that man does not destroy one herring for every fifty destroyed by other enemies...nothing that man has hitherto done....or is likely to do, has produced, or will produce, ant appreciable effect on the number of fish in the sea."

I include this in full because it bears all the hallmarks of Buckland's brand of Victorian sophistry that is part science, part pulpit, and part music hall. At its heart, it is an observation just as empirical as those of an uneducated fisherman, who claims he can tell the temperature of the sea just by looking at the colour of it.

Yet, Buckland's ready reckoning of the natural predation of herring by competitor species, which is actually second-hand, contains a solid grain of truth. It is sourced from direct observations that anyone can make. Other animals besides humans hunt for fish, and are probably better at it than we are.

There are so many other things that percolate through his narrative. There is the pervasive air of unchallengeable patrician authority, yet numbers are assumed and estimated with scant use of known facts or reliable scientific references. The authors of the report disregard the question of whether the herring populations are static in the sea around Ailsa Craig, or whether they constantly migrate and fluctuate in number. In fact, the original source for the numbers of gannets on Ailsa Craig and elsewhere in Scotland came from a Captain MacDonald of the fishery cruiser *Vigilant*, a man who appears nowhere in history as an ornithological authority.

It's all anecdotal, but it's effective as a piece of pseudo-scientific propaganda, and instantly recognisable as the hyperbolic, television narration of the last twenty years. This is a class of storytelling that is intent on gripping the audience at the expense of a tight hold of the facts. I find it admirable though for its suggestion that there is more than enough of nature's bounty for all to share among God's creatures; men, dolphins, gulls, seals and gannets alike. Buckland's only fault, I think, is being blind to the evil that men *can* do, even though there had been evidence enough of it in his day.

Peterhead Prevailing

If Buckland, Walpole and Young were to return to Peterhead today they would find the place not so terribly changed, but the attitude of the fishermen utterly altered. This is an industry no longer touching its forelock for visiting toffs, but holding the whip hand. Herring isn't quite a thing of the past at Peterhead, which has, on and off for the past twenty years or so, been the largest whitefish port in Britain.

The temperature controlled covered market there boasts a footprint in excess of 2,500 square feet with double doors to keep the cold in, and cctv cameras to keep a watchful eye. Inspectors and examiners are on hand, in what is a strictly controlled environment in every sense. These measures are as much about protection as they are about control. The high-value market at Peterhead handles almost a quarter of the total fish landings in Britain and is one of the town's main employers.

The 2016 Sea Fisheries Statistics from Aberdeenshire Council, published in December 2017, calculated total landings at Peterhead to be 161,235 metric tonnes, a catch valued at £174,000,000. The dominant species, by far, was mackerel at 56,800 tonnes with haddock (18,100) and cod (10,400) a distant second and third.

For the year ending 2017, the industry press estimated that a combined catch of approximately 175,000 metric tons of fish and seafood to the value of £198 million was landed at Peterhead. This far exceeded the previous three years, but it remains to be seen how much further it can grow in the face of aggravated competition from Europe, and the penchant that supermarkets have for importing fish from the far-east.

Recent figures for Herring from Peterhead are indicative of a fishery that is holding its own in the face of such pressures. In 2017, more than 24,000 tons of herring were landed at the port, with a slight increase in 2018 peaking at 26,338 tons. These numbers are down from a bumper year in 2006 (44,557 tons), but up from a low of 19,000 tons in 2011.

It is still the case, nevertheless, that fresh fish in Scotland, especially the northeast, is exactly that – fresh as the day it was caught. More often than not, it goes from boat to plate faster it took a nineteenth-century salmon to land on a Balmoral platter. There is much blather and palaver around Scottish cuisine at the moment, with workaday hotels and pedestrian restaurants footering around with 'imaginative dishes'.

It seems a travesty that so much wholesome food such as herring and mackerel are essentially an export crop, the best of it going to Asia but the vast bulk of it sold to traditional markets in Europe. Give me a nice smoked kipper for breakfast, or a grilled mackerel on toast, washed down with sailor-strength tea at a table overlooking the sea. I will show you what fine dining is all about.

When it comes to modern fishing, the old tensions still remain. Inshore fishermen resent the incursion of trawlers. Trawlermen, and the small handful of trawlerwomen, are as forthright in asserting their rights as ever they were. The industry also enjoys the same civil, but distanced relationship with science as they did in Buckland's day. All of them need each other, but they are only ever united in their criticism of politicians of whom they make the most unrealistic demand to please everyone all the time.

The fact is, that fishing in Scotland is as healthy as it can be, but is impacted by the same things that affect everyone else. It is, perhaps, the beginning of a new era for all of us, informed by fluctuating resources, rising prices, disappearing jobs and seismic shifts in the global economy.

Most people just want food in their bellies and a roof over their heads, but fisherfolk have worries that others don't. It's been an uncertain occupation at the best of times, but the greatest concern still is that not everyone who goes out to earn their living on the sea comes home again.

Peterhead, like neighbouring Fraserburgh, is a working town that has always needed to reaffirm its strategic importance in order to keep working. When the fish faded, a terminal was built at Peterhead and the harbour filled with oil tankers. Now that oil has lost its lustre, the port must increasingly consider diversification.

It may even transpire that the times will come full circle should the Peterhead Port Authority think to make more of the marina there. It's a wee bit hard to believe that in the 18th century, Peterhead was a spa town that once attracted "the flower of Scottish nobility", but apparently it was quite the place to gad about back then.

The port authority's official website text reads like the Victorian post office directory adverts referred to in this book, while the kind of 'leisure sailor' it is designed to attract could easily be describing Archibald Young himself.

'Peterhead Bay Marina is a purpose built leisure facility offering a comprehensive range of services and facilities for the leisure sailor....(it's) ideally located to act as a safe stopover point for vessels heading to and from Scandinavia... and is used by vessels heading for the Caledonian Canal and the popular sailing areas on the Western coast of Scotland. Peterhead Bay Marina has earned a reputation of being one of the friendliest and cleanest marinas in Scotland. Vessels of up to 22 metres in length can be accommodated.'

As one who is familiar with how the other half live, I can faithfully report that an influx of 22-metre motor yachts into Peterhead is almost certainly going to arrive with considerable disposable income aboard. Potential whale watchers, however, will need a good pair of sea-legs if they are to be sure of sighting David Gray's fin whales. They are a deep-water species more commonly seen in the North Sea beyond the continental shelf. Closer inshore, Minke whales are more common, as are bottlenose and white-beaked dolphins and harbour porpoises.

Organised whale watching from boats is, however, a growth activity in the reasonably sheltered waters further afield in the Moray Firth. It's, therefore, unlikely that Peterhead will experience a growth spurt in ecotourism anytime soon, but by all means keep a weather eye from the shore. You might be there at exactly the right moment to witness a passing pod of itinerant killer whales, or confirm the much more recent phenomenon of the wandering humpback, a species that is essentially a tourist in eastern waters. It would require a good, sea-going vessel to follow such a fascinating creature on its leisurely meanderings, but that kind of high-end, sight-seeing is, perhaps an enterprise vacuum waiting to be filled.

Buckland, Walpole and Young had to settle for an ex-navy paddle-boat, but the 'Jackal' would be substantial enough for the seaborne leg that would take them to Shetland and Orkney. Before that, they had to visit the communities of the Moray Firth and travel on to Wick. It's a challenging enough journey today and, once again, we have to wonder at the ground they covered on a daily basis in order to create a comprehensive picture of the herring fishery in Scotland.

Fraserburgh and The Moray Coast

Various Locations, 29th August – 1st September 1877

"They come, they come—the herrings come;
   They're growing every day;
   From many an off-shore bank they come,
   From many an in-shore bay.
   The merchant buys; the merchant sells;
   The merchant gets his gain;
   The sailor leaves his home and dwells
   Away on the lonely main"
   – from The Herring Song by Fraserburgh fishcurer James Ritchie in John Cranna's 'Fraserburgh Past and Present'.

I have mentioned Fraserburgh very little, although it merited a chapter of its own in the 1878 herring report. The lines above are taken from an extraordinary book by the town's harbourmaster John Cranna. It was published by The Rosemount Press and it faithfully records everything you ever wanted to know about Fraserburgh prior to 1915, but were perhaps too afraid to ask. The fishcurer's lyric was not only charming, it was popular too, and according to Cranna's meticulous chronicle, it was a hit song in the making.

   "The song was so much esteemed when it appeared, that it was set to music by the late Mr. Robert Anderson, Fraserburgh, and published by Mssrs Novello, Ewer

and Co. of London."

Fraserburgh was every bit as productive as Peterhead, and no less in need of a new harbour, for it attracted just as many boats. James Couper, the local fisheries officer, offered evidence at the Saltoun Arms Hotel on 29th August 1877 that shows the 1876 crash in stark numbers. The take plummeted from a four-year high of 165,000 crans in 1875 to 75,002 the following year. It's doubly perplexing that the fishery could be so precarious when you consider that the fleet that year numbered more than 790 boats at sea.

The concentrated nature of the fishing frenzy and the rush to market is almost dryly observed when Couper submits that, *"The summer fishing commences about the middle, or the 20th of July. It closes in the middle of September. The contract is for eight weeks. Nine-tenths of the fish are small and immature. The fish do not cure well. A proportion of these are sent away fresh, but the great bulk are salted and sent away unbranded."*

Incidentally, it's not evident from the report how far the identity of the boats at Fraserburgh were investigated, or whether many were the same ones recorded on different days in different places around the north-east coastline. Nevertheless, hundreds of thousands of crans of herring were landed at Fraserburgh between 1872 and 1875, and the fishing fortunes of the town mirrored those of Peterhead.

More importantly, there is no sense that improvements at one port could of benefit to a neighbouring one. An 'our little town' mentality prevailed, no doubt encouraged by autocratic landlords who invariably owned not only the harbour, but much of the property in the community and pretty much all of the surrounding estates. Even today, it's possible to consider the Moray Firth communities as highly differentiated, even though they are superficially similar. Each locale intimates a sense of isolation from its neighbour, but scratch the surface and you will find relatedness.

Throughout the twentieth century, the towns of Peterhead and Fraser-burgh came quickly to be conjoined in the mind as improved communications made the seventeen miles between them utterly insignificant. Yet, it's just as easy to see Fraserburgh as the gateway town to the Moray Firth, rather than an adjunct to Peterhead and Aberdeen in the south.

At least, that's been *my* feeling whenever I've visited the region. There is a sense of calm descending as you pass through Fraserburgh and out along the suddenly small B9031 coast road towards New Aberdour, Pennan, Dubford, and the first port of call at Banff.

The fishery along this stunning stretch of sheltered coastline has always been small-scale compared to Aberdeen and Peterhead, but it remains locally important. Indeed, It's very hard to think of characterful places such as Banff, Buckie, and Lossiemouth without thinking of fishing.

The smaller links in the thinly populated chain of communities facing into the Moray Firth include evocative names such as Gardenstown, Portsoy, Cullen, Findochty, Port Gordon, Hopeman, Burghead and Findhorn. Few of these unassuming coastal villages prosecute much fishing now, but in 1877 they were dependent upon it, and felt they were facing a crisis.

The handmaiden of crisis is confusion, and the farther north the commissioners travelled, the more confused some of the evidences became. One problem that will perhaps confound modern readers is why these places do not seem to have been considered by their inhabitants as economically mutually dependent, and collectively productive. One reason could be that the railways had not yet joined Aberdeen to Inverness via the Moray coast, thus perpetuating a sense of splendid isolation and time captured in a bottle.

The Moray Coast Evidences

The commissioners convened at the Fife Arms Hotel in Banff on the 30th August 1877, where the local fisheries officer James Gow delivered a report that they included verbatim, although it might seem only to undermine confidence in his abilities. A document like the commissioners' report is bound to record disparate views, with a clearer picture emerging from consensual opinions on the moot points. Gow, as a fishery officer, might reasonably be expected to reflect consensus rather than his own personal views. Instead, he sounds, to our ears, more like someone who thinks his knowledge superior to the experiences of others.

Some of his more eminently challengeable declarations are that he "*is in favour of free trade in fishing with no restrictions on the fishermen".* Today, this would put him out of job, and he seems oblivious to objectivity when he says, *"the fishery for the herring fluctuates with the movements of the enemies of the herring"* and obstructive when he disavows himself of wider debate, stating that he's *"not acquainted with the sprat fishing in the Beauly Firth."*

Year	Boats	Crans
1866	159	17,690
1867	172	19,308
1868	159	12,097
1869	167	9,120
1870	150	19,824
1871	156	22,360
1872	187	19,980
1873	213	30,585
1874	212	34,960
1875	210	31,690
1876	150	9,530
1877	151	13,593

Table 4. Report of James Gow Fisheries Officer at Banff.

Gow, who had been in post for only three months, seems very little engaged or in agreement with the most pressing questions of the day, and it's a bit surprising to have our faith in Victorian administration undermined by someone so blissfully unaware of his own ineptitude. He is quite alone when he states that the 1876 failure was due not to storms (which is universally agreed everywhere else) but the *"greater attractions of the fishery at Fraserburgh and Peterhead"*. If only he'd actually read the records he submitted to the commission. He'd have seen that there were only fifty fewer boats out that year, and that the take from the same number of boats in 1877 (to date) was consistent with previous years.

The uneven quality of some of the evidences doesn't invalidate Buckland's report, far from it. But it's worth running the rule over a selection of varying ideas, suggestions and notions from the Moray Firth communities. They show three things that help us to understand the aims of Buckland's commission. These are: the most pressing concerns of the industry, the range of contrasting opinion, and the relatively broad terms of reference for making submissions to the commissioners.

The evidences may appear a little chaotic at times, but Buckland, Walpole and Young weren't going to repeat an exercise like this with any frequency. It was clearly better to write everything down and sort it out later.

Some statements are more considered than others, but all of them are interesting in their own way. It's possible that Buckland's inter-laced addenda have the effect of putting words into the witness's mouths. Take for instance Alexander Simpson, a fishcurer of fifty years standing, who combines natural history with xenophobic jingoism in just three sentences, *"Spawning is all over in two days...the take of herring in the North Sea by foreigners is not equivalent to the take on the northeast coast of Scotland...the Scotch fishermen are beating the foreigners."*

Simpson's views may be based upon long experience on and about the quayside, but as a native son of Banff and Buchan, he's unlikely to have described his fellow countrymen as Scotch. That's a term that applies in Scotland to no other thing than the water of life.

William Patterson of Macduff, and a fisherman for fifty years, said something interesting when he reported that, *"If there is a storm from the north and he herrings are in shoal water near shore, they retire into deep water. This may account for the failure in some years, (but) it will not account for the failure every year."*

Some thought the decline simply a symptom of macro-economics. As Robert Clarke, a fishcurer speaking at the Station Hotel, Lossiemouth on 1st September remarked *"the immature fish for the fresh market were worth more than the mature fish for the curers. The fish up to the 1st July were sent by passenger train, and reached London in a day."*

It's an observation pithily echoed by James Scott who says, *"Since the opening of the Highland railway in 1863, the herring fishing has decline one half. If you kill all the children then there can be no men and women."*

Also at Lossiemouth, a different notion of sustainability came from Hugh Ross, a buyer and curer for McEwens of Glasgow, who said, *"the government gives the crown brand to full herrings, each of which contains 35,000 eggs"* and postulated that there was a great (natural) waste of spawn. He doesn't offer his ideas about the causes of this waste, but he's satisfied that there is *"no harm in killing full herrings."* In his mind, the herring is a species capable of replacing itself in perpetuity, and in spite of super-massive egg mortalities.

Earlier in the report, and frustratingly out of sequence for the purposes of this book, the fishcurer from Banff provided a quite different account of super-abundance. The aforementioned Alexander Simpson reported that in 1843, the first year he cured at Burghead, the boats took 130 crans each in 30 hours on Guillam Bank.

Buckland concluded, *"This is a remarkable instance of the fluctuations in the herring fishery for which it is impossible to account. There were some 60 boats on Guillam Bank in 1843 when this remarkable take was made. Guillam Bank is near Tarbert Ness (sic), near the shore. The bottom is rocky. The nets were covered with spawn. The nets could not have taken the whole shoal of herrings on this bank."*

The records from Buckie, one of the few sets of annual returns that are woefully incomplete, show that the fishery there did indeed fall off sharply in the following year. Subsequent years also describe fluctuations with a short sequence of good years punctuated by very poor years, but the pattern is of a fleet that is dwindling towards extinction.

The story of Guillam is, to this day, an anecdotal leitmotif for our entitled attitude towards nature, and our bewilderment when we find that absolute control of it is an illusion. Indeed, science has shown that with modernity comes a particularly misplaced sense of ownership that affected Guillam Bank for very modern reasons.

In 2009, the Fisheries Research Service (FRS) was merged with the Scottish Fisheries Protection Agency and the Scottish Marine Directorate, and re-named Marine Scotland. Prior to that, in 2004, FRS surveyed the environmental health of Guillam Bank and found that sediments there contained increased concentrations, *"above generally accepted background, of polycyclic aromatic hydrocarbon (PAH) compounds within and outside the boundaries of the sea disposal sites."*

It transpires that in the decade between 1973 and 1983 the British Aluminium Company had used Guillam for the disposal of solid industrial waste from their Invergordon smelter. The FRS report further stated that although high concentrations of PAHs were routinely reported from sediments around smelters, the increased PAH concentrations in the sediments of Guillam Bank disposal site was *"surprising, because the last disposal operation took place over 20 years previously"*.

While no evidence was found to support any significant "biological uptake" of PAH, a 1998 map of herring spawning grounds shows the Moray Firth devoid of meaningful spawning activity on the part of North Sea herring.

There are, of course, productive spawning grounds around our shores, but the data confirms that the entire embayment of the Moray Firth, inclusive of the Cromarty, Beauly and Dornoch Firths, is one of several substantial nursery grounds for juvenile herring around the coast of Scotland.

Whatever the reasons for desertion of former spawning grounds in the nineteenth century, the environmental violations of the recent past more than justify current policies of continuous monitoring and research.

In light of the preceding, thought-provoking facts, the four witnesses at the Drill Hall in Burghead (also on 1st September 1877) seem, with hindsight, possessed by a degree of wishful thinking. There, the mood was more belligerent and confrontational as the blame was squarely put upon *"overfishing"*, a happenstance characterized as an *"evil that will correct itself"*.

If ever there were fishermen who wanted to be left well enough alone, then it was the men of Burghead. David Mackenzie, a skipper and fisherman with 42 years at sea behind him, saw little merit in regulating mesh sizes, boasting that he was *"a much better judge of a net than either the commissioners or the House of Commons...the nets should not be regulated"*.

In fact, the data from Lossiemouth alone flatly contradicts the traditional naysayers such as Alexander Cook who tried to rationalize the perceived decline in herring landed on the Moray coast as due to: *"1) the garvie (sprat fishing, 2) the bait fishery and 3) the early fishing."*

The commissioners' report clearly shows there were far fewer boats

107

leaving from the tiny harbours along the Moray coast, but no fewer fishermen in the loop. They were deserting their home ports for places that could accommodate bulk catches from bulkier boats. It was left to the Fisheries Officer at Lossiemouth, John Murray, to complain that, *"The best men leave the district, and those who stay here are the least equipped."*

Increasingly though, the commissioners found the discussion inevitably led back to the thorny issue of remedial harbour works. Speaking at Barclay's Hall in Buckie on the 31st September, Alexander Grant, a fishcurer, described Cullen as being, *"very deficient in harbour accommodation. There are 106 boats belonging to Cullen, but they are all fishing elsewhere because the harbour is so bad."*

Yet the response to this deficiency, so widely reported everywhere, was uneven and not always down to an abdication of governmental responsibility. Lord Seafield owned the harbour at Cullen, but calls for improvements were met with selective deafness. He instead sought to offload the expense by offering to *'give over the harbour and its dues to the town council'*, knowing full well that the costs would be prohibitive.

Others were more opportunistic in outlook. Sir Robert Gordon turned up at Buckie in person and virtually petitioned the commissioners when he announced a plan to improve his *'deficient harbour accommodation'* at Nether Buckie. He'd already won a total of £25,000 in grant aid, which he topped up with £8,500 from his own pocket. Now, he returned to the well seeking another £10,000 to finance a deepening of the harbour and the construction of a breakwater.

It's hard to know whether Sir Robert suffered from a deficit of acumen, or whether he'd been too clever for his own good. His grants from government and the Fisheries Board came with the caveat that no dues would levied on fish, boats or men. He must have agreed to that in the first instance, but later changed his mind when he realized the harbour was a money-pit.

He told the commissioners, *"such a stipulation would prevent the further improvement of a fishing harbour"* and the Nether Buckie men would, in any case, be *"willing and glad"* to pay reasonable dues for the sake of improvement."

Gordon may well have felt his own pocket had been picked by his namesake, Mr. Gordon of Cluny, whose resident engineer, James Barron cheerfully reported that a new harbour was being built at Buckie. It was to 'cover eight acres' and consist of 'two basins, (comprising) an inner and an outer harbour. The inner harbour was to have 'a depth of 10 feet at low water' and the outer 'a depth of 6 feet at low water'.

Overall, the new port would 'accommodate 400 boats at an estimated cost of £50,000'. Barron gave Sir Robert's rival project short shrift when he declared, "This harbour will have no connection with Nether Buckie, which is a mile off. There is, therefore, no immediate necessity for improving the harbour at Nether Buckie."

This prompted James Innes, a fisherman of Port Gordon to pipe up. "There is a first-class harbour at Port Gordon built by the Duke of Richmond three years ago (and) will hold 150 boats". The Duke, may have been a man with an eye for the main chance, but he signally failed to foresee the determined rise of Buckie, a mere two miles distant, as the dominant port on the Moray Firth.

Fishing at Port Gordon went into decline after a brief flourish, and there followed a familiar tale of financial failure, crippling death duties and a once serviceable harbour left to the elements for decades. Port Gordon harbour is now owned by the Crown Estate, whose commitment to the cost of maintenance, much less regeneration, seems to be similarly conditional on contributions from the public purse. But at least civic oversight comes with some expectation to fulfil the potential of such a pretty place.

Moray - The Sunshine Coast

In recent years, Moray has been very good at marketing itself once more as a holiday resort, with its heritage coastline as the star attraction. It helps a great deal if you have resident pods of playful Bottlenose Dolphins cavorting in the bay on a regular basis. They attract not only tourist coin, they also bring researchers, conservationists, journalists and natural historians to the shoreline, and invite them to climb aboard a chartered boat for a closer look.

Buckland does not mention these delightful cetaceans in the report other than recording their status as predators of herring. Neither does he reference viewing the Moray dolphins for pleasure in his essays. That does not mean that he did not write about them at all. His thoughts may still float diaphanously among the voluminous papers and correspondence yet to be uncovered.

I like to think of Buckland taking a day or two off to whale watch while Archibald Young footslogged from one village to the next. The commissioners actually covered the Moray coast in the course of three days, visiting Lossiemouth and Burghead in a single day on 1st September, and again the suspicion must be that they split up to gather evidences. They did not appear in Wick until the 4th September, so there was ample time for sightseeing.

If Buckland were alive today, a visit to the Moray coast would undoubtedly see him liaising with the Whale and Dolphin Conservation Society (WDC) and gaining an appreciation of the Moray Firth as a cetacean hotspot. Several species can be seen in Scottish waters, at least for the time being, but the Moray and Tay estuaries are among the places where Bottlenose Dolphins are conspicuous from the shore.

The Moray dolphins are, in fact, the most visible manifestation of a resident Scottish population of *Tursiops truncatus* that ranges up and down the northeast coast from Moray to the Firth of Forth. They only number around 200 in total, but their rise to stardom owes a great deal to global press coverage, and an endless stream of shared images across the internet. Certainly, their importance to the local economy underscores the value of carefully managed eco-tourism.

The WDC operate the Scottish Dolphin Centre from Spey Bay, which is six miles from Buckie, and a fifty-minute drive from Fraserburgh. There, visitors can enjoy free entry and learn more about these intriguing mammals and the wildlife of the area. The WDC also provides a list of accredited whale watching boat operators and essential information about where and when to visit.

There is no shortage of dolphin-related advice in the area, but it's the third sector organisations that now fill the interpretation vacuum, arguably the official preserve of government-directed conservation agencies. Research has repeatedly shown that dolphins, and other cetaceans such as Harbour Porpoise, Risso's Dolphin and Killer Whales, persist on the eastern seaboard despite industrial pollution and biohazards. It may need a great deal more than the incentivisation of tourism and gazetting marine conservation areas to maintain the Moray Firth as a safe haven for dolphins.

Our travels with the commissioners , both then and now, are informed by logistics. There is, today, no rail connection north of Aberdeen to Fraserburgh, so we cannot trace their journey from the Silver City to the end of the line at Portsoy. The rail network did not extend to Banff, Buckie, Lossiemouth and Burghead (much less Wick) so Buckland, Walpole and Young were as reliant as we are today on the state of road transport along the Moray Coast. Let us start then in Banff, which no doubt looks enviously upon the Marine Aquarium across Banff Bay at Macduff, and strike seven miles along the coast towards Portsoy.

If you are there in July, you might be in time to catch the annual Portsoy Boat Festival. If not, you can always visit the restored Sail Loft where three generations of sail and rope makers once practiced their trade. Other interesting features at Portsoy include the former salmon bothy (now a community resource) and the boatshed (a working volunteer centre). These properties were bought from the Seafield Estate and restored through the efforts of the local community and their partnerships with funding agencies.

Further on, at Cullen there is a holiday park at the eastern end of a long, unspoiled sandy beach, overlooked by the Cullen Bay Hotel where 'Cullen Skink', a specialist variant of fish soup, is as freely available as it was in Buckland's time. The recipe could easily be found in Mrs. Beeton's cookbook, and it is hard to imagine that a gastronome with Buckland's reputation had no previous experience of the dish.

Barely a ten-minute drive away is Buckie, whose Cluny Harbour has all but acquired iconic status. It dominates the literature and defines the appearance of the town, but its impressive scale looks today quite disproportionate. At first glance, it appears to be the result of a massive miscalculation with a slide rule, an error so off the scale that one that no one dares to admit responsibility for it.

A few minutes' walk away in Cluny Place, you'll discover The Fishermen's Heritage Centre, a small local museum that tells the story of Buckie with pathos and charm. It rather dwells on the fate of those lost at sea, but that is perhaps to be expected in a community exhibition that faithfully reports the events of the past that speak, as they do elsewhere, to the collective memory.

Buckie also boasts *'the second-largest town hall in Moray'* in the shape of The Fisherman's Hall, built in 1886 to the civic benefit of *'the fisherfolk of Buckie'*. It's pretty much always been a community hall for meetings, events and concerts and, for a period during the 1920s, it also hosted the *'penny cinema'*.

Golf courses proliferate along the Moray coast with eighteen holes for virtually every town between Fraserburgh and Lossiemouth. It shouldn't be surprising, therefore, to find yourself following any number of SUV's bristling with bolted-on mountain bikes and laden with golfing parapher-nalia. There are also likely to be performance saloons sporting roof racks rammed with windsurfing gear, and sleeping bags rammed up against the rear and side windows. Be sure to give them a wide berth, for they are certain to be texting scenic images to distant friends over their mobile phones as they drive along.

Lossiemouth is, of course, synonymous with the RAF combat base and so has less immediate need of the tourist buck. All the same, it too has mustered a fisheries museum, a caravan park, and is home to yet another golf club. The landscape is resilient, and it will always be possible to find an unspoilt view somewhere along the Moray Firth, but the prevalence of golf as a hybrid cash-cow/business-hub located in blandly gardened ground is becoming overbearing. It amounts to little more than paving our native wild lands with sterile boulevards of manicured grass, and will, if unchecked, alter the outward looking face of Scotland.

Seven miles on and we reach our terminus is at Burghead. The sheltered harbour there could comfortably accommodate HMS Jackal, and is still in steady use today, but I suspect they parked the boat at Lossie and once more worked separately.

The commissioners enjoyed a three-day spell between Lossiemouth and Burghead on the 1st September, and the forward trek to Wick on the 4th, which would square with the time it might take them to ergonomically cover the ground along the Moray coastline. They had heard evidences in town halls, but used hotels only at Banff and Lossiemouth.

A small, but important point to note though, is that the 2nd of September fell on a Sunday, a day that is consistently set aside for worship among upstanding figures in society. If I had been among their number on Saturday 1st September 1877, I'd have offered to scoot Frank Buckland in the pony and trap along the coast road to Burghead. He might talk all the way there and all the way back, but he wouldn't be stuck for something interesting to say.

Burghead today is one of those planned places that is more substantial than it looks on the map. Built between 1805 and 1809, it sits on a modest headland that is as broad as it is long, thus creating an impressive footprint, criss-crossed by a grid of intersecting streets. Grant Street, a wide, main thoroughfare, runs its length and leads from the main road directly to the harbour area, where inshore fishermen routinely land their catches and moor alongside the growing number of pleasure craft taking the coastal tour.

It would be worth visiting Burghead for the street names alone. In the old town, they obey convention with a 'King', a 'Church', and a 'Park Street'. Nearer to the sea, 'Granary Street' and 'Station Road' skirt the quayside, but things get more opaque further out in bungalow-land, where we find unexpected holiness in 'St. Aethan's Drive', high status inferred on 'Mason Haugh Road', and Nordic suggestion in 'Sigurd Way'.

Perhaps it's only in locations situated, by accident or design, at the edge of things that we see the past and the present conjoined in the naming of places. It's a means of both preserving and commemorating things that we feel are significant, either by reason or by instinct. This could explain why customs such as 'The Burning of the Clavie' continue in places like Burghead. It is a very old tradition, and a rare thing as one that is rooted in folklore rather than a community's desire to re-state its identity.

113

Buckland recorded the event in his 'Notes and Jottings", although quite when or where he actually conducted the interview isn't given. His description is authentic enough to have come from the mouths of locals, and Buckland rarely omitted to credit his sources. Interestingly, he adds to our understanding of the ceremony as it was practiced in a way that is close to the ancient than the modern.

"One of the most interesting facts that I came across in Scotland was the remains of fire-worship at Burghhead (sic) near Forres. A very ancient rite is there still carried on, called the clavie. On the last day of the old year, old style, which falls on January 12, a large tar-barrel is set on fire and carried by one of the fishermen round the town while the folks shout and halloa.

If the man who carries the barrel falls, it is an omen of misfortune to him or his family. The circuit of the town having been made by the man with the burning barrel, it is placed on a large stone on the top of the neighbouring cliff and more fuel is added. The sparks as they fly upwards are supposed to be witches and evil spirits, the town and the populace hoot and execrate them accordingly."

If you're in town on the 11th January (the 10th if the 11th falls on a Sunday), you may find yourself bringing in the New Year in the 'old way' with a burning of symbolic, inanimate objects; in this case, split wooden casks.

One of these casks is placed on a pole, filled with tar and set alight. It's basically a very large torch, which is carried through the town by the Burghead born-and-bred and used to light a large bonfire.

En route, the *'Clavie Crew'* hand out pieces of smouldering wood to any householder in need of luck. The climax of the tradition is the raising of the pole on Doorie Hill where it sits as like beacon lighting the way into an imagined past.

I like to think of Buckland, Walpole and Young feeling moved by Moray, but perhaps looking into the future rather than contemplating the great mysteries. We can only wonder what they'd think about the 'come and go' decades of the twentieth century, which saw fishing, shipbuilding, manufacturing and oil production wax and wane in importance. We remain an industrious species that still thinks big, but to what purpose? The

114

Victorians can show us many things; one of them is that you can pursue your goals to fast and too fiercely.

Beyond the bluster and blow of the east coast proper, the Moray Coast, faces northwards into a Firth protected from the elements by the fertile hinterland to the south, and the expansive promontory of Caithness to the north-west. It has a Riviera touch about it that began with the arrival of the railways in the 1850s that it has never lost. It has something for everyone from golfers, sailors and whale-watchers to new-age mystics and little kids with buckets and spades. Perhaps, the only thing that's really, truly important is to remember that life is for living.

Wick and Lybster

Town Hall, Wick, Friday 4th & Saturday 7th September 1877

"When walking down the pier through Pultneytown (at Wick), I was perfectly amazed at the wonderful fleet of herring boats in the harbour; they were so close and thick together that it would not have been difficult to walk from one side of the harbour to the other across the boats without seeing the water. The quays were also covered with herring barrels, all disposed orderly and in due form......each set bearing its own peculiar brand as affixed thereof by the Government authorities."
– Frank Buckland in Notes and Jottings.

Frank Buckland was a man who believed in living life to the full. There was little that did not excite his curiosity, and his principal passion was the natural history of fish. His appointment as an official HM Inspector of Fisheries in February 1867 came just in the nick of time for him, for it represented the culmination of his ambitions and just reward for all his prior exertions in pursuit of such a goal.

Buckland seems to have been a robust character, save for the last few years of his life when his health went into a steep decline. He was obviously a good travelling companion, and the few complaints he makes appear at odds with his otherwise avuncular disposition. Buckland's entertaining memoirs and journals are the prosaic product of a butterfly mind, but his good-humoured inquisitiveness also bubbles up through the stodge of the herring report.

I cannot say whether Buckland looked at the world through rose-tinted glasses, but his perambulations around Wick do not seem to have taken him past the shanty town that grew up around the annual herring fishery. The boats he idly observed in the harbour had to be crewed by more men than Wick alone could muster, and the farlings had to be attended by more herring maids than lived in the surrounding area. Wick was, therefore, a magnet for migrant workers.

If the harbour was overcrowded with boats during the herring season, then the town itself was quadruply compromised. There was no room at the moorings and no room at the inn either. The herring rush northwards of itinerant fisherfolk created overcrowding and insanitary conditions of such squalor in Wick that it led to several recorded outbreaks of typhoid and cholera.

Far from initiating suspension of fishing activity and commanding effective quarantine, everyone kept right on fishing until declining takes influenced a slight re-calibration of the workforce on the beach. Quite how Buckland failed to notice all the people swarming around the narrow streets of Wick is a mystery that has gone with him to the grave.

It's true, though, that the late 1870s marked a period of transition at Wick. The town became less dependent on migrants as the home fleet grew in size and competence, and Peterhead and Aberdeen were beginning to lure away large numbers of fishermen and fishergirls. In 1877, incomers at Wick were still a challenging burden. They numbered in excess of 5,000 souls over a concentrated period of no more than two or three months and their presence, welcomed by some more than others, would have been hard to ignore.

We are more than halfway through our journey with the commissioners, and Buckland shows no sign of flagging. The disease that manifested itself shortly after he completed his Herring Report in 1878 had yet to take hold, and if he felt unwell or fatigued fulfilling this exhausting schedule, it's not mentioned. It's possible that he thrived on good company, and if he found Young tiresome, or Walpole aloof, then he seems to have found a kindred spirit in Captain MacDonald of the *Vigilant.*

Macdonald is presented to the commissioners as the senior officer on board a vessel described as a 'Fishery Cruiser'. He is the same Captain MacDonald quoted in Buckland's problematic equations pertaining to gannets, fish and men, and he has a lot to say for himself in his evidences.

He took the floor to make an extremely lengthy speech, or else he submitted a written report that fleshes out the Wick evidences by a good four pages. In fact, his testimony coupled with an equally verbose statement by James Mackie, the editor of the *Northern Ensign* newspaper, together account for the first part of the extensive Wick evidences gathered on 4th September at Wick Town Hall.

The commissioners split their evidence gathering at the Caithness town with an excursion to Orkney and Shetland, returning to Wick on the 7th September to sit for the herring fishery professionals. There will be more to say about the management of the tour in the next chapter, but we should first look a little more closely at Captain MacDonald, for he is not recorded in the Navy List as captain of the *Vigilant,* a vessel that was a dispatch ship in 1877, and not *officially* in the service of the fisheries.

The Navy List is essentially a compendium of all things under the governance of the Royal Navy, including the complement of fully described ships, their locations, duties and functions. It also includes the men of the Senior Service (active and retired), their roles, duties and remunerations. MacDonald is not mentioned in the Navy List for 1877, and HMS *Vigilant* is identified essentially as a cargo vessel based in China, captained by Commander Hugh C.D. Ryder.

There is no reference at all to vessels on fisheries business in the Navy List, but HMS Jackal, is in there; an armed, paddle steamer, itemised simply as 'an iron vessel based on the West Coast of Scotland'. Buckland, in his personal account of his experiences on board the Jackal, does, however, make it clear that the ship was essentially on secondment from inshore policing duties at Loch Fyne.

Looking at the history of fisheries protection is a little more revealing, as a single paragraph on a Scottish government webpage explains, *"The first vessel that the Fishery Board of Scotland (established in 1882) took over was a former Royal Navy sailing cutter (sic) Vigilant, which had worked for some years on protection tasks. Over the years, new ships were added to the fishery protection fleet (along with) responsibility for managing the task of fishery protection."*

In the Herring Report, the Jackal was *'put at the disposal of the commissioners'*, and *'fisheries vessels'* in use prior to 1882, are consistently framed as armed, protection ships charged with policing inshore waters. The Fishery Protection Squadron (FPS) of the Royal Navy is in fact, the oldest front-line squadron in the service and can boast Lord Horatio Nelson among its many alumni. Yet, The FPS is nowhere mentioned in the 1878 report and rarely called by that name in fishing references that examine this period.

The late nineteenth-century regionalisation of fisheries protection evolved organically according to local need, until the Scottish industry eventually justified a protection fleet of its own. It's strange to sit here today in 2019, amid the fallout from 'divisive' referenda and see such a clear example of devolved administration in key areas of law, order, economy and, by extension, defence. The separateness of Scotland is already evident, but so too is the distancing of responsibility in London. Then, as now, the former is to do with blood, history and identity, while the latter, as James Mackie was keen to point out, is a matter of money.

The Wick Evidences

Captain MacDonald, according to Buckland, was a fisheries protection officer who commanded *'Fishery Cruisers for 20 years, and was, before that, commanding Revenue Cruisers for 20 years'*. There can be no doubt that MacDonald was a very experienced seaman whose observations have great merit. He was not, as far as we know, officially engaged in the gathering of quantitative data, and he presented few figures, if any, to back up his qualitative evidences. But he was a captain, and on the sea, the captain's word is the last word.

To be fair to MacDonald, he may have been reporting direct observations after the fact, but his natural history is generally sound. His understanding of the spawning habits of herring squares with ours, *"There are two spawning* seasons, one in August and September, and one in February and March", he reports without fear of contradiction. Also, his similarly terse description of spawning grounds is hard to fault, "(Spawn) adheres to the bottom and is usually from half an inch to five eights of an inch thick...they always spawn on shelly sand or shingle...all deposited in depths varying from 3 to 30 fathoms."

MacDonald may be very direct and to the point, but he also paints a compelling picture of super-abundance and limitless supply, 'a fortnight ago, while cruising off Helmsdale, the witness fell in with a shoal of herrings in 18 fathoms of water, extending for four miles in length along the coast and two miles broad; a solid mass of herring.'

He was less impressed by the behaviour of the fishing fleet, which at times could verge on the chaotic, "I saw 600 boats shooting their nets an hour before sunset on ground which was not enough for 100 boats. The destruction of nets that night was enormous, as the nets got jammed together". MacDonald didn't seem to mind the spectacle so much as the unseemly disorder, for he proposes only to "have a universal law that no nets should be shot till half-an-hour before sunset", a law that he naturally saw no difficulty in enforcing.

If MacDonald was even-handed about competition among fishermen, he was dismissive of their methods. "The shoals of herrings in the spawning season are in a solid phalanx. The (number of) nets may be increased in particular places so much that they spoil the fishing...500 boats each with a mile of nets shot clear of each other, will catch more than 1,000 boats with a mile and a half of nets, possibly rolling up (inside each other)."

The tangle of nets, and subsequent cutting, clearly represents a loss to all, but the nightly 'herring grab' each season between June and September also indicates indifference to the environmental consequences. Abandoned nets, often full of fish left to rot, sank to the bottom where they spoiled the very spawning grounds that gave the fishermen their living.

Captain MacDonald, with a voice that sounds tired of repeating itself, bemoaned the waste when he said, "Wherever the ground is polluted by great quantities of nets with dead fish in them, the herring leave the coast".

When the matter of the spurious garvie/herring debate is raised, he can no longer hide his scorn, "a garvie is a sprat, and a sprat is not a herring".

120

After forty years at sea, he may have been entitled to find fishy obfuscation wearisome, and he sounds impatient when he says he could *"distinguish them blindfold by three senses – touch, taste and smell".*

It's hard to divine whether Macdonald really cared much for fishermen as much as he aspired to keep all things in sensible order. He was obviously engaged with the natural history of Scottish inshore waters and could see the common sense of exploiting the productivity of the sea.

In general, he supported extending the harbour at Wick as a matter of good practice, pointing out that the entire town depends on good health of the herring fishery. Nevertheless, he saw equal benefit to empire by the government *'advancing money on easy terms to the local authorities and supplementing those loans with grants'* for *'harbours of easy access where boats could float at all times, would do more than anything else to develop the herring fisheries. The Scotch fishermen furnished four-fifths of the Naval Volunteers when they were established in 1857.'*

The next witness was the local newspaperman, James Mackie. He submitted a contrasting statement that was far wider in scope and made an appeal that became increasingly politically charged, and overtly polemical in tone. He too was energised by the momentum to extend harbour facilities at Wick; despite previous, failed attempts that saw nature prevail over Victorian harbour engineering.

Mackie comes across as something of a firebrand editor with views that he is at pains to share candidly without fear or favour. His newspaper, along with the John O' Groats Journal, has since been widely sourced for its social and historical commentary.

In many ways, he's so vociferous it's easy to forget that the Northern Ensign is a local paper serving miles-out-of-the-way Wick and isolated Caithness. Mackie got his chance to reach a much wider and more influential audience when he came before Buckland, Walpole and Young. He seized the opportunity and, leaving nothing to chance, submitted his own written evidences.

Unfortunately, Mackie rather likes the sound of his own voice, and modern readers would long lose interest before giving up on his opening remarks.

We can, therefore dispense with the first five paragraphs of hyperbole that preface the nitty-gritty.

James Mackie, in short, advocated restrictions all round, from a firmly enforced close season and policed night-fishing to the regulation of net mesh sizes at the point of manufacture. He liked to use the word 'illegal' a lot, a term that was unlikely to advance his case very much among the fishing community. His most useful contribution, though, is an impassioned plea to renovate the harbour.

Earlier in the century, Wick had been one of several locations vying for the title of herring capital. At its frenzied peak, the town was bloated with incoming fishers, gutters, curers and coopers, with little enough room for the boats wedged into the harbour, and less room still to accommodate the concomitant migrant labour. The impossibility of the situation ought to have been realized much sooner, following the repeated instances of typhoid in the town and a nasty outbreak of cholera in 1832.

The chaos was compounded in 1848, when the violent storm on the eastern seaboard killed a total of ninety-one fishermen from several communities, with thirty-seven lives alone lost from Wick. Yet, here was Mackie in 1877, still trying to impress upon the commissioners the need for a safe harbour and an improved landing facility at Wick.

Mackie also mounted a frontal assault on the unequal allocation of resources south of the border. *"It appears by a Parliamentary return recently issued that, while during the present century there has been expended, as voted by the Parliament, for harbours in England, Wales and the Channel Islands, upwards of seven millions, for Ireland nearly two millions...the sums voted for Scotland amount to only £613,000; and out of the sum expended in Scotland, not a farthing has been laid out in Sutherland or Orkney, only £416 in Shetland, and but £13,537 in Caithness."*

The commissioners, however, appear to have found this part of his statement wanting, and went out of their way to point out that expenditure in England was mainly on national harbours, although they did concede that, *"the Select Committee on Harbours of Refuge of 1857-58 recommended Wick as a harbour of refuge, half the cost to be at the expense of the Government and half of the locality."* Still, they could not fail to sense the feelings of resentment in the hard-done-by Highlands, or overlook the slow pace of improvements in the far north.

On the other hand, the almost casual mention by James Mackie that nearby Lybster harbour was *"in ruins"* evidently caused particular consternation among the commissioners. The harbour had already received government money as a *'special case'*, but the £6000 expended would be wasted in the absence of urgent remedial works. The Herring Report contains several interesting appendices, one of which is the tetchy correspondence between the commissioners and the owner of Lybster harbour, the 5th Duke of Portland.

William John Cavendish-Scott-Bentinck inherited his title by accident on the unexpected death of his brother. He was notorious eccentric who frittered much of the family fortune away on spendthrift building projects at his Welbeck Abbey estate in Nottinghamshire.

These included a riding house which was 400 feet long by 110 feet wide and 50 feet high, which was lit by 4,000 gas jets and an enormous wall 1000 feet long for the sole purpose of growing peaches 'in which braziers could be placed to hasten the ripening of the fruit'. More extravagant, and stranger still, was the bizarre network of wide tunnels and underground rooms that he had constructed underneath Welbeck.

The 5th Duke's building projects provided local employment, which naturally made him popular in his home county. There was no escaping, however, the offence caused by his attitude towards the fishermen of Lybster. Walpole was liberal in heart and mind, but he was also a government scribe, well used to addressing the high and mighty. He appears to have been given the matter some priority too, for the letters start flying only a week after the commissioners' visit to Lybster on the 8th September, and long before their return to London.

All three commissioners put their names to the correspondence, with Buckland at the top, but Walpole must be the prime candidate for lead author. Apart from the fact it's sent from the corridors of power in Whitehall, it's full of things like *"We have the honour to inform Your Grace"* and *"We beg earnestly and respectfully to inform His Grace".* The exchanges begin cordially enough on 15th September with a polite but unambiguous opening shot from the commissioners, *"We understand Your Grace is proprietor of the harbour, and that no one but Your Grace is competent to make the necessary repairs to the pier."*

The duke did not deign to reply, prompting a sharper follow up two month later on November 15th expressing a hope that, *"Your Grace will be good enough to inform us whether you intend to take any steps to repair the pier, which owing to the damage caused by last winter's storms threatens to fall into decay, and to choke up the harbour with its ruins."*

Cavendish-Scott-Bentinck never did reply in person, but instead delegated his factor in Edinburgh to deal with the irritation. James Lindsay (junior) a Writer to the Signet sought to obfuscate, *"The duke does intend to take steps for repairing the pier",* but… *"provided he shall have first obtained the consent of the Board of Trade and formal and binding agreement to entitle his Grace to levy increased harbour dues in consideration of the large expenditure that will be needed to restore the harbour."*

If the aim was to add insult to injury, then Lindsay succeeded admirably with a crudely attempted brush-off. *"I may add farther, that the preliminary procedure considered necessary in such a case as this will be attended to in the proper time".* In other words, 'sometime-never'.

Walpole shot back with a zinging riposte. The commissioners he says, *"did not contemplate a large expenditure…we had satisfied ourselves, by careful personal examination, that a moderate outlay would be sufficient…What we wished especially to urge was the necessity for immediate repair to guard against the possibility of the winter storms of 1877-78 completing the ruin already begun."* The commissioner's reply also pointed out that the duke was already charging ten shillings per boat for 'weirage' five shillings *on top* of mooring fees for 'room to lie in winter'.

Attempts to winkle empathy from the duke by pressing him *"to lose no time in repairing Lybster Harbour…upon which the whole population of Lybster depends"* fell on deaf ears. He had, it seems, *"been advised by practical men, and in whose opinion he has confidence, that a large expenditure (at least £6000) will be needed for restoration of the harbour…and that a moderate outlay will not suffice...this would be just a throwing away of money."*

There is also something chilling about the disdainful tone emanating from the 5th Duke of Portland, which is undiluted by his man in Edinburgh when he writes, *"If you shall not forthwith hear to the contrary, you may take it for granted that his Grace adheres to his views and intentions expressed in my letter of the 4th (September)."* The matter is effectively ended with Lindsay's final sentence, *"I need not to tell you that many others who now pay no dues frequent and make use of this harbour which is... a public benefit and not merely...a private harbour belonging to the Lybster Estate."*

Walpole was an historian whose studies eventually led him to embrace fairer, if not greater, parameters of social justice. Buckland, regardless of his ambitions in public life, was at heart a humanist, primarily in the service of a pre-ordained, greater good. Archibald Young, himself an Edinburgh advocate, may have respected Lindsay's position, but he can't have been impressed by the duke's abdication of responsibility. All three were deeply God-fearing men, who daily sought to separate right from wrong, albeit governed by a sense of moral and actual superiority. It's easy, with reputations at stake, to see why this spat should be preserved in a government document. It places on record who acted honourably and who did not.

The attitude of the 5th Duke of Portland, a man famous for 'throwing away money' seems to have particularly offended the commissioners. His responses constituted a persistent wrong that ran like a worn thread through certain sections of Victorian society. The duke, a recluse and an obsessive, continued in his self-indulgent fantasies until his death in 1879. In the meantime, Lybster and everyone in it could go hang.

When the commissioners included these letters in an appendix, they were bending over backwards to make it clear where faults lay and remedies could be found. More than that, they saw this kind of impasse as worthy of historical record, a decision vindicated by the need to return to it here almost 150 years after the fact. Wherever inward investment in infrastructure fails, there is only so much that local authorities can do to ameliorate that failure. It is the road not built, never mind taken, that makes all the difference between a prosperous community and a forgotten backwater.

The commissioners heard many more evidences when they returned to Wick on the 7th September, much of it presented by James Cleghorn, an ironmonger, who had a bee in his bonnet about overfishing. He'd presented his hypotheses to an earlier commission in 1866, and turned up again in 1877 with the same suggestion that the *'falling away'* was due to overfishing. It's remarkable too that this testimony, written by a nineteenth-century ironmonger, should become the premise for a modern scientific paper, and one in which our old friend Captain MacDonald also appears.

Early evidence of the impact of preindustrial fishing on fish stocks from the mid-west and southeast coastal fisheries of Scotland in the 19th century (Jones, P., Cathcart, A., and Speirs, D. C. 2015) was published by the International Council for the Exploration of the Seas (ICES), one of the foremost scientific authorities on fishing in Europe. The paper mines a similar seam as this book by examining fishing reports, in this case those published between 1854 and 1895, and it highlighted Cleghorn's apparently prescient concerns. The ironmonger loudly and persistently contended that the voracious offtake of immature herring would undermine the ability of the population to replace itself, leading inevitably to a collapse in stocks.

Cleghorn's choice of words may be anthropomorphic and his metaphors mawkish, but his views, music to the modern conservationist's ears, made him something of a *cause celebre* when they were published in The Times.

He concluded that, *"..massing was necessary to fecundity....our time of fishing them is that which gives least chance for the herring to be permanent in any locality; and their mode of love-making taught me that the herring, above all other fish, was the most amenable to be fished up."*

So far, so innocuous, but Cleghorn went on to undermine his own credibility by proposing a closed season in July, August and September. It's hard to see how such a move would advance commerce in Scottish towns and villages reliant on the seasonal abundance of herring.

As John McCormack, a fish curer and Chairman of the Wick Chamber of Commerce was quick to point out, *"A close season in July, August and September would end his business at once...there are 66 curers in Wick...the adoption of Mr.*

Cleghorn's close time would be a national calamity."

The population biology of herring, and that of many other exploited wild stocks of wild animals, concentrates the minds of modern researchers everywhere. The phenomenon of 'sudden collapse' is often exposed as fallacy when underlying trends relating to life cycles, anthropogenic forces and stochastic events are examined more closely.

Cleghorn, quite unscientifically, alluded to this, and flagged up processes that lead to desertion of breeding grounds and local extinction. Researchers in the twenty-first century interpret this as prescience, but inshore fisheries have shown they can recover over time. It's been said many times before, and will be said again, it's not the fish that need managing; it's the fishing.

The Far North

Neither Wick nor Lybster harbours prospered, although they were eventually repaired and restored. It was too little effort that came too late to compete with Aberdeen, Peterhead, Fraserburgh and Buckie. Today, these communities, smiling through the tears of the past, have long shaken off feudal overlordship, while Wick inches along the path towards re-invention.

The Caithness coast faces the easterly gales with a combination of fortitude and acceptance, but gathering publicity pictures for the area is strictly a summer job. Wick is, nevertheless, a pretty place for being unspoiled by too much 'progress', although it suffers a little perhaps from a lack of economic diversification.

The town is a photogenic attraction in its own right, amenable, walkable and obliging from every angle. Yet, the train still stops at Wick, which is more than can be said for Kirriemuir, Brechin, Forfar and Laurencekirk, four Angus towns that are the same distance from Glasgow as Wick is from Inverness.

The way to Wick by train is long, for it takes the same scenic, but circuitous route as it did in Buckland's time, from Helmsdale on the coast, via the remote hamlet of Altnabreac. As we travel farther north in Scotland, we inevitably find the weather wilder, the days longer, and the summer sunshine somewhat rationed.

Perhaps it is the typically townie, prejudiced perspectives that make Wick appear like a mere speck on the map, far distant from the nearest skinny latte. It may sit sixteen miles short of John O' Groats but it's still only 200 miles from Perth. This in an age where people in the Fair City of Perth, and nearby Dundee, think nothing of coaching down to Newcastle, and Manchester and Liverpool for Premiership football, horse-racing and music events.

It is resources that are unequal, not the distances. If communications are slow and congested, then inward investment in infrastructure is slower still, and it's hardly the fault of the location. The failure to open up the Highland coastal routes and provide the same connectivity that is enjoyed elsewhere is reminiscent of Cavendish-Scott-Bentinck's constipated worldview. When proposals do come, they are in the shape of (yet more) golf courses, bloodsport holidays, and luxury cabin complexes. These are not solutions to persistent isolation, they encourage it by making access as exclusive as a Victorian hunting lodge.

It is perhaps for those reasons that Wick is like a photograph of an imagined past; a picture postcard image of life as if heavy industry had never happened. Big oil did not come to stay in Wick. That juggernaut merely rattled windows and loosened masonry as it battered up and down the A99.

This is the main road that links the Far North to the Inverness with mostly a peaty wilderness beyond. It's slow as sin, and marvellous if you like looking at miles of moorland, but you have to get down to the coast to experience wild Caithness at its best.

The precipitous cliffs and sea stacks that overhang the North Sea along the Caithness coast are made of stratified sandstone, which is constantly battered and holed by the elements. Elsewhere, there are long sandy beaches where waves hurtle to the shore as if desperate to escape the clutches of the merciless east wind. There are gentler spots like the salmon-rich River Helmsdale, which finds an outlet to the sea at the sheltered village of the same name.

Caithness is a favoured destination for hardy souls such as climbers, surfers, ramblers, fishermen, photographers, note-takers, writers, poets, artists and amateur historians. It's also still a stronghold of the large estates, where development proceeds and/or preservation is maintained at the discretion of the laird. You can pan for gold in the Suisgill and Kildonan Burns just as they did during the unlikely gold rush of 1869. It's an activity offered free of charge, and by 'kind permission' of the owners of Estate, who may well change their minds should the price of gold change markedly.

We next turn our attention to the commissioners' amazing journey from Wick to Shetland and the Orkneys. It's a chapter full of marvellous detail, primarily because Buckland and Young appear to be excellent sailors and diligent diarists. Buckland, in particular, is like a schoolboy out to earn his 'Blue Peter' badge by describing everything he saw and experienced on the way. There is little mention of Walpole on board the Jackal. Perhaps, he was lying below, sick as a dog. There is, however, the first mention in *Notes and Jottings* of an interesting fellow traveller who appears to be a busman's holiday.

Orkney and Shetland

Station Hotel, Kirkwall, Wednesday 5th September & Zetland Hotel, Lerwick, Thursday 6th September 1877

"In the following pages, no attempt is made at fine writing, and the matter is put down much in the order that it occurred to me. I trust it may afford some amusement, perhaps instruction, to those who take an interest in the curiosities of Natural History." - **Frank Buckland in his own Preface to Curiosities of Natural History.**

Frank Buckland was really very famous in his own lifetime. His popularity as a lecturer, journalist, editor and author is comparable to many contemporary wildlife commentators, but he was also a credible scientist whose work was valued.

Buckland was also acknowledged for his skills as an anatomist. He was a schoolboy dabbler in dissection and later trained as a surgeon at St. George's Hospital. He subsequently became, principally through his own self-taught efforts and a network of useful contacts, a noted animal pathologist.

In the nineteenth century, the process of describing animal anatomy was almost a competitive sport, with everyone from clergymen amateurs to aristocratic auteurs seeking to get into the annals of scientific discovery. Frank Buckland, on several occasions trumped them all, mainly because he proactively sought specimens to examine from a wide variety of sources.

He dissected everything from monkfish to rhinoceros in the basement of his house in Albany Street, an address that quickly became the destination of choice for the disposal of strange animals, recently, and not-so-recently-deceased. He also lived within walking distance of Regents Park Zoo, where one of his best friends and closest colleagues was the collection manager and Zoo Superintendent, Abraham Dee Bartlett. This relationship afforded him ready access to creatures that many others could not name, much less explore with a scalpel.

Buckland juggled several careers, but he gave equal weight to every one of them. He wrote constantly, and provided great detail in his scientific contributions, the most important of which are undoubtedly his reports for H. M. Fisheries. He expanded just as much energy on his popular accounts of nature, and corresponded incessantly. But he also exaggerated for effect and made schoolboy errors, some of which may be down to a lack of editorial oversight. Most of them are simply the product of a butterfly mind that cannot wait to properly cultivate one topic before moving on to the next attractive flower.

He also pursued an endearing line in self-deprecation, not least in the preface to the first edition of *Curiosities of Natural History*, quoted at the beginning of this chapter. There were four volumes of this popular compendium of his collected writings, most of which were previously published in *The Field*.

The critics at *'The Saturday Review'* did not disagree with Buckland's self-assessment, but that didn't hinder our indefatigable hero. He cleverly turned a bad review into an entertaining piece of self-satire by quoting freely in a footnote to the second edition, *'Mr. Buckland's book reads like the contents of a note-book, thrown out pell-mell'*.

Buckland was, at the time, an Assistant Surgeon with the 2nd Life Guards at Knightsbridge Barracks and Windsor, and his address is given as The Athenaeum Club in London. In the 1850s, he may have felt himself sufficiently ensconced in the bosom of the establishment to turn ridicule into an amusing and effective riposte.

Later in life, Buckland increasingly sought academic recognition and credibility as a leading authority on natural history. His appointment to the role of Inspector of Fisheries gave him the opportunity to do just that, and the contrast between his work for government and his popular writing becomes more striking as his career progresses.

This is plain to see in his extensive *Natural History of the Herring*, included as Appendix II of the 1878 Report. It is detailed, insightful and enthusiastic, but it is also ordered and disciplined. His account of the multifaceted life of the herring runs to twenty-seven pages, and it stands up as a more than decent monograph.

There is nothing left unsaid about this fish, including the 'Cry of the Herring' of which he writes, *"It is stated that herrings when first caught utter a little cry, which sounds like the word 'squeak', faintly pronounced. I have ascertained that the air-bladder communicates with the conical bottom of the stomach by means of a slender tube. The herring has no larynx or organ of voice. I conclude that this peculiar squeak is caused by the action of the air-bladder, the gaseous contents of which are suddenly altered by coming in contact with the external air."*

As far as the herring's hearing is concerned he remains open-minded to a fault, *"The herring has also the bones of hearing, but they are not easily found except by boiling the head. The presence of these acute organs of hearing also corresponds with the nocturnal habits of this migratory fish, and abundant evidence was given during the course of this enquiry on the effect of noise...upon the shoals of herring. Thus at Dunbar, blame was laid upon the firing of guns by the artillery...The guns of the Volunteers at Dundee were also looked upon as a cause why the herrings had gone away."*

Frank Buckland's surveys and written contributions to the various fisheries reports bear witness to the scientific rigour and accuracy that these tasks required. They contain concise writing and demonstrate the serious intent behind his passion. Yet, his work as a prominent servant of the Crown and his efforts as a populariser are equally driven along by his seemingly boundless energy.

There are certain anomalies in Buckland's herring report, which are compounded by discrepancies in *Notes and Jottings from Animal Life*, a collection of natural history vignettes published two years after his death in 1880. The report offers few, if any, details about the logistics of the 1877 hearings. Buckland, on the other hand, refers to them in his lightly written musings largely to set the scene for an entertaining anecdote. In fact, he usually crammed four or five quite unrelated stories into a single chapter, a trait that irritated his critics, but kept his audience entertained.

An important piece of writing is Buckland's account in *Notes and Jottings* of 'The Cruise of the Jackal', a travelogue that describes the next part of the commissioners' 1877 sojourn in Scotland. It contradicts not only the chronology of the commission's travels, it also trips over its own feet in its urgency to move the story along. We can easily forgive such discrepancies if they make it easier to digest a complex narrative, and turn it into a page-turning adventure.

In *Notes and Jottings*, Buckland first gives the *"exact order in which the courts were held"* on the eastern seaboard and clearly itemizes each village between Aberdeen, the Moray coast and up to Wick. He then states that, *"The Jackal first met the commissioners at Aberdeen on September 4th 1877"*, but he then goes on to describe how prior to their departure for Orkney, *"We held our court at Wick early on the morning of September 4th and started to board the Jackal, then lying with her steam up"*.

Moreover, the Herring Report firmly places the hearing at Aberdeen on 27th August, and has the commissioners travelling onwards from there to hear evidences on a daily basis at Peterhead, Fraserburgh, Banff, Buckie and Lossiemouth, until they reach Burghead on September 2nd.

This impossible schedule gives credence to the theory that the commissioners separated from time to time, but it may also be a case of poor editing executed in haste in order to capitalize posthumously on Buckland's name. Worse still, this same chapter has Buckland describing the Jackal *"passing Ailsa Craig"* on the journey between Orkney and Shetland.

It's a nice trick if you can pull it off, for as every Scottish schoolboy knows, the islet of Ailsa Craig lies sixteen miles off the Ayrshire coast. It's a bit of a howler, and one that Buckland, even at death's door, was unlikely to make.

Elsewhere in 'The Cruise of the Jackal' there are charming glimpses of life on board with Buckland enjoying every minute of the experience. He waxes lyrical about the *"boatswain's merry pipe"*, closely observes the crew at work, and wonders in awe at the *"tremendous force of united tides"* that flow through the Pentland Firth, the *"narrow opening between the mainland and the Orkneys – an awful place, where King Neptune lives, and where his racehorses frequently get loose and have a stampede"*.

There is no mention at all of Walpole, who may have been seasick, or simply keeping himself to himself. At one point, Buckland borrows Archibald Young's barometer and *"vowed a testimonial"* to it *"if it gave good weather during the cruise of the Jackal"*. This promise to an inanimate instrument of a good review, perhaps in Buckland's own magazine *Land and Water* had the desired effect, *"for we escaped bad weather throughout our wanderings in Scotland"*. The three men, by their own account, had a good working relationship, but the dialogue and inter-action between them is tantalizingly scant.

Indeed, Buckland only mentions in passing that his friend from the Zoological Society of London is also on board when he relates, *"We adjourned to the captain's cabin, and, after hearing many interesting stories from our friend Bartlett, coiled up for sleep."*

We don't know whether Bartlett was an extra participant on professional secondment, a substitute inspector for an absent Walpole, or merely a guest, but he re-appears later in the narrative inspecting captive beavers with Buckland on Bute. That story will have to wait for the moment.

The Orkney Evidences

The commissioners convened at the Castle Hotel in Kirkwall and, given the eccentricities of the story so far, readers will not be surprised to learn that they found Kirkwall Castle long gone. There was no herring fishing there either, for that was prosecuted out of St. Mary's, also on mainland Orkney; Carra, Hoxa, and St Margaret's Hope (Burra) on South Ronaldsay; and at Stronsay. Most of the fleet was, however, moored at Burra, and its ranks were most likely swelled by herring fishers from elsewhere.

The herring fishery operating out of Orkney was never considered significant and is described by the Campbeltown officer Robert Hendry as, *"local to the district, not large...and falling off during the last two or three years in consequence of storms."*

All the same, the dataset he provided indicated that around 232-317 boats were consistently active between 1865 and 1875. Moreover, the Orkney fishery enjoyed an eminently sustainable catch throughout a six-year period of plenty between by landing over 20,00 crans of herring annually. According to fisherman John Harcus, all of these herring were immediately cured at St. Margaret's Hope and sent to the profitable markets of the herring-loving Baltic states.

The most interesting thing to emerge from The Kirkwall hearing has more to do with technology than ichthyology. John MacCrae, identified as a 'Clerk of Supply', first of all clarified the dependency of the Orkney fishery on outside help, stating, *"most of the curers here are non-resident"*, and came from Wick, Glasgow and Leith. There was in fact only one local curer based on Stronsay, probably the least convenient location a fish curer could choose to establish his business. MacCrae then went on to blame the more recent post-1875 decline of the herring fishery at Orkney as *"owing to storms"*.

This last statement, heard often throughout the hearings, is a bit insubstantial for a scientific report, but MacCrae elaborated by explaining that the fishing boats stayed in harbour as a consequence of uncertain weather as much as obviously hazardous sailing conditions. He also put forward a useful and practical proposition, and brought some much-needed vision to bear on the proceedings.

"For a whole week this year, most of the boats were unable to put to sea. Weather signals are telegraphed from London to Kirkwall. There is (also) a storm signal at Kirkwall. These signals are of very little use to the herring fishermen, for Kirkwall is not a herring station.

A telegraph station at St. Margaret's Hope is of the utmost importance to the proper working of the herring fishery. The existence of a telegraph station at Stronsay has had much to do with the success of the fishery there this year.

I there had been no telegraph station at Stronsay, the news (of herring in the vicinity) might have taken two or three days to in reaching the South Isles, and the men (there) would have lost the best part of the fishing. The fluctuation of the shoals is a strong argument for telegraph stations."

Perhaps MacCrae was one of those entrepreneurial types so beloved of newspaper editors forever seeking an amazing story of rags to riches. He may well have imagined himself at the head of the queue for the position of Telegraph Officer for the Orkney Isles. It would certainly explain his motivation for having it all worked out in readiness for Buckland *et al.*

"The telegraphs wanted are: - 1. From Kirkwall to St Mary's; 2. A cable from St. Mary's to Burra; 3. From Burra to Water Sound; a cable from Water Sound to Carra; and a land line from Carra to St. Margaret's Hope. The telegraph would accommodate a population of 4,000 and...would greatly develop the fisheries."

The landed gentry in the shape of Colonel Burroughs, proprietor of Rousay, perhaps fearing an upstart in his midst, chimed in with his own advice on the telegraph provision. He also suggested that the herring fishery would benefit from a telegraph station at St. Margaret's Hope, but proposed, less helpfully, that, *"the route of the cable should be from Gills Bay on the Caithness Coast to Scapa",* which was (and still is) virtually a suburb of Kirkwall.

In fact, the telegraph cable that had been laid between Dunnett Bay in Caithness and Kirkwall in 1876 was a relay for the indirect telegraph service to Shetland. Its history was chequered, with a number of understandable breakdowns. But quite why Burroughs thought that building another telegraph station at Gills Bay, eight miles from the existing one is a form of reasoning that only makes sense to the military mind.

The commissioners kept their own counsel in the course of the hearings, but MacCrae's testimony must have rung bells. Frank Buckland was certainly already aware, many years previously in 1857, of the advantages of the telegraph enjoyed by the Norwegian herring fishery.

In, 'A Hunt on the Sea Shore', (Chapter IV of his second series of 'Curiosities'), we find Buckland in correspondence with a 'Mr. Roberts', who seems well clued-up on herring fisheries.

"A Worthing boat sets out to the north for herrings. The skipper depends on the accounts of what is doing off many ports. He looks for his penny letter, sent by some friend, advising him whither he shall steer." Roberts evidently feels that this isn't a terribly modern way of doing things. He continues by looking a little enviously at the *modus operandi* in Norway, *" The necessity for early information so that the fish do not stay in the fjords uncaught... has caused the Norwegians to establish an electric telegraph, so that the herring fleet may sail at the earliest appearing of the fish."*

The Shetland Evidences

In Shetland, the picture was quite different and informed by the method-ologies of the Dutch herring fishery. Every year towards the end of June, Dutch factory ships, known as *busses*, would set sail for the coastal waters off Shetland, arriving on or about the 24th June. They'd been harvesting herring in the area since the late 16th century and the practice of catching, curing and barrelling the take on board these large vessels had been extremely successful for more than hundred years.

The local fishery on Shetland specialized in the long-line catching of cod and ling, while the pursuit of herring was a marginal occupation. Shetland fishermen landed paltry catches of *Clupea*, although fishcurers in the isles seem to be present in numbers. These curers were there primarily to serve the white fish industry, but later development of the herring fishery in Shetland delivered a bonanza beyond their wildest dreams.

In 1877, the commissioners found that the herring take from Shetland had dwindled from a one-off peak of 13,275 barrels in 1866 down to around 2,500. The locals were rather stoical about it, if the scant testimony is anything to go by. It's also evident that the Dutch fleet was still active in Shetland, and appeared able to violate territorial waters pretty much at will.

Buckland, Walpole and Young may have felt they'd travelled a long way to gather very little information of any great worth. Looking back now, Shetland gives every impression of being a community a little locked in its own past, and quite unaware that it is sitting on the cusp of far-reaching change.

The observations of Robert Hay, a fishcurer at Lerwick, are short but very much to the point, *"The herring fishery has diminished from what it was forty years ago. Of late years it has revived a little. For the last few years the boats have come from Orkney and Wick. Some boats also come from Holland. The Dutch cure their herrings on board. The Dutch boats are 100 tons."*

It's hard to know whether Hay is insightful or just a good guesser when he says, *"..if the herring fishery were prosecuted here at the proper season, they would get plenty herrings, and good herrings."*

Fisheries officer Alexander Milligan fleshes out Hay's submission by explaining that, *"The (herring) fishing begins on 10th June and is prosecuted by Orkney and Caithness men, but the boats soon leave for the home fishing. The herrings do not get a fair chance of being caught. The men come here at an off-time when they cannot get the herrings at home. The native boats are engaged in the cod and ling fishing. They use herring and conger for bait."*

The words of Joseph Leask might ordinarily be overlooked, for his profession is not given and he seems to have severed his any previous ties he may have had with the fishing industry. He had evidently made substantial losses from his prior involvement in the herring fishery and, perhaps understandably, didn't mince his words.

" The herring fishery was never prosecuted here to any extent, except by the Dutch. There are more than 100 Dutch boats in the Lerwick district every year. The Dutch fishermen come within the three-mile limit (and)..are not so numerous as they use to be. The Dutch do not come in such numbers as formerly."

At this time, the domestic herring fishery in the Shetlands was undoubtedly insignificant, but the Dutch had troubles of their own. The offshore buss system was good for getting the notoriously delicate herring cured quickly and preserved fresh from the sea. It wasn't so good at getting the finished article to markets and dining tables.

The Scottish inshore method of fishing at night and landing early in the morning resulted in the happy confluence of supply meeting demand in a timely fashion. Better still, the rapid expansion of the rail network and steamship services to all corners of the British Isles meant that herring caught the night before in far-flung Shetland could be on the boat and/or train to Edinburgh, Glasgow and London the very next day.

The Shetland herring fishery, from 1880 onwards rose on a tide of technology that swept aside the practices of the past and powered an unprecedented boom. The fishery grew and grew, and more than four hundred boats could be counted by the end of the decade. That number more than doubled in the ensuing years, until Lerwick became the undisputed twentieth-century capital of the Scottish herring fishery. Between 1900 and 1914, there were never less than 400,000 barrels of herring cured in Shetland, hitting over a million in 1905, with regular peaks in excess of 700,000.

As Cinderella stories go, it's pretty spectacular. Yet, the herring boom of 1880-1914 doesn't quite match the sprinkling of fairy dust that followed in the wake of another twist of fate. This time, good fortune came much later in twentieth-century, but it wasn't in the shape of silver, or even gold. It was the black, black oil and it is oil, more than all the fish in the sea, which has made Orkney and Shetland what they are today.

North Sea Oil is a massive subject, well beyond the scope of this book. Long before the discovery in 1969 of the Montrose Field, 135 miles east of Aberdeen, oil firms had been issued with exploration licences. North sea oil was always a known quantity, but then, as now, exactly how much and how long it would last was less certain. As it turned out, UK oil production peaked in 1999, and is today an industry that describes itself as 'stressed'. That has been enough to prompt an exodus of contractors and companies whose revenue generating activities had, for more than forty years, propped up the economy of northern Scotland.

The Orkney Isles

If you 'google' The Orkney Isles today, you will be rewarded with hits that most prominently feature the words *accommodation, attractions, holidays, wildlife* and *wilderness*. That may be the result of Visit Scotland's hyper-active SEO tactics, but oil isn't the big noise it once was. It's true that the black stuff is still pumped ashore from the Piper and Claymore fields into the Flotta terminal, but its current operators have more recently tasked themselves with 'decommissioning' and 'robust management of change' in a time of company buyouts and assets changing hands.

It's a good thing then that Orkney has another natural asset, altogether less finite than oil; and that's wind power. The Scottish government has a declared stake in renewable energy, but for Orkney it's a vested interest. The isles may still be wired to the grid via the mainland, but it's wind turbines that now generate 100% of the net domestic supply. Nature has been harnessed before, but there is more equality in the relationship this time around.

There have been many objections to wind turbines on environmental grounds. Many of them have more to do with spoiling the view rather than despoiling pristine habitat or environmental pollution. Visual pollution is a poor excuse on Orkney where the landscape retains most of its character in vistas of romantic desolation, interrupted only by the call of a distant shorebird piping somewhere overhead. In fact, the isles are tailor made for ecotourism because they offer a deceptive diversity of sights, sounds and experiences that are peculiar, if not unique to the locale.

The bird list for Orkney is remarkable, and that alone makes it a destination of pilgrimage for both the professional ornithologist and the amateur naturalist. Species uncommon elsewhere in the UK, such as waxwing, red-throated diver, hen-harriers and Great Skua, are seen more readily here. If you want to be sure of your 'tick' however, then tour guides, excursions and birding advice are almost as abundant as the birds themselves.

Orkney is also famous for its seabird colonies, although the more complex Shetland archipelago hosts the largest numbers. These are the breeding grounds of scores of kittiwakes, guillemots, gannets, fulmars, razorbills, puffins and the rarer resident 'tystie', or black guillemot. If you're still in any doubt about Orkney's importance as a wildlife destination, then be informed that the RSPB manage a total of thirteen reserves there. It's evidence perhaps of nature's last stand from a vestigial, defensible position.

Shetland

The Norse heritage on Shetland is very much a living thing. It courses through the veins of native islanders and is expressed in language, culture, identity, and in their genes. It is well-known that Scandinavian characteristics make up around 25% of the Shetland genome. More than any of these things, it is not the perceived isolation of Shetland that defines the *differentness* of this astonishing place. These isles lie bang in the middle of the North Sea, virtually equidistant between Aberdeen and Bergen, and they must appear to the mariner more like an international hub than an imperial outpost.

Shetland had been the scene of human settlement long before the Vikings set foot on this sub-arctic archipelago with evidence of human occupation dating from the Mesolithic period (4320-4030 BC). The Orcadian site at Skara Brae, a virtually complete Neolithic village dating from the 4th century BC, is perhaps more familiar than Scord of Brouster, Northmavine and Jarlshof on Shetland. Taken together though, they have shifted our perceptions of prehistory from the conceptual to the physical.

Antiquity may be less mysterious as a result, but it is no less fascinating for that. It is this tangible connection to our collective past that draws visitors into Orkney and Shetland in their droves. Orkney may be nearer to mainland Scotland, but Shetland is more ideally placed and better resourced to net the cruise ships that have now replaced steam drifters and supply boats in Lerwick harbour.

These vessels disgorge tourists who, on a daily basis, come to graze on archaeology and make the tills of local shops ring with joy. The large number of large ships arriving on a daily basis delivers more of a stampede than enhanced footfall. This kind of tourism has a tendency to create antipathy amongst the invaded locals, but Shetland has been invaded before and survived to keep its character intact.

There are other kinds of visitors, of course. The birders and wildlifers come to worship at the stone stacks colonized by internationally important breeding populations of seabirds such Puffins, Black Guillemots, Gannets,

Kittiwakes, Razorbills, and both Storm and Leach's Petrels. The visiting archaeologists, film crews, reporters, travel journalists and broadcasters come to tell and re-tell the truths and half-truths about Vikings, Druids and pottery people who may or may not have been more or less civilized than we are now.

Perhaps the most important visitors are those who come to seek solace in solitude somewhere on an empty Orcadian beach, or looking out to sea from A Shetland clifftop, dreaming of some other *Ultima Thule*. These northern isles are more than a window into the past. They offer a spiritual compass that points from the past, though the present and into an unknown future. It evidences human persistence with relics from the Neolithic, through the Bronze Age, the Iron Age, Roman occupation, Viking colonisation and, more recently, the Industrial Revolution.

There is, however, no benefit in being too misty-eyed about the past if you are a Shetlander. Living there requires commitment and hard work, for no one can afford to be idle for long in circumstances that demand self-reliance. Shetland's attitude to the oil boom was to negotiate the best possible terms and create a hedge against the inevitable. An oil fund was established that today stands at around £217,000,000, and the response to the downturn in the North Sea has been to keep re-investing in a diversified economy dominated by, you guessed it, fishing.

The economic statistics for 2015-2016 (Shetland Islands Council, 2017) show that the white fish and shellfish take, more than half of which was mackerel, totalled 129,000 tonnes to a value of £82,000,000. In terms of income, it is important, but it's an activity that only employs around 386 people.

In contrast to the commissioners' view that the supply of fish from the sea is limitless, the watchword now is sustainability. Fishermen will inevitably disagree in principle with quotas, regulations and restrictions, echoing their ancestors by persisting with the self-generated myth that they know what is best. In practice, however, history has told the northern fisheries time and time again that nature knows best, and to ignore her signs is folly.

Agriculture, particularly the practice of crofting and tenant farming, remains important on Shetland and it's suggested that employs about 2,000 people. The breakdown of this statistic rather muddies the water in the Shetland pony trough, for only 179 souls are listed as full-time working occupiers. There are 1,425 part-time working occupiers, while the rest are made up of full-time, part-time and casual employees working on the land.

Farming is a notoriously precarious occupation, and low-value work compared to, say, working at the oil terminal on Sullom Voe. On Shetland, you really have to know what you're doing if you want earn a living from livestock, or else learn quick. The methods are different and specific to local conditions, most notably blistering changes in the weather, and a fickle macroclimate.

However sceptical we may be of statistics (and I am), a rebalancing is evident on Shetland as the oil slowly dwindles, and the salient features of island living are restored. These features are common to many islands, some more prosperous than others. Those who are best placed to guarantee their future understand that to be reliant on one, single enterprise, however lucrative, is ultimately fatal. Diversity and flexibility are the twin turnkeys of a successful mixed economy, even if it means getting up early in the morning and going to bed late at night.

The Highlands and Islands

Inverness, Fort William, Tarbert (Harris), Stornoway (Lewis) & Ullapool, 11th – 18th September 1877

"If the members of the party have different tastes, all may be gratified during a journey through the Caledonian Canal, or among the western islands and lochs of Scotland" – **Archibald Young in 'Summer Sailings'.**

This next stage of the commissioners' undertakings began in the most comfortable of lodgings at one of the finest hotels in the Highlands, the Station Hotel in Inverness. It was built in 1855 and, in its day, it was a byword for commodious accommodation for the weary rail traveller. It is also indicative of a town that had finally come of age as a railway terminus and a civilized destination for gentlefolk. It must have felt to our cultivated commissioners like landfall to a trio of shipwrecked sailors.

One of the most curious things about the report is the apparent lack of logistical and planning reportage. The commissioners would have had to account for every coach, carriage and telegram, but those records are now, we have to hope, filed away in the depths of the national archives. Neither is it clear whether the map, which is included as an insert in the 1877 Herring Report, was drawn up as an aid to forward planning, or as a final cartographic record of their travels.

It's worth pausing then to catch our breath after the exertions of the trip to

Orkney and Shetland, and look ahead at destinations down the line. It takes only a little imagination to eavesdrop on Buckland, Walpole and Young, perhaps sharing an aperitif and a cigar in the hotel's smoking room with a map spread out before them.

They mention it nowhere in the text, nor in their personal writings, but they certainly took the Jackal down the Caledonian Canal to Fort William, then onwards to Tarbert on the Isle of Harris. They subsequently sailed to Stornoway on the Isle of Lewis, Ullapool in the north and back down to Balmacara on the shores of Loch Alsh, just across the water from the Isle of Skye. The same sequence of visits via the alternative route around Cape Wrath in the Pentland Firth would have been impossible according to their calendar of events.

It's an especially puzzling omission, given the status of the Caledonian Canal as a visual spectacle and an historic, new route through the Highlands. It was also of interest as a major feat of engineering. Construction began in 1804 of a man-made waterway to conjoin a natural loch system that included Loch Dochfour, Loch Ness, Loch Oich, Loch Lochy and seaward Loch Linnhe. This initial ambition was achieved in 1822 with further improvements made later in the century in order to make the canal fully navigable for larger steamships.

By the mid-1800s, the eight locks that comprise Neptune's Staircase at Benavie was an attraction in its own right. The canal not only constituted a trading conduit for eastbound and westbound maritime traffic, it kickstarted Highland tourism. It then became a simple matter to mythologize the mysterious Loch Ness, amplify the majesty of Ben Nevis, and exaggerate the wild, sweeping landscape as very real selling points.

It's here that we must turn to Archibald Young for a portrait of the Caledonian Canal in order to set the scene. Young was never as famous as Buckland or Walpole, but he was able to juggle careers as an advocate, an outdoorsman, a fisheries inspector, an angling correspondent, a writer of letters and an author. He was even a fair watercolour artist, and the illustrations in his book 'Summer Sailings' (1898) could easily be collectibles today, if any of the originals have survived.

The second chapter of his charming book, which is really an edited anthology of previous magazine articles, is entirely devoted to his experiences on and around the Caledonian Canal. '*A Yacht Cruise Through the Caledonian Canal*' gives us a sense of Young as a fit, quick-witted, and energetic younger man who lives country life to the full, but who looks on it with the intellect of the educated, metropolitan mind.

He describes contrasting activities such as wildfowl shooting, sea and freshwater fishing, walking, sketching, climbing and, of course, visiting ruined castles. Nothing escapes his eye, and no item is too trivial to report.

'*At the point where the canal and the River Ness flow out of Loch Dochfour, the landscape assumes a charming, sylvan aspect. Dochfour House is a spacious and elegant, modern building in the Italian style, surrounded by woods, but commanding a fine prospect over Loch Ness, from which it is only a mile distant.*'

There are also descriptive passages that are a great deal more evocative and persuasive than much of the tourism blurb we churn out today. I'd certainly want to take a moonlight cruise past Castle Urquhart after reading this:

'*As we pulled away from the ruins, the moon had begun to appear above the hills, and was shedding a long pencil of silver light across the calm waters of the lake. The donjon tower soon intercepted our view, but we still saw her beams through the shattered windows – as if a bright lamp had suddenly been kindled from within by an unseen hand – when all at once the light vanished, as a cloud crossed the disc of the moon. The effect was startling; and a superstitious Celt might have fancied some old warrior tenant of the castle revisiting the earth by the pale glimpses of the moon.*'

The Highlands and Islands Evidences

Station Hotel, Inverness, 11th September 1877

The evidence gathering at Inverness was a rather meek affair compared to some of the more vexed sessions that took place elsewhere. Nevertheless, the first witness turned out to be a famous and eminently credible witness who immediately re-returned the conversation to the question of harbour accommodation. More pertinently, he did not mince his words when identifying those responsible for their construction and upkeep.

Joseph Mitchell was a retired engineer living at Inverness who had been responsible for the design and building of no less than sixteen harbours situated all around the country. He spoke with considerable authority when he said, *"There would be nothing unreasonable in compelling the proprietors of a harbour to keep it in repair".*

Neither does he shirk from berating the Duke of Portland, a character who is emerging from the report with his reputation pretty much in shreds.

"The engineer of the Fishery Board ought to have the power to go down to Lybster to repair the harbour, and to charge the work to the proprietor", declared Mitchell tersely.

Joseph Mitchell was perhaps able to be forthright because his reputation was unassailable. He was born on 3rd November 1803 in Forres and educated at Inverness Academy. He later studied in Aberdeen, but he served his apprenticeship under Thomas Telford on the Caledonian Canal project. Mitchell's obituary, published by the Institution of Civil Engineers, has Telford taking Mitchell very much under his wing, and essentially launching his successful career.

Mitchell became a sought after surveyor and civil engineer continuously working on a large, community and infrastructure enterprises for, among others, the Church of Scotland, the Fisheries Board, and the Highland Railways. He had homes in Inverness and London, and was an hospitable, if outspoken, public personality. It is clear from the very candid obituary that when he spoke, he expected people to listen.

'On many points he was unbending, for when once he saw what ought to be done, nothing would turn him aside from his position. Sanguine in temperament, and confident in the ultimate success of his schemes, he had scanty patience with those who did not at once recognise the benefit of his proposals, and often he too keenly urged his views on men not ripe for such changes.'

Mitchell was not the only one lying in wait for the commissioners, and it's worth mentioning here that the local and national newspapers at the time widely circulated advance notice of the commissioners' scheduled visits to each town and village, the length and breadth of Scotland. Certainly, there were dozens of publications, and they had acres of broadsheet newsprint to fill, but results from the archives amplify the public interest in their investigations, and the status of the commissioners as notable people.

Among those itching to state their case were the sprat fishermen based in and around Inverness. Donald Sutherland a fisherman of Avoch who *'fishes in the Moray Firth from Helmsdale to Lossiemouth'* pre-emptively put up an immediate defence of his industry.

He was '*anxious that the garvie (sprat) fishing would continue, and is certain that it does not injure the herring fishery.'*

It appears that fishermen who depended upon a localized sprat fishery had begun to suspect that the herring lobby meant to put them out of business. Their testimonies are defensive, and largely designed to defuse the increasingly combustible relationship between the two fisheries.

Sutherland continues, "*..the garvies are sold in Inverness market and (with the advent of the railways) sent to England. The railways increased the demand for garvies.*"

William MacDonald, a fisherman from Clachnaharry, also took the opportunity to affirm that the innocuous sprat fishery offered no threat to the mighty herring industry. His contention that "*The fishing for garvies does not interfere with the fishing for herrings*" is fully supported by Alexander Dugal, manager of the Highland Railway, '*since its opening'*. He submitted a table summarizing the quantity of garvies carried by the railway over the proceeding three years, providing a total figure of 801 tons.

"*The sprats chiefly go by the 10.18 mail train, which reaches Euston at 4.00 p.m., and (the passenger train to) King's Cross at 6.40 on the following morning....the sprats that are sent away go almost entirely to London.*"

The comfort of the Station Hotel encouraged the commissioners to tarry in Inverness for an extra day before going onwards to Fort William. Perhaps, Archibald Young gave the others a guided tour, first of Inverness, and then along the way as HMS Jackal retraced his earlier journey.

In *Summer Sailings*, his only reference to Inverness is short, but somehow loaded with inferences that may not have played so well to his government employers. Perhaps that's why he waited until the relative safety of retirement to write his otherwise innocuous memoir.

"...the town of Inverness, its gaol and court-house and the spires of its churches stands out in bold relief, backed by a range of richly-wooded hills; while the gray (sic) forms of loftier mountains fill up the extreme distance. We spent a forenoon at Inverness, where recruiting parties, flaunting in ribbons, and accompanied by bands of music, were actively endeavouring to procure men for the militia, now a difficult task in the Highlands, no longer the nursery of soldiers which they once were."

Archibald's personal politics were conservative, so we can't tell whether he's lamenting to the point, or pointing out a consequence of recent history. In any case, the commissioners arrived in Fort William refreshed and ready for the order of business, only to find sensibilities offended and tempers somewhat frayed.

Caledonian Hotel, Fort William, 13th September 1877

We can be grateful to the 'assistant inspector' George Rieach for his succinct overview of the fishing stations associated with Fort William. He usefully reported that, *"The principal stations are Loch Ness, Loch Linnhe and Loch Eil, but the fishery is scattered over the whole district."*

Despite his grand title, an inspector rather than an officer, his duties appear light. No branding of herring barrels was carried out at any of the lochside stations and his work is described as limited to collecting statistics, ensuring that boats were properly numbered, and arbitrating over minor squabbles between fishermen.

Some of these antipathies spilled over into open hostility towards the changes that modernity had wrought upon an area that in the early 19th century was characterized as the epitome of unspoilt Scotland. The principal causes of offence in the eyes of local fishermen were plain for all to see. Steamships, trawlers and strangers were to blame for virtually all ills, but the concerns raised, although generally empirical in nature, were genuine and completely credible.

The canal had not brought the envisaged levels of commercial traffic to make it a going concern. By the time it was built, larger, faster, commercial vessels had been developed and built to routinely, and quite easily, circumscribe the coast. The Pentland Firth was no longer the challenge it once was, and the canal had become the slow road from one side of the country to the other. It might have been redundant altogether, but for the inshore coastal trade and the growth of tourism in the region.

The pleasure steamer on the loch was, by 1877, a fixed feature in the Highland milieu and it remains one of the strongest images of the northern idyll. The fisherman who met with Buckland, Walpole and Young saw things quite differently.

"..the steamer traffic is against the fishing, railed John MacDonald, 45 years a fisherman. Steamers came here in 1826, but only once a week. Now, five large steamers call here every day, besides small screw steamers."

He's also affronted by the godless behaviour of incomers and does not hesitate to point an accusing finger, "Strangers now come here and go out on a Saturday night and on a Sunday morning. All the fishermen here desire that this should be stopped. The strangers come from Ardrishaig."

It reads very much like a Buckland insert, much less Walpole or Young speaking, when the text continues with 'When a Scotchman is away from home he is not so particular about the Sabbath as while he is at home.' It is one of the few occasions when the condescending, patrician voice, so strongly associated with the Victorian social order, comes through. His intention might have been to introduce a little levity into the narrative, but it jars with the overall purpose of gathering facts without fear, favour, or prejudice.

Alexander Clark, an agent for Lloyds, steered the discussion towards the hot topic of trawling.

"..the failure is due to the trawl net...There were many failures of the same kind before, but (not) such a continuous blank as there has been lately." Over and above advocating the prohibition of trawling on spawning beds, he suggests that, "it would be beneficial to put it (trawling) down in a small place like the upper *parts of this upper loch. The trawlers are strangers. There are none (resident) here. They come the moment they hear of fishing."*

Archibald Fraser, of Fort William, is happy to name names when he reports, *"the Barra fishing is injurious to this fishery. The fishermen here believe that the Barra fishery is the cause of the failure here...Strangers used to fish on the Sunday, and at all hours."*

George Rieach intervened at this point to flatly contradict Fraser's aspersions about the fishermen of Barra, *"It is a complete delusion to say that the Barra fishery has any effect on the fisheries in the west coast (sea) lochs."*

On the other hand, Fraser does find an ally in the unsurprising shape of the Reverend Patrick Gordon, the minister at Fort William for the past twenty-three years. He is evidently *'scandalized'* to have heard even of *"the few cases of strangers coming in and fishing while his own men were asleep or keeping Sunday. There is no resident officer to stop this."*

Again, an addendum, or perhaps an aside from Archibald Young wearing his advocate's hat, looks suspiciously like it has been sneaked into the text when we're told, *"the law does exist, and was tried to be enforced in Mull, but without success, from deficient evidence."* That remark isn't qualified in any of the appendices, although there was a law, indifferently and inconsistently enforced, that specifically prohibited fishing on a Sunday.

This reference to the law masks an on-going argument about the extent of the Church's influence on the legislature, and in particular the observance of the Sabbath. What was once a strict edict had been diluted over time, and become devolved to the jurisdiction of local authorities. An interesting report from researchers at Glasgow University (Brown, C.; Green, T & Mair, J., 2016) contains a reference to a test case in Dundee that involved an apprentice barber who *'refused to shave customers on a Sunday on the grounds of religious conviction'.* He was found in the first instance to be *'in breach of indenture',* but his appeals went all the way to the House of Lords where his actions were finally vindicated.

Tarbert Hotel, Tarbert, Isle of Harris, 15th September 1877

The HMS Jackal must have been a well-made craft. It was built by Napier's at Govan in 1844 and saw continuous deployment in some of the most challenging seas around in the world.

It was launched on 28th October, and equipped with a two-cylinder steam engine, a single 18-pounder carronade, and two 24-pounder carronades. It was also a two-masted vessel measuring 142 feet in length and 22 feet across her beam.

She looked quite sleek in side elevation and, as a sailing vessel, handled more like a schooner than a steamer. The Jackal was commissioned at Plymouth in 1846 and, having performed impressively in sea trials, subsequently saw service first in the Mediterranean, and then as a store ship based at Ascension Island in the South Atlantic.

HMS Jackal was formally seconded to the Fisheries Board from around 1864 onwards and would have been a familiar sight along the coasts, on the lochs and among the islands. It cost around £15,000 to build her, and she was eventually sold for scrap in 1887 after a long, hardworking life that lasted more than forty years.

The good ship Jackal was, therefore, more than capable of transporting three fisheries inspectors (and Bartlett the Zoo Man) across the Minch to the Isle of Harris and the Tarbert Hotel where the turnout was disappointing, but the testimony revealing.

Buckland, Walpole and Young had previously heard widespread criticism of the 'early fishing' that began yearly in May in the Minch; the amorphous expanse of water between the outer isles and the heavily inleted west coast of Scotland. If they thought they'd hear local fishermen defending their right to fish when and where they pleased, then they were about to be educated.

George McLeod, a fisherman, put them straight on the matter when he explained, *"There are about fifty boats from Harris fishing for herrings; there are five men to each boat. The fifty boats fish here from 1st June to the 15th July. After that, forty of them go to the east coast, most of them to Wick."*

Who, then, is fishing in May, if not Tarbert men?

George is quick to point the finger. *"The Stornoway fishing..commences on May 15th...it breaks up the shoals in the butt of Lewis."*

Norman McLeod (jr.) agreed wholeheartedly adding, *"The May fishing is doing harm to the curers and the markets. The May fish are immature. It would be necessary to appoint someone specially to enforce the close season."*

Kenneth McLennan (occupation unknown) warmed to the theme, *"It would be necessary to have a government steamship to enforce the law."*

He was, presumably, thinking of a vessel very similar to the Jackal moored down at Tarbert harbour. In any case, the other witnesses present; John McLeod, Norman MacFie and John MacKay lined up to concur with him and are recorded as *'agreeing with the previous statements.'* One other witness, Norman McLeod senior, offered an interesting aside about the particularly poor catch of the previous season.

"There was falling off in the Minch fishing in 1876, which was, however, attributable to the very stormy character of the summer."

This indicates that the summer storms that year were significant all around northern Scotland, and taken together, the overall take from coastal communities must have appeared like a sudden, inexplicable and alarming decline.

Lewis Hotel, Stornoway, Monday, 17th September

We might reasonably expect the Stornoway fishermen to have been on the defensive, given the blunt accusations made in Tarbert. Any suggestion of mutual antipathy was quickly dispelled by one statement after another blaming strangers for the May fishing.

Thomas Macdonald, fisherman of Broad Bay, placed the facts firmly before the commissioners when he said, *"The generality of the fishermen would be in favour of a close season not extending beyond the 23rd May. The fishermen cannot establish one themselves because the east coast fishermen come here and fish, and the local men are obliged to do the same. The east coast men come from Wick, Peterhead and Fraserburgh....It does not pay the curers to get herring before the 20th May, and the better price the curer receives, the better price he can pay the fishermen."*

Alexander McLean, a fisherman from Poolewe in Ross-shire, added, *"The*

fishery (in the Minch) commences at the beginning of May, which is too soon."
He also volunteered a morsel of natural history, no doubt for Buckland's
delectation. *"The whales usually feed on the outside of a shoal, occasionally in
the very middle of them."* The species of cetacean is not specified, which
is frustrating. Buckland, writing in Notes and Jottings, gives a similar
description of fin whales hunting herring, but it does sound tantalisingly
like an ambush at sea involving toothed whales, perhaps killers, working
co-operatively.

It was always the case, then as now, that people in the rural and remote
communities in Scotland did not rely so heavily on one occupation or
industry as larger, more centralized populations.

Norman MacDonald, also of Broad Bay, spoke at length and questioned
the economics of the May fishery, *"A close season is desirable, among other
reasons, because in early summer the weather is cold, and the weak and the poor
fish alone are near the surface. The fish rise gradually from the bottom as the
temperature increases. Another reason for the close season is that the Lewis men
would be able to work their crofts in May. The quality of the herrings is of very
little value...the fishermen usually get only 10 to 15s a cran for the early herrings
(half as much as they might expect for mature herrings)."*

It's clear that some thought has been given to the issue and there is
widespread recognition that a law without enforcement would be ineffective.
As Kenneth Smith, a curer, says, "It would be possible to enforce the close
season. *"The fishery officer might be aided by a revenue cruiser...the fishermen
will submit to the law. When the close season was instituted in 1861, small boats
went out in the parish of the lochs. A policeman went over and stopped their going
out. The law was enforced."*

Kenneth Murray, a fish curer of Stornoway and Ness, was as dismayed by
the situation as anyone else, *"The fishing commences too soon. Some years the
herring are unfit to eat on the 20th May, when the fishermen wish the fishing to
begin."*

Murray actually seemed more vexed by yet another unhappy circumstance
relating to harbour accommodation.

"A new harbour would create a new industry at Port Ness. A petition was

presented to Sir James Matheson's factor on the subject last year. It would be easy to make a good harbour there.

There have been frequent occasions when lives were lost at Ness trying to get into the harbour. In 1862, thirty lives were lost and at a later date seven lives were lost.

A harbour would immensely develop the fishery, and would lead to the construction of new curing houses, and almost a new village. It would ultimately develop the property of the proprietor."

Sir James Matheson was always going to be the kind of proprietor possessed of a large pair of deaf ears. Matheson bought the Isle of Lewis in 1844 for over half a million pounds and cleared dozens of families off the land, shipping them to Canada. He went on to become the governor of the Bank of England and the second largest landowner in Britain.

The business empire he built with his partner William Jardine was based first on slavery, and later consolidated by trade in silks, tea, spices and opium throughout China and the Far East. The firm continues today as a *'British conglomerate incorporated in Bermuda'* with its head offices located in a Hong Kong skyscraper.

There is no evidence that the commissioners petitioned Matheson over Port Ness in the way that they pursued the Duke of Portland over the harbour at Lybster. Perhaps, they expected more of Portland and very little of Matheson.

Upon his death in 1878, at the age of eighty-two, Matheson bequeathed £1,500 for the building of a harbour at Port Ness, one-fifth of the estimated cost. It may have been enough to assuage his conscience, but probably too little to guarantee a place in heaven.

Royal Hotel and HMS Jackal, Ullapool, 18th September 1877

Two sessions were held at Ullapool on this date. One at the Royal Hotel and the other on board HMS Jackal. The commissioners met first with locals at the Royal, and later that day heard from Captain Digby. As a methodical and assiduous naval officer, Digby perhaps submitted extracts from his log rather than sat formally before the commissioners. In any case, his testimony refers primarily to the spawning grounds at Ballantrae Bank and so is presented in the next chapter on Loch Fyne.

The witnesses at the Royal Hotel comprised mainly local, inshore fishermen plying their trade in and around Loch Broom. Their submissions are short and to the point, reiterating much of the testimony previously heard on Harris and Lewis. The consistency of these witnesses serves to underscore the value of the herring report as an impartial record that resists the influence of hearsay and the voicing of petty enmities.

Alexander Fraser, a 78-year-old fisherman, took aim at the trawlermen and scored a direct hit when he drew a bead on cause and effect.

"Trawling; i.e. circle trawling, was introduced a good many years ago...The fishery has fallen off since trawling was introduced....the steam yachts carry beam trawls and sweep up all before them... they (the herring) spawn on the bank between Loch Broom and the islands...the trawl and yachts trawl on the spawning bank."

William McKenzie, a fisherman at Ullapool, supported by, Duncan McKenzie, John McKenzie, Allan McKenzie and John McLeod, perhaps in organized revolt, spoke as one when William announced, *"The fishing in the Minch is prejudicial, and there should be no fishing before the 26th May."*

The commissioners went on to *'Balmacarra'* (sic) on the last leg of their Highland tour, and there found Gordon of Cluny's factor had followed them from east to west talking up his Barra fishery. In fact, it was James Methuen of Leith who, in 1869, set up a fishing station at Castlebay on Barra that employed thousands of migrant workers and extended the season from May through June and July.

Cluny had owned Barra since 1838, and one of his first acts (like so many others before and after him) was to expel most of the resident population. Little wonder then that the salient feature of this marine harvest was a massive seasonal influx of *'strangers'* from all over Scotland in spring and summer each year.

It also may explain that the principal contrarians who met with Buckland, Walpole and Young in these communities were merchants or fish curers. They sound a bit like present-day climate change deniers. Still, it is much to the commissioner's credit that they give equal weight to the six fishermen of Balmacara who were caught in the crossfire of the battle between subsistence harvesting and industrial exploitation of a shared natural resource.

Donald Matheson put it succinctly for the local fishermen when he saw, *"trawlers in Loch Hourn in 1872 destroying herrings in the daytime. There were 200 crans landed that day, and there was no fishing afterwards. The 200 crans came in one trawl."*

Cluny's agent and factor, Ronald McDonald, was clearly sent miles out of his way to divert the commissioners' attention, and his crude attempts at misdirection are included in the report verbatim. He begins by needlessly magnifying the economic importance of Cluny's Barra, South Uist, and Loch Boisdale fishery as, *"a comparatively new industry (that) has assumed considerable proportions... The fishing is reckoned to include 5000 strangers in the fishing season."*

It also seems likely that Buckland, Walpole and Young, already experienced fisheries inspectors and men of the world, were unimpressed by sophistry such as *"...these fisheries fluctuate according to the state of the weather"* and, more desperately, boasting that he, *"got the very finest herrings he ever tasted in South Uist in June."* Perhaps, Cluny's man was acutely aware that local curers had already declared these herrings as *"inedible"* and *"unfit for curing."* Alongside the sober representations of the fishermen, McDonald sounds a little shrill and his testimony little more than marketing speak.

The Highlands and Islands in the 21st Century

One of the tender mercies of the nineteenth-century herring boom is that it left few physical scars visible on the landscape. Other wounds, such as sunken boats, wrecked lives and everlasting sorrow are, by their nature, less obvious. They are left either to self-heal, or be eaten by time and rust.

The migrating herring factories that made up a peripatetic caravan of gutters, salters, curers, labourers, fishermen, coopers, traders, merchants and hangers-on worked in the open in the most temporary of conditions. There is, therefore, little trace of them except in photographs from late in the century, in street names, and in the many maritime museums that mourn their passing.

The prevailing image of the Highlands and Islands of Scotland persists as an exemplar of iconic, unspoilt natural landscapes, peopled by unpretentious folk leading an almost pastoral existence. This has much to do with the resistance of the landscape to the deep penetration of industrialization as it does to marketing myths. It is still a world of winding roads, train tracks that end abruptly, and ferries that are subject to the tender mercies of the weather. The area has isolation in abundance, but it lacks many of the certainties of modern life.

Highland traits and Island manners may be charming features, but they only serve to contribute to the same separateness of the Highlands and Islands that permitted the clearance of people from their homes, with barely a murmur of protest from the Anglicized Lowlands. The Highland welcome can be forgiven for being more guarded these days, although that hasn't discouraged the continuing inward migration of strangers from the South.

In 2018, there is a distinct sense of opening up the Highlands and Islands for development, but it's hard to know at this stage whether this constitutes reparation of a sort, or merely more exploitation. The wind farms on Lewis have the effect of altering a picture after it has been sold to the mug punter, gulled into buying what he thought was a pastoral masterpiece.

The fish factories are busy, but the inshore fishermen are still waiting for proportionate recognition and support in pursuit of an authentic, subsistence livelihood. Their contribution to the tourism purse also seems strangely unmeasured. What, after all, is a pretty coastal village or town without harbourside creels and the comings and goings of the small, brightly painted boats?

The romantic, windswept beaches of the western isles have as much plastic (if not more) strewn about them as anywhere else, while the pristine sea lochs that perforate the mainland on its west side can measure discharged fuel, carelessly discarded rubbish and invisible chemical pollutants as comparable with many a despoiled rural idyll.

One thing that has been preserved in the Highlands and Islands to a greater extent than many other parts of Scotland is its *inherent* value. It is easier to make a case elsewhere for digging something up, chopping something down, or ripping out something centuries old that won't be missed until it's gone.

Keen observers of attempts to subvert this holistic sense of worth have seen them met with concentrated resistance that depends entirely on legislation and enforcement of the law. One recent example of this has been an application for licences to dredge pristine kelp beds among the western isles. This kelp, protected by the law, is a major ecological feature that is essential to the health of inshore waters, and the creatures that depend upon it for shelter, breeding, and rearing of young in a safe nursery environment.

It is habitat that is of crucial importance to the inshore fishermen who depend on the crustaceans, cephalopods and smaller fish species for a living. Moreover, the destructive nature of mechanised kelp dredging was as obvious to the fishermen, scientists and the green lobby, as trawling was to the men of Tarbert, Stornoway and Balmacara.

In the end, an impressive online campaign held the Scottish government to account for its own stringent legislation around marine conservation areas. The applications were refused, not because government inspectors spent weeks on site taking evidences, but because Ailsa McLellan, an oyster farmer from Ullapool, built a watertight case against an exploitative practice that was obviously wrong, and ended up further strengthening kelp bed protection in law.

This has been a rather storied chapter, and we now find ourselves approaching the sharp end of the pointed differences that exist in Scotland about nature, resources, and sustainability. Tourism and the 'selling of Scotland' exemplify the nation's pent-up ambition, but it doesn't always fit neatly into a working landscape. The fundamental questions persist, 'What kind of Scotland do we want' and 'Who is it for?'

There are profoundly conflicting 'solutions', which are mooted almost on a daily basis, and there is still a great deal of external interference in Scotland's internal affairs. As I write this, a government enquiry is underway to examine an application to build a golf course at Coul Links in Caithness.

The area in question is a Site of Special Scientific Interest within a National Reserve, which embraces an internationally gazetted wetland site. It couldn't be better protected, but, in reality, it isn't. The developer's application should have been thrown out, but it wasn't. The enquiry shouldn't be happening, but it is.

In stark contrast, there are numerous proposals to give over the existing landscape to 're-wilding projects'. These are 'plans' that form no part of long-term Scottish government land use strategies. Yet, reintroduction of iconic species is well understood to require long-term commitment. It shouldn't really be allowed to happen, but in one part of Scotland it already has, with the accidental release of beavers 'into the wild'. In this particular case, the return of the native has gained acceptance, but it its tenure is conditional.

It is a species whose potential for conflict with human interests is so significant that management measures are already in place. A 'licence to cull' may even be issued in circumstances where the beavers threaten to cause significant damage to property an/or watercourses. A recent BBC report suggests, however, that some people are prepared to shoot first and ask for a licence later.

The introduction of the European Beaver in upper Tayside does nothing to restore 'the wild'. That no longer exists. The beavers currently roaming the quasi-countryside in Scotland are nothing more than naturalized aliens. They are strangers in a strange and hostile land, and I think it questionable that Scotland is capable of accommodating a free and expanding population of such large and highly fecund rodents.

Too many essential stories remain untold, and too many urgent issues find themselves outside the scope of this book. It has been important to dwell on some of them here though, if only to remind ourselves that our principal obligations are to future generations if we want to pass on the treasures and pleasures of The Highlands and Islands intact and fit for purpose.

Loch Fyne

Inverary, Crarae, Lochgair, Ardrishaig, Tarbert, Campbeltown & Girvan, 21st – 28th September 1877

"Vast as are the resources of the sea, yet it is possible that modern appliances and want of scientific cultivation for fishing may draw too much upon the general stock in certain localities." – **Frank Buckland (in Burgess, 1967, pp 168).**

The commissioners travelled to Inveraray fully aware, and perhaps better informed than anyone, of the notorious incident that took place in 1861 at Loch Fyne. The death of trawlerman Peter McDougall from Ardrishaig was a tragic error, but it quickly became emblematic of a conflict that fomented strong feelings in the community and provoked the strong arm of the state.

Trawling had been practiced at Loch Fyne for many years before the introduction on 1851 of an experimental ban that lasted until 1867. In the meantime, recalcitrant trawlermen, perhaps encouraged by the hitherto light-touch enforcement of the law, carried on regardless. This, in turn, enabled a somewhat romantic view of the Loch Fyne trawlerman as a Victorian anti-hero, punished out of all proportion for simply scraping a living.

"They were harassed on land and sea, jailed, and had their nets and boats confiscated", reports Angus Martin in his useful booklet *Fishing and Whaling* published by the National Museum of Scotland in 1998.

The evidences put before the 1877 Commission offer a more rounded perspective, not least from fishermen who were around at the time, and epitomize to a continuing, polarized debate about the virtues and vices of inshore trawling.

"The breach of the law was winked at", testified one old salt, only too happy to remind the Commissioners that indifferent policing had contributed to a sense of entitlement amongst the trawlermen.

The trawling continued at Loch Fyne illegally for ten years, but against a backdrop of ineffective enforcement and a highly productive business model that could more readily absorb the odd confiscation or fine. At Loch Fyne, the herring fishermen spoke to the Commissioners about the affordability of buying a boat and nets, and reported the lucrative returns that could be expected from such a relatively modest outlay. This is in contrast to their cousins on the east coast who were more commonly 'fee'd' to a curer, boat-owner, or merchant.

It is often the case, that legislation may be viewed with scepticism, or even treated with contempt, but sooner or later, the state will feel the need to lay down the law and make an example of someone. MacDougall was involved in a deadly confrontation with the crew of the *Jackal*, not yet seconded to the fisheries board, but one of a number of vessels periodically deployed by the navy on fisheries enforcement tasks.

A previous, violent incident in 1853, in which a gunner and a marine from *HMS Porcupine* shot and wounded a fisherman, was deemed use of excessive force. Both servicemen were tried and sentenced to three months imprisonment, but it only served to foreshadow the inevitable. The general account of the McDougall tragedy is framed as a predictable outcome of a bad law poorly enforced, but is also a story of implacable resistance to the sudden imposition of immovable authority.

The subsequent inquiry heard that the marines on board the Jackal felt sufficiently threatened to break out arms, but it was the suggestion of summary execution that agitated the authorities. Perhaps unsurprisingly, the nervous young seaman who discharged the fatal shot in the midst of a general melee was cleared of murder, but found negligent. Nevertheless, the trawlermen at Loch Fyne had their martyr, and so occupied the better part of the high moral ground when they met the commissioners.

"The state of things and the bad feeling which it created were so serious that in 1862, a Commission was formally appointed to enquire into the operation of the laws relating to trawling for herrings. The commission reported strongly in favour of the trawlers."

When the commissioners convened at Inverary they found that controversy, contradiction and conflict persisted around what is really a single issue; the benign offtake of a natural resource by subsistence methods versus the rapid, mechanised removal of biomass. Their conclusions await us in the final chapter of this book, but first we have to hear what the fishermen of upper and lower Loch Fyne have to say for themselves.

The Upper Loch Fyne Evidences

Inveraray Town Hall, Friday, 21st September 1877 & Argyll Arms Hotel, Inveraray, Saturday 22nd September 1877

It fell to R. A MacFarlane, Provost of Inverary (pop ca 580) to hand in a 'memorial', which had *'previously been ratified at a previous public meeting'*, and represented the *'whole fishery interest of Inveraray'*. Its tone suggests the signatories subscribed to attack as the best form of defence, and a fusillade of text fires across four full pages of the report.

It states *'emphatically'* that the herring fishing in Loch Fyne has been a failure *'compared with what it used to be in former times.'* At times, the language is a little overheated, but the argument is cleverly structured. It avers that regulation isn't necessary to maintain the prosperity of the fishery but *'free trade'* does not mean that you can go where you like, do what you like, and take what you want. They advocate rigid rules and close management over enforcement while at the same time bemoaning, *'..the comparative ignorance of, and indifference to, the future consequences of their reckless action upon...other people's interests.'*

Other food sources are closely managed, they argue, so why not the herring? *'The supply of lobsters, crabs, oysters, salmon and grouse is now not held to be inexhaustible...the supply of herring is exhaustible in the same manner.'*

There is also a pretty fierce swipe at those who contended there was insufficient knowledge to justify legislative interference with the modes of prosecuting the herring fishery. Buckland must have winced, or perhaps rankled, as he read the following,

'Those who make such statements are either ignorant of the amount of knowledge of the habits of the herring possessed by all practical fishermen.'

The 'memorialists' instead assert that empirical observations alone don't constitute a valid assessment of the reasons for the failure of the fishery at Loch Fyne. They urge *'careful enquiry'* but submit their own theories, many of which had merit and sound terribly familiar to modern ears. In the main, they echo much that the commissioners had heard before, namely: disturbance on or near spawning grounds, excessive offtake of immature fish, trawling, overfishing, small mesh sizes, water pollution, putrid fish rotting in lost nets, noise, and daylight fishing.

It is all very detailed and thorough, and much of it reads like a discussion paper that Scottish Natural Heritage might produce. All of these negatives occurred at Loch Fyne, and were partly corroborated by Captain Digby in evidences from his log book presented on board HMS Jackal at Ullapool only three days before on 18th September.

In particular, he noted *'large quantities of herring in the lower waters of Loch Fyne...very few of these came above Ardrishaig where complaints of the trawl net..are most rife.'* Perhaps more damningly, he reported finding drift nets in huge numbers full of rotten fish and dead gannets that had been left out for days at a time on the spawning bank at Ballantrae.

In one instance he found they'd been left out for a week because the weather was deemed too bad to retrieve them. *'Nearly 300 boats were fishing last year with drift nets from Ballantrae...The boasts do not lie with their nets...Ballantrae bank is one of the chief spawning grounds at Loch Fyne...the parent herrings are destroyed in the act of spawning.'* Interestingly, he seemed to think that the trawlers stayed out of the area because *'the bottom is 'too foul' for this method of fishing.'*

The recommendations of the 'memorialists' were simple and straightforward. They advocated protection of spawning fish, protection of young, immature herring, prohibition of trawling at all times between Mull of Galloway and Mull of Cantyre, prohibition of day fishing, a close season from 1st February to 1st June, and a close time to cover observance of the Sabbath laws.

It all seems perfectly sensible, because it clearly speaks to effective management of fish stocks that any government agency would recognise today. Yet, these folk were not conservationists. They were protectionists seeking to ring-fence their share of a profitable enterprise, and they had their sights firmly fixed on trawling.

There is a turn in the memorialists' narrative with *'Trawling is peculiarly destructive...vast quantities of spawn are destroyed...immense quantities of young and useless herring are taken'*, that continues with *'Fish in large quantities are left to putrify and pollute the waters...the herring are ultimately driven away from such grounds'*...contributing to a *"shocking waste."*

Furthermore, *'Trawling is conducted in daylight...by the method of trawling the fish are frightened and scared away.'* Finally, and perhaps hoping to drive a stake through its black heart, trawling was deemed to be, *'...to a large extent, answerable for the depressed state of this fishery.'*

It is possible, though, to overstate your case, and Buckland can't have been best pleased when he came to the passage that rubbished his own proposition that it would be impossible to fish the herring to extinction, *'Your memorialists consider it judicious to dispose of certain crude statements which have gained currency...in influential quarters.'*

The reference, none too oblique, is to Buckland's calculation that because the herring's natural enemies take so much more fish than fishermen, then human depredation must be inconsequential.

The counter-argument they make is recognisable today as the hot topic of species extinction driven by anthropogenic disruption of natural systems. Where the herring is heavily preyed upon by a cohort of natural enemies, the memorialists argued, it follows that further predation at human hands interferes with the delicate balance of nature. There is, therefore, the potential to undermine survivorship and recovery of local populations.

Someone with a gift for the persuasive metaphor concluded, 'If the candle is burning so fiercely at one end, lit by nature's hand, (then) there is all the greater reason why the flame at the other end kindled by man should be regulated.'

The evidences at Inverary rather fizzle out with a series of seemingly inconsequential remarks that are nonetheless evocative of times changing and old ways giving way to the shock of the new...'"There are three steamers now plying Loch Fyne. 'The Lord of the Isles' daily, one luggage boat thrice, and one twice a week" (John MacFarlane, fisherman for 20 years)."

John McKellar reportedly declared Loch Fyne fish, 'a distinct fish' with a better flavour. Although he thought trawling the 'chief cause of the failure', he was, nevertheless, 'interested in acquiring his own boat.'

On 22nd September the commissioners met Quentin Montgomery Wright, a writer and bank agent who described the virtual collapse of the Inveraray economy and attributed the failure, "entirely to the advent of trawling." There was a time, according to Wright, when fishermen could deposit savings of "20 to 40 pounds after the close of the fishing season" something he implies rather than states is a thing of the past.

It was from here that Buckland, Walpole and Young either divided their labours, or else together undertook a whistle-stop excursion down the western edge of Loch Fyne from Crarae to Ardrishaig. If it were my decision to make, I would certainly have left one of the others at Inveraray to endure the rambling historical digressions of the very Rev. Neil McPherson, and the dreary unpicking of Fisheries Board figures by the pedantic fisherman Martin Munro.

Free Kirk, Crarae, 22nd September 1877

The best use of time and resources would, to my mind, involve placing Archibald Young on a hired pony and trap and sending him forthwith to Crarae. Once there, he needed only to spend a pleasant hour in the company of the local schoolmaster Daniel Thompson who spoke on behalf of the community. As it turned out, also present were the Reverend John Clark and thirty-eight fishermen who *'unanimously expressed their concurrence in the evidence.'* It was also claimed that those in attendance represented *'one half of the fishermen of the village'* who *'would agree with the views expressed.'*

Clark's evidence is a succinct summary consisting of four paragraphs that essentially presses a singular case. *"The fishermen are all of the opinion that the failure is due to the trawling."* Nothing less than the prohibition of trawling all year round would do. It's not uncommon, in a polarised debate, to hear an over-amplified argument, but Thompson certainly warms to his own oratory as it builds to its conclusion.

"The herrings have fallen off in the last 12 years...there is no doubt that the trawl nets have destroyed the herring fishery...the trawling kills all the herrings, young and old, little and big."

There is no doubt who is to blame. *"The trawlers come from Tarbert...and cut the drift nets. The Loch Fyne fishermen are, therefore, compelled to use the trawl in self-defence."* The solution is even clearer, *'The suppression of trawling is the only point he wishes to impress upon the commission'.*

Nevertheless, Thompson goes on to make his *'only other point'*, *"The fishermen now report all instances of Sunday fishing and the minister writes to the delinquent's minister to use his moral influence to stop it."*

The lack of individual evidences from any of the thirty-eight fishermen present is a clear departure from the principle and practice in the Herring Report. The idle interrogations of Buckland, and Walpole's remit for statistics are similarly absent. It was the same at Lochgair where the impression that information is being relayed to the commission through an educated and trustworthy administrator such as Archibald Young.

Lochgair Hotel, Lochgair Saturday 22nd September 1877

John Mackillop was the schoolmaster at Lochgair and had been in post since 1864. He repeated the litany of complaints against trawling generally, and the *'Tarbert men'* in particular. The trawling needed, in his view, (and in the view of *'all the fishermen present'*) to be prohibited *'from the Mull of Galloway to the Mull of Cantyre.'* Daylight fishing also needed to be curbed.

No numbers are given for the fishermen in the room, but three men, one of whom seemed to be a former fisherman and another who was '*81 years old*' were inclined to add their twopence worth. Having said that, Archibald McEwan of Kames who '*was fishing for 20 years previous to the trawl net being legalised (in 1867)*', quite consciously, described subsistence fishing and a pastoral way of life as profoundly under threat from modernity

"*Formerly, no boat need leave Loch Fyne...old infirm men were able to maintain themselves comfortably by fishing quite close to their homes. Now, if a family should lose the head of the family, there is nothing for them but the workhouse.*"

The octogenarian Archibald Bell chimed with his testament that '*There were more herrings in the loch when he was a lad.*' In a rare editorial oversight, it's recorded that he '*approves of Mr. McCulloch's recommendation to prohibit trawling.*' It's not clear if this is an typographic error, or whether Bell misheard MacKillop's name and his words faithfully recorded. Certainly, there is no McCulloch recorded as present and the mistake is very much out of step with the attention to extraneous detail that defines much of the recorded evidences.

Ardrishaig Hotel, Ardrishaig, Saturday 22nd September 1877

The commissioners, working together or separately, covered a lot of ground on 22nd September. The distance between Inverary and Ardrishaig is about twenty-five miles, and even with horse-drawn transport and a naval gunboat at their disposal, they worked efficiently to get gather evidences from a dispersed community.

The contrast between the snapshot evidences taken at the previous three locations in the course of the day and the more involved deliberations at Ardrishaig is also significant. It is at Ardrishaig that the various conflicting issues and interests within the Loch Fyne herring fishery intersected with the laws of nature and the rule of law. It's hardly surprising that the individual evidences were relatively lengthy and complex, but they were also comprehensive and complete.

"*The herrings 20 or 30 years ago used to spawn at Loch Fyne; they do not spawn*

168

now except at Ballantrae. The destruction of spawning herring at Ballantrae prevents the fish from coming up Loch Fyne. The herrings in Loch Fyne will not be so plentiful if the spawning herrings at Ballantrae are destroyed" - Donald Munro, fisherman for 45 years.

"The fish in May are not fit to cure. They are sent to Glasgow and there is no difficulty in selling them" – Stuart Hamilton local fisherman, who was, *'not in favour of prohibiting trawling, either experimentally, or at all'.*

Hamilton refers to a catch worth £400 and may have been alluding to the whole season's take, but he also adds that *'some boats at Tarbert have got £300 with one shot.'*

It is facile to patronize the simple fisherman from a bygone age, so any temptation to think Hamilton's claims an exaggeration ought to be resisted. He is merely describing the beginning of industrialised fishing, and the 'smash and grab' economics that eviscerates nature, first locally and then regionally, in the course of rapid, mechanized harvesting.

John Bruce, a fisherman for 40 years described the incentive in arithmetical terms so simple that even the allegedly innumerate Frank Buckland could grasp, *"A boat for trawling can be got for £30, a trawl for £20. A boat for drift fishing would cost £90 and the nets £50….the trawl-net fish get quicker to the market than the drift-net fish."*

Bruce is hardly a visionary but to his way of thinking the need for oversight in the face of year-round fishing, both night and day, seems obvious. *"The drift and trawl nets are in a free-for-all. There is no one to look after the fisheries. There used to be a cutter to do this kind of work and to regulate the fishery. There is no protection of any kind."*

In circumstances such as these where an immediate business opportunity conflicts with long-term sustainability within an economic matrix, there is always the voice of the obdurate, unreasoning misdirection.

In this case, it was Duncan MacGregor, a trawlerman, who declared that he, *"never saw more fish in Loch Fyne than he saw last Friday, 3 miles north of Tarbert."* He also claimed to have caught 20,000 herring at Otter Spit *"at a shot".* Unsurprisingly, he was in favour of *"free trade"*, and though that, *"every man should do as he chooses."*

Lower Loch Fyne Evidences

We must now turn our attention to the lower reaches of Loch Fyne where it is confluent with the Firth of Clyde and its umbilical relationship with Glasgow becomes self-evident. It's also plain to see that the commissioners' itinerary once more becomes a little counter-intuitive. On the 24th and 25th September 1877, they visited Tarbert and Campbeltown respectively, where they found a concerted lobby very much on the side of the trawlermen.

Common sense would suggest they should complete their investigations on Loch Fyne at Girvan, a trawling community on the Galloway coast, and at nearby Ballantrae. The evidences from these locations could only be pivotal to the fractured debate among fishermen about the wisdom of fishing on a significant spawning bank.

Instead of pressing on to get answers to pressing questions, they diverted themselves to Glasgow where, on the 27th September 1877, they spoke to fish curers, salesmen and merchants. The Empire's second city would also have been the most logical terminus at the end of their long sojourn in Scotland, so the detour is doubly puzzling.

They don't reach Girvan and Ballantrae until the 28th September where they conducted the hearings on the same day. At this time, the commissioners still had HMS Jackal at their disposal so the logistics of travel were straightforward. So, why go to Glasgow first? Perhaps, the VIP on board had to check in with his superiors at the Zoological Society of London that everything was tickety-boo at the zoo.

Documented evidence tells us that Frank Buckland and London Zoo's Abraham Bartlett were more than just professional acquaintances. They were cronies, and there are several candid references to support that view in Bartlett's autobiographical, 'Wild Animals in Captivity', published in 1899.

"Of all the persons I have ever met or associated with, I know of none who possessed a more amiable, good tempered and kinder disposition than the late Frank Buckland. Of this I had many opportunities of judging, having on several occasions accompanied him on his duties of Inspector of Salmon Fisheries."

As previously stated, Bartlett, aged sixty-five but still very much in charge at the zoo in Regents Park, is recorded on board the Jackal for the Orkney/Shetland evidences. He also travelled with Buckland to Bute from Ballantrae at the end of the evidence gathering. The reason for this will be explained in due course. In the meantime, we return to the proper sequence of events to hear quite contradictory evidences from Tarbert.

The Good Templar's Hall, Tarbert, 24th September 1877

If the Reverend Roderick Morrison, minister at Tarbert, was put forward as a neutral spokesman then he was either very naive, or complicit in a clumsy attempt to ambush the Commissioners. He produced, *'a memorial...agreed to by a large meeting of Tarbert fishermen'* and *'signed by 240 persons'*, which contained one statement after another rubbishing any criticism of trawling.

William Bruce, a fisherman for 40 years, offered this breathless testimony, *"The men watch for bubbles in the water made by the fish breathing..the net is drawn in towards the shore, and lifted into a boat. The fishermen must be very silent the whole time this is being done."*

If Bruce's description of trawling by stealth lacks credibility then his claim that *'there are more herrings in Loch Fyne now than there have been since I was a boy'* sounds flimsier still. In many ways, his evidences are characteristic of the 1877 report, which seeks to record the voices of the participants regardless of their obvious partiality or prejudices.

Certainly, the witnesses at Tarbert were more intent on discrediting others than they were with presenting the Commissioners with useful information about fish and fishing.

"Strange fishermen from Ardrishaig..are more given to ringing (i.e. trawling in pairs in the middle of the loch)..Ringing is more injurious than shore trawling", volunteered Archibald Campbell, adding, *"The upper Loch Fyne fishermen only wish to prohibit trawling for the sake of the easier work of drifting."*

John McGeogan moved to dismiss the case against trawling with, *'There is no ground for the statement that herrings are injured by the trawl net...drift nets make more noise and do more harm than trawl nets."* His sentiments were echoed by William Hay who declared, *"there is nothing to show that trawling has been prejudicial to the fish."*

Neither of these fishermen referenced the inconvenient truth in the figures of George Reiach, '*27 years in the service of the (Fisheries) Board*'. His tables on pages 133 and 135 of the 1877 Report suggest that the situation was more complex, and vulnerable to speculative interpretation. They show that the average take from the area in the decade 1856-1866 was half as much again as the average take for the previous decade, with peculiar dips in 1852 and 1863.

More importantly, the need for the fisheries men to arbitrate by means of separating potentially credible fact from preposterous fiction fully justified the reach and extent of their evidence gathering in the summer of 1877.

White Hart Hotel, Campbeltown, Tuesday 25th September 1877

The fishermen at Campbeltown had not prepared a script but they were, if anything, candid to a fault. Their alacrity is unlikely to win the hearts of modern conservationists, but they have unwittingly left to posterity a reliable memoir. We can divine from a simple sequence of quotations, a condensed oral historiography of Loch Fyne in the late nineteenth century.

'All herrings caught from here to Inveraray are known in the market as Loch Fyne Herrings', so said Dugald Robertson, indulging in an early example of marketing hype. *'There is a herring fishery all year round'*, he assured the commissioners. This particular fisherman had *'been in Ireland from April until June'* and *'uses a trawl net (at Loch Fyne) from August to December.'*

In January, Robertson concentrated his efforts at Ballantrae Bank where he switched from trawling to drift-netting. He might appear to be industrious and conscientious by using *'a common drift net'*, but he was one of many who fixed their nets at night and left them until the next morning or, as Captain Digby testified at Ullapool, a negligent week or more, by which time the catch was literally dead in the water.

It was common knowledge that the *'fish at Ballantrae are in the act of spawning'*, but Robertson, rather disingenuously, *'could not say whether the destruction of spawning herrings is injurious to the fishermen in Loch Fyne'*, adding rather cynically, *"There is no difference in killing a herring the day before it spawns, or a month before it spawns."*

The mindset of the fishermen at lower Loch Fyne may seem short-sighted, if not downright exploitative with little regard for future outcomes. They fished at every opportunity, by every available method as long as there were fish to catch. The depredations of the spawning banks at Ballantrae are a case in point.

William Sharp was *'in favour of continuing the Ballantrae fishing.'*

Malcolm Mclean, *'would allow the Ballantrae fishing to go on.'*

"A great deal of money is earned by catching the spawning herrings at Ballantrae" said Neil Brodie, who added bluntly that he, *"...would not spare the spawning fish. They might only be spared to be eaten by dog-fish and other vermin."*

There was only one, very muted, dissenting voice among them, John Martin who squeaked that he was *"opposed to the Ballantrae fishing at any time."* What became of him afterwards is perhaps mercifully, has gone unrecorded.

Town Hall, Girvan, Thursday 28th September 1877 and Ballantrae Hotel, Friday 28th September 1877

The outlook for the spawning herring on the banks was even bleaker at Girvan and Ballantrae, where opposition and obfuscation took precedence over self-evident facts of natural history.

Yet again, a 'memorial', signed by 108 fishermen, was presented at Girvan It opened appositely enough, with three, numbered points summarized here as follows:

1. 'The taking of herring at the banks of Ballantrae...does not injure the herring... product.'

2. '...trawling of for herring is unimportant.'

3. '...herring should be allowed be allowed to be taken at all times'

There follows a seemingly contradictory passage that refers to an experimental eight-year fishing ban at Ballantrae during which time the locals enjoyed *'splendid (line) fishing of cod and stenlock.'* Those halcyon days were brought to a premature end by the incursions of *'large beam trawling vessels.'*

The verbatim reporting of the commissioners leaves us to work out for ourselves that trawling mattered much less than unfettered access to a shared resource.

John McQuistan of Girvan, a vocal advocate of a wholly, totally unregulated fishery, claimed that, *'herring never spawn at Ballantrae in summer'*, while the fisheries officer at Girvan, John Melville, opted for a diplomatic fudge, reporting, *'There is a good deal of spawn destroyed by the stones and ropes of the nets'*, but he could not bring himself to say, *'whether this practice is injurious.'*

At Ballantrae, there was yet another deposition, this time from John McWilliam, *'a former fisherman'* and Inspector of the Poor, whose long, pedantic submission need not detain us here. Suffice to say it is more notable for stoking disaffection between communities with repeated references to *'Argyllshire men'* he accuses of trying to shut down the fishing station at Ballantrae. *'Truly, it would surely be well if they would cease their croaking against Ballantrae at once and forever and attend to their own affairs.'*

The view from Ballantrae is unremarkable, for the general position of the fisherman there was that no close season, or ban on fishing the spawning banks were the least bit useful or desirable. It does, however, feature a consistent failing of the report, which is the credence it gives to the tedious representations made by *'prominent citizens.'*

In addition to John McWilliam, we also hear from the Ballantrae postmaster, a surgeon and the local minister. Much of their evidence is irrelevant, and they quote pedantically from data already known to the Commissioners. Elsewhere, they digress into long excerpts from redundant historical accounts by other members of the clergy and middle classes. They are, at best, a distraction from more important considerations, one of which was a collective failure to consider the long-term implications of unregulated fishing on the Ballantrae Banks.

Modern Loch Fyne

One of the ills of the internet age is the way in which a manufactured identity can suffocate its individual components. Loch Fyne is famous today as a fairly upmarket tourism hotspot with a magical mix of esoteric wildlife, high-end watersports and fine dining. Yet, most Scots would struggle to find on a map many of the communities that Buckland and his colleagues visited in 1877. Fewer still would have good reason to visit Crarae or Lochgair, unless it came as part of an 'experience'.

Loch Fyne is a rich and beautiful place. Otters sport and play along its shores, while dolphins leap and seals dip and dive in its crystal waters. There is still good fishing to be had, although the occasional basking shark that wanders in from the open sea might be a fish too far for most sea anglers. The land around the loch, as is often the case, remains the preserve of the estate owner, rather than the commoner or, better still, an NGO like the RSPB or the Scottish Wildlife Trust.

It could be argued that nature has already been privatised at Loch Fyne, with many of its most interesting features visible only from a hired boat or on a manicured woodland walk. There are countless operators who think generically of wildlife and promise visitors they will see '*lots of squirrels, birds, seals and deer.*'

It seems negligent not to share a more complete understanding of how nature is preserved in places where development has been slow, low-key and minimally invasive. Perhaps the proximity of nuclear submarines at Holy Loch has been a deterrent to development, more than it has disturbed the sleep of Russian leaders.

The Argyll Bird Club usefully explains that Loch Fyne is better understood as part of the wildlife-rich Cowal Peninsula where golden eagles, ravens and peregrine falcons enjoy an uncommon stronghold. There are various vantage points around the peninsula from which to look for birds, but Otter Ferry on Loch Fyne proper is singled out as a place of interest.

There, with luck, the keen birder might spot a Red-throated Diver, a Hen Harrier, a Peregrine Falcon or, seasonally, Ringed Plovers, Dunlin, Eurasian

Curlew, Common Redshank, Common Sandpipers, and Turnstones. It might even be possible to see an otter there, but it's far from guaranteed. It's regrettable that there are few wildlife organizations on the ground providing interpretation. Apart from enhancing the experience, it's necessary to debunk the artificial re-branding of nature with a pseudo-Gaelic natural history that is pure invention.

If the outdoor life of leisure makes you feel peckish then have no fear. It would be difficult to starve to death on Loch Fyne these days, given the sheer number of pushy restaurants, cafes and bars. This, though, is how and where a settlement gives up its identity to the business with the biggest sign above the door, or the topmost hit on Google. Soon it becomes known only as the nearest place to the important eatery or the exclusive inn, or the branded leisure complex.

The Loch Fyne Oyster Bar at Cairndow began life in the late 1970s as an oyster farm feeding a culinary speciality into elegant, fashionable restaurants. It soon became a smart restaurant brand itself, and expanded into a shoal of outlets, later swallowed up by an even bigger fish. The original oyster bar remains and, although oysters are, for many, an acquired taste, we can be confident that Frank Buckland, were he here today, would almost certainly pay a visit.

Loch Fyne was a brand as much as it was a place long before the advent of online communications. In 1877, the witnesses from Inveraray to Ballantrae were tripping over themselves to claim uniqueness for Loch Fyne herring. They may well have been justified because the fish arrived in Glasgow more or less fresh off the boat, and was immediately sold as street food, ordered for breakfast in the hotels, or served at lunch in a fine overcoat of oatmeal or breadcrumbs.

The nineteenth-century curer, merchantman, shop owner or restaurateur would be alive to the marketing opportunities and unique selling points presented by Loch Fyne herring. Better still, the coming of the steam age meant that the loch almost immediately became a tourist destination for day-trippers.

The explosion of interest in such excursions virtually guaranteed Loch

Fyne its place in the iconography of idyllic Scotland, with its romantic landscape and its oneness with a 'Highland' world of untroubled nature.

To this day, it is easy for television presenters and newspaper columnists to perpetuate this illusion simply by ignoring the fact that Ardrishaig lies further south than Dunfermline. It is a six-minute drive from the nearest Indian takeaway at Lochgilphead, and only an hour or so in the car northwards to the nearest pubchain food outlet at Oban.

It is, perhaps, a little too soon though to mourn the complete demise of Scotch myths. It's entirely possible that Archibald Young, or perhaps even all three commissioners, passing through Crarae, would recognise it today as largely unchanged and still a place of splendid isolation.

Glasgow

The Royal Hotel, Glasgow, Thursday, 27th September 1877

"There are two classes of persons who are perpetually agitating and bringing forward proposals on the subject of fisheries. One of these classes seems filled with the constant apprehension that the fish in the ocean are likely to be almost immediately exhausted by the operations of man. The other section of the community to which I have referred seems also to be filled with the notion that the fisheries cannot flourish without the direct patronage and encouragement of the State or individuals." – **Sir Spencer Walpole addressing The Great International Fisheries Exhibition, 1883.**

It's fairly safe to assume that Buckland, Walpole and Young sailed from Campbeltown to the Broomielaw on the HMS Jackal on Wednesday 26th September. An unhurried round trip on a pleasure craft from Glasgow to nearby Arran took a glacial twelve hours in 1877, so it's safe to say that the Commissioners opted for a leisurely cruise.

It also made sense for them to rise from a comfortable hotel bed in Glasgow on the 27th, well-rested and ready to meet the *nouveau riche* merchant curers of the Empire's second city. The men they would meet carried on their businesses within walking distance of The Royal Hotel at 50 George Square. There would be time enough, before and after the hearing, to eat well and enjoy the sights and sounds of a city on the move.

It may have been a short voyage in nautical miles, but it covered an ocean of time. It's easy to visualize the Jackal steaming away from the dying light of a gentler era towards the dawning of the modern age. It's easier still to look at photographic images from that period and see the changes as they were occurring. We have, among others, the famous firm of George Washington Wilson to thank for startling pictures of the quayside clamour on the Broomielaw. The sense of excitement is palpable. These boats are going somewhere, and everyone wants to be on one of them.

The Broomielaw in 1877 was the main route that ran alongside the Clyde on its north side, much as it does today between Anderston Quay and Clyde Street. Behind it lay the busy shopping arcades of Argyle Street, running parallel with the neatly mapped grid of streets and squares around St. Vincent Street. Anyone shadowing the fisheries men would, like them, be stepping onto the quay and into a maelstrom of mercantile activity. The place was buzzing with business as ships constantly arrived to disgorge their cargo, and wheeler-dealers conducted their myriad affairs, accounts and transactions.

The Broomlielaw was the profit motive personified. Then, as now, it was all about the right product in the right place at the right time. The Glasgow Post office directory of 1877 shows the Broomielaw clearly dominated by more than a dozen wine merchants, a likewise number of steamship agents, and three or more ship's chandleries. It also demonstrates that opportunity is the midwife of diversity. There were coal merchants, sailmakers, clothiers and commission agents aplenty, but there were other curious enterprises too.

At 54 Broomielaw, the enterprising Mr. J. Green sold gutta-percha, a rubber-like material manufactured from natural latex and used primarily to insulate telegraph cables. There was a solitary restaurant and two pastry makers on the Broomielaw for people with time and money to eat, and a temperance hotel for those with an aversion to the demon drink. In amongst the artisan flag makers and brassfounders there were suppliers of ship's instruments, a photographer, a 'ship's chemist and druggist', and one Archibald Dewar, advertising himself as the 'Superintendent of the Sailor's

Home' and an 'emigration agent for New Zealand.'

Aside from the flight from poverty, travel for its own sake was also a money-spinning commodity. The age of steam had reinvented the Firth of Clyde and the Kyles beyond as a busy, bustling, multi-lane highway on the water. The steam engine was a firmly established technology, but it was improving all the time. By the middle of the nineteenth century, city sightseers could affordably see Scotland at its best; and steam helped to create a tourism offer that marketed itself. Steam power also generated a brisk coastal trade, giving birth to the iconic 'puffers', small steam vessels that carried mixed loads of goods, freight and folk on highly circuitous routes around the inner isles.

More importantly, the New World had been brought closer to home with the development of ever-faster trade routes and the long-established demand in Britain for tobacco, sugar and cotton from the former colonies. America was a lucrative project still in development, and Glasgow, facing the Atlantic, grabbed on to its coat-tails with all its might.

It's somehow apt that Buckland, an enthusiastic, lifelong smoker should, at the end of this long undertaking, find himself almost completely surrounded by fine tobacconists. A Glasgow directory from 1869 is, as you would expect, a voluminous guide to a huge and ever-expanding merchant's city. The directory's listings are packed with a tremendous variety of enterprises, but it's the supply of wine and tobacco that catches the eye.

There are *countless* tobacconists in a city not yet full-grown, and the list of wine merchants runs to almost ten pages of tightly-packed, single-line entries. Glasgow was evidently a place for those looking for the sporting life, or else a ticket to a better life elsewhere.

The commissioners' visit to Glasgow was also coincidental with events that came to shape the city's history and future identity. There were steamships travelling to every corner of the empire, but the traffic closer to home made Glasgow's close relationship with Hibernia an umbilical connection. Services were running to and from Galway, Limerick and Larne bringing cheap migrant labour from Ireland to supplement the Highlanders similarly displaced by famine, poverty and patrician cynicism.

It's at Glasgow that we see a perfect storm of capitalism where exploitation is recalibrated as a perverse 'New Deal' for the poor, and an investment opportunity for the rich, with the merchants in the middle taking a percentage from everyone. It was the epitome of an imperial metropolis; vibrant, exciting, fast-moving and full of risks for all.

Buckland Walpole and Young met no fishermen in Glasgow. They exclusively met with individuals at the very top of the food chain, blandly described in the 1878 Report as *'fishcurers and salesmen'*. Until this point, fishcurers had been represented in the report by agents and functionaries, or else characterized as former fishermen with a head for figures and an aptitude for negotiation.

The fishcurers that emerge in Glasgow were high-status individuals who capitalized on King Herring by delivering fresh, ready-to-eat, street food to the masses and exporting the cured product as delicacies to the foreign market. The silver darlings poured daily onto the quayside at the Broomielaw, travelling mere yards to the curing houses in Fox Street, Jackson Street and East Clyde Street. Anything that did not go to the fresh fish market was salted, barrelled and despatched to London, Hamburg and Stettin.

The ergonomy of year-round supply from the west coast, the islands, Loch Fyne and Firth of Clyde through centralized distribution from the heart of a rail, sail and steam hub of Glasgow made these men very rich. You could say it turned humble, silver fish into ingots of gold. These 'fishcurers' may have conducted their business on the Broomielaw, but they lived elsewhere, far distant from the dirt, the smell and hubub on the quayside.

Hugh McLachlan, is a typical example. His premises, located at 18 Jackson Street, were situated between Stockwell Street and Dunlop Street, quite near the Trongate. His curing house was almost equidistant between the 'Steam Boat Quay' on the Broomielaw and the Caledonian Railway Station (Glasgow Central). St. Enoch's Station was on his doorstep, the Glasgow and South Western Goods Station on his flank, and the North British (Queen Street) Station was a ten minute cart-drive up Buchanan Street.

McLachlan is part of a community of fishcurers. They are all operating within a few streets of one another, and prosperous enough to live in mansionhouse apartments or, like MacLachan, in a large, detached villa in leafy suburbs on the south side of the city.

McLachlan lived at Lewis Villa, in Pollokshields, a bespoke estate built from scratch, which grew into a significant satellite just outside the city limits. Other Glasgow fishcuring moguls lived in similar growth areas such as Crosshhill and Kinning Park. These middle-class suburbs were no doubt idyllic, but they also earned a certain notoriety as self-governed, police-boroughs.

The influential residents of such communities could petition the authorities to protect their idyll and preserve autonomy by self-financing and enacting the administrative functions of their respective enclaves. This included not only municipal management responsibilities such as water, gas, lighting and maintenance, but also policing in the area.

Police boroughs, which persisted well into the twentieth century before their final abolition in 1975, were relatively commonplace as an instrument of governance in a decentralized Scotland of the nineteenth century. In the case of well-to-do suburbs, however, it looks more like a means of further consolidating grandiose notions of exclusivity and, by inference, social exclusion.

Pollokshields became a police borough in 1876 even though it barely qualified as 'a populous place'. It certainly could not boast the stipulated figure of 3,000 inhabitants required for a successful petition.

It's not recorded whether any of the Renfrewshire boroughs campaigned for full independence, but the manoeuvrings of community leaders were satirized by one contemporary wit named Archibald McMillan in his collected humourous sketches *The Adventures and Opinions of Jeems Kaye'* (Pugh, 2011).

As I said in my introduction, this book is about nineteenth-century voices that challenge contemporary misconceptions about oral and written communications during the reign of Queen Victoria. The aim is to let these voices speak for themselves and allow readers to listen for the modern elements in their modes speech, and the continuing influence of their concise, expressive language on our own vernacular.

In McMillan's writing, we can read and understand the dialogue spoken in this exchange between his characters as the kind of Glasgow dialect that is indistinguishable from the one we hear on the streets today.

'*What are you (in Strathbungo) noted for?*"

'*The finest park in Scotland, the Crossmyloof bakery, (and) the only place in the three kingdoms whaur ye will see a baronet selling coals by the hunnerwecht...*'

'*You don't wish to be annexed to Glasgow?*'

'*Annexed tae Glesca? I should think no. The Glesca folk come rinnin' oot tae us lookin' for hooses. Ye never hear o' Strathbungonians wanting tae flit intae Glesca.*'

[Eventually] the Chairman said,

'*Whatever we do with Crosshill and Govanhill, and all these mushroom burghs...*'

'*Stra'bungo must be free..An' unfettered', says I.*'

'*An' unfettered!', says he,*'

'*Free as the ostriches or the eagles that soar in the heavens!' says I.*'

'*As free as them!', says the Chairman.... So we adjourned, an' that's the way Stra'bungo wis saved.*'

McMillan is a Victorian, yet, like Buckland, Walpole and Young, he very rarely uses any of the affected and flatulent phraseology reserved for addressing the monarch, parliament or the newspapers. When we set aside the grandiloquence of court etiquette, the showmanship of Disraeli or the hyperbole of the papers, we can begin to separate the affectations of 'Victoriana the Brand' from a more authentic account of the nineteenth-century authored by those who lived it.

The Glasgow Evidences

The curing magnate Hugh MacLachlan spoke plainly enough when he addressed the commissioners. He began by speaking with the authority of one who had been "*35 years in the trade*", but by the end of his oratory he sounds merely authoritarian. He claimed to cure more herrings than "any other curer in Scotland" including the take from "200 boats from Barra Head and the lower part of Lewis", but he also stated that these fisheries had "decreased since he commenced business."

He made the general observation, already established elsewhere from Scotland, that general improvements in the fishing industry, especially boat-building, had resulted on more bounteous catches. MacLachlan went so far as to quantify the phenomenon saying, "If the fishermen had the same materials for catching (herring) 10 to 15 years ago...they would have caught a third more herrings."

Since then, in his view, a decrease had been "ongoing year by year" concurrently with ever more aggressive fishing tactics; but he also intimated the underlying cause to be "the taking of immature herring."

What follows is a strange turn in the discussion when Hugh McLachlan says,

"Trawled herrings are better for fresh markets as they are got in earlier.."

And then, somewhat surprisingly,

"Trawling is most injurious for the fishing and should be prohibited altogether...it leaves many more dead in the sea as are taken ashore."

There may be some truth in his words, but why should a fishcurer in Glasgow seek to land fewer fish by prohibiting trawling? He then seems to be interrogated from the floor or, more likely, by the commissioners themselves. He's evidently asked about the use of lethal force to put down trawling; a line of questioning in the report that emerges wherever objections to trawling are made. MacLachlan, though has come prepared to answer the charge.

He was "aware that the Commissioners' Reports in 1856, 1862 and 1864 were against repressive measures to put down trawling." His response to that was to propose possession of trawling gear and/or trawled fish as the principal offences. Fishermen would somehow have to demonstrate they were not trawling, or face "forfeiture of boats and nets...a £20 penalty for fishermen"...and a penalty of "not less than £50 for buyers and others."

It's unlikely that the Commissioners particularly warmed to MacLachlan's attempted inversion of the principle that offenders are presumed innocent until proven guilty, although possession of a beam trawler and huge pile of

184

herring on the quayside is a little more persuasive than a smoking gun.

To our ears, MacLachlan's words sound like nothing more than an argument for sustainability but there is reason to be sceptical of the curing baron's motives as he presses home his argument. He was absolutely in favour of a *"closed time"* extending 5-6 months along virtually the entire western seaboard (but presumably *not* The Minch), with similarly draconian punishments for those breaking the law. He though the garvie fishery *"injurious to the herring fishery"* and he even has it in for the hapless gannets. He would, given half the chance, repeal the Sea Birds Preservation Act *"as there are thousands of Solan Geese and other birds at Ailsa Craig, which consume as many herrings as the boats actually catch."*

There is compelling evidence in the next chapter of this book that Glasgow curers and merchants were at odds with their would-be masters in London. MacLachlan can't have been terribly popular with anyone else in the room either.

William Rafferty, an equally prosperous, merchant fish curer, came out vociferously in favour not only of trawling, but a comprehensive policy of non-interference. He told the commissioners that he *"believed the take on the west coast to be increasing"* and that he would *"give fair field and no favour to both drift and trawled herring."*

He wasn't in favour of a close season either declaring *"the herring make a law for themselves"*. The prohibition of daylight fishing he thought would *"act unfavourably to the trawlers"*, and would (conveniently) leave observance of the Sabbath to the fishermen. Rafferty's position on fishing at Ballantrae Banks is equally prejudiced in his own favour when he tells the commissioners that he *'supports the fishing at Ballantrae'*, reasoning that *"There is no more reason why full fish should not be caught at Ballantrae than at Wick."*

Aside from a general argument about the use of trawlers, the issue of quality control rears its head more than once at Glasgow. James Carsewell, a fish curer from Rothesay, commenced fishing in 1826 but noticed that the herrings were *"not so regular"* as they were before trawling. There would always be slim pickings for him at the end of the line, given Rothesay's location on the tip of Bute, yet he *"did not want to buy trawled herring for curing purposes...the herring will not keep when cured."*

William McLachlan (sic), a fish salesman in Glasgow, no doubt a 'humble' one, parroted Rafferty's opinions. It's uncertain if he is related to Hugh MacLachlan but he is just as sure of himself when he pronounces *"the fishery in the Minch....and at Loch Fyne to be in a very satisfactory condition"*. He was very much in favour of *"leaving things alone"* although the commissioners can't have appreciated the tone of his closing remark, *"The herrings are better able to make a law for themselves than Her Majesty's government."*

At first glance, the men who met the commissioners in Glasgow look a little like a dysfunctional cartel, squabbling over the spoils on the quayside. It's more likely that the competition between curers at Glasgow's fish market, a half-square mile of vested interests between Clyde Street and the Trongate, was driven by conflicting imperatives. The trawled fish provided cheap, edible, fresh fish, in great volume and of reasonable quality, to the fastest-growing metropolitan population in Europe. The long-established, 'traditional', drift net fishing supplied branded barrels of quality controlled 'matties' to rich, mature markets in Europe.

This ought to have piqued the inspector's interest because they had earlier heard reports from the east coast about periodic complaints heard at Stettin and Hamburg about the questionable quality of some shipments of quality-assured herring. There is no doubt that Scotland caught, supplied and sold some of the finest fish in the sea to markets with an almost insatiable appetite for a quality assured product. At the same time, it's obvious that fishermen, boat owner/operators, merchants, agents and salesmen were hostile to anything that might interfere with the way they conducted their affairs.

In the next chapter, I will describe and evaluate the findings of the commission and the manner in which it was set down in 1878. It will surprise many who might associate government examination with government control. It might even disappoint many who confuse government control with the sensible management of finite resources. For one thing, few of the principals considered nature's bounty in finite terms. We flatter ourselves today into thinking that we know better, but all too often our actions are far less excusable for they way we simply choose to ignore that most bothersome of inconvenient truths about the nature of nature. It bites back.

The most extreme outcome of unchecked harvesting of a species is extinction driven by anthropogenic activity. This is not, by any means, true of herring in 1877, but it was hardly unthinkable, even where the likelihood of such a thing appears remote.

This is where we leave Glasgow and its confrontational curers, and join Buckland, Walpole and Young on a post-evidence gathering excursion to Bute along with Frank's old friend Abraham Dee Bartlett. They can only have undertaken this 'beano' *after* visiting Girvan and Ballantrae on the 28th September, because they not only commandeered the Jackal and all its crew for two whole days, they descended on Bute, mob-handed.

The ostensible purpose of this jaunt was to follow up on the advice Buckland and Bartlett had previously given to the Duke of Argyll on the colony of beavers they'd supplied in 1875 via the animal dealer Charles Jamrach. Abraham Bartlett, alongside Frank Buckland and, to a lesser extent, the animal dealer Charles Jamrach, represented a seminal breed of kind of 'hands-on' animal person. Their practical synthesis of empiricism and scientific understanding made them reliable sorts that dabbling dukes could turn to for sound advice. It is fair to say that the three of them helped to shape vocations that we might recognise today as the skilled wildlife communicator and the scientifically-informed zoo-keeper.

The European beaver *Castor fiber* was a species that had, by the 12th Century, been hunted to extinct in England and Wales, and wiped out in Scotland by the end the 16th Century. In fact, Buckland more than anyone, ought to have been alert to the fact of accelerated extinctions by human hands. He had a good working knowledge of palaeontology, an intimate understanding of rarities in nature and a keen interest in acclimatization of non-native species. All the same, Buckland seems quite untroubled by the fact Bute's beavers belonged to a different species, *Castor canadensis* sourced from North America.

When they got to Bute, they found Argyll's beavers in good condition, well-fed, properly cared for, and with ample opportunity to fully express their natural behaviours within a large stone-walled enclosure. They had destroyed trees, moved large logs and built lodges and dams. We can almost forgive Buckland's taxonomic irreverence and the duke's indulgence when we read some of Buckland's typically charming prose describing a scene of domestic bliss in the beaver colony.

"HMS Jackal in her cruise anchored at Rothesay and the morning after our arrival, Captain Digby, the officers, my colleagues and myself, chartered a carriage to pay a visit to the beavers.

At some little distance from Mount Stewart House there is a lonely pine-wood. Through part of this wood runs a natural stream. In the centre of the wood a stone wall has been built....to keep the beavers quiet and undisturbed.

As far as I could be ascertained from the curator of the beavery, there were twelve beavers. There were certainly one or more young ones in the big house, which these most intelligent animals had erected.

On entering the enclosure one might easily imagine that a gang of woodcutters had been at work felling the trees around them."

With work and play behind them, the most ergonomic return journey to London for Buckland, Bartlett, and Walpole, and the most sensible course for Young, would be to return to Glasgow and catch a train back to their respective homes.

It is worthwhile to imagine good friends on the last night of their Scottish project sharing a drink, a cigar and an anecdote or two. All of them led rich lives, full of experience and fulfilment, and could feel justified in feeling a sense of accomplishment.

We could fill four books writing about these four individuals and their intersecting relationships with the great, good and merely indifferent minds of the nineteenth century. None of them were converted Darwinians even though Darwin's ideas not only held sway, but the implications of his theory were clear to anyone tutored by nature.

Walpole, Young, Buckland and Bartlett were as concerned with that debate as the next God-fearing Victorian. Bartlett especially had a great deal of communication back and forth with Darwin, whose questions and queries were answered with courtesy, but very little deference. Buckland disparaged Darwin, while Walpole and Young seemed to sit happily on the fence.

It can be a hard truth to accept, but even today, people who are passionate about animals are not, in every case, equally engaged with 'big ideas' about wildlife preservation, nature conservation, and environmentalism. They *should* be energized and informed about those issues, and most of them are, but mostly they are like our commissioners, focused largely on the job in hand.

We have to remember when we discuss their contribution to a scientific understanding of nature in the 1878 Herring Report, and elsewhere, that the commissioners' brief was to feed the nation as effectively and as profitably as possible. The following chapter must, therefore, be read through the prism of economic imperatives. But before we go there, we can usefully look at the Glasgow of recent times, and see just how quickly imperatives can shift and change under our feet.

One View of Glasgow

The Broomielaw still exists as a main artery hugging the Clyde, but it's much changed since Buckland's time. It is still part-quayside and part-thoroughfare, but it is no longer a hub of transatlantic trade. The warehouses, steamship offices and chandleries have long disappeared, replaced by gleaming office blocks of a nascent financial district that hasn't quite delivered on its promises. The Broomielaw of old now exists only in sentimental folk songs, but Glasgow's history shows that the city has always favoured the main chance over sentiment.

Glasgow's capacity to tear itself down and rebuild again from the ground up is a recurring phenomenon in the history of Scotland's largest conurbation. Despite this, it has also displayed a remarkable aptitude for preserving enough of its past to maintain the outward appearance of an historic Scottish metropolis.

Today, the most prominent buildings on the photographed landscape are the cathedral and the university. They are Glasgow's most constant features and, alongside Kelvingrove Art Gallery and Museum, they represent the civic and civilized face of a city that rescued itself from terminal regression.

The postwar slums, crime gangs, violence and urban degradation that dogged Glasgow all the way into late 1970s and 1980s is well documented elsewhere. We pick up the Glasgow story on the cusp of regeneration with the 'Glasgow's Miles Better' campaign, which took a smiling, outward-facing Glasgow as the leitmotif for a city keen to attract inward investment. It was the turning point for a town stained black with petrol exhaust emissions and the negative connotations of ingrained criminality.

It is to Glasgow's credit that it built solidly on the initial suggestion that the city could be an immersive experience; a place where art, architecture, heritage, education commerce, enterprise and blue-chip events intermingle freely to their mutual benefit.

An evolving strategy of riverside re-development, and the appearance of high-status and highly visible civic and commercial marques delivered an unexpected bonus for Glasgow as a year-round destination. It became in the 1990s and early 2000s a place that many people visited for its own sake, in addition to those who came to do business, to study or to work.

They say that nothing succeeds like success, a phrase not far distant in spirit from the city's official motto, 'Let Glasgow Flourish'. It is beyond doubt that the twenty-first century has seen Glasgow prosper once more, but it has gained as much by mining its own story as it has from hosting international televisual events such as the Commonwealth Games.

The prospective visitor to Glasgow is spoiled for choice when it comes to art, heritage, culture and history, but you have to get out of the traffic first. The best way to do that is to think about Glasgow as a place where the past and the present interleave with one another to such an extent that you can feel yourself moving backwards and forwards in time.

The way that the two Glasgows, ancient and modern, interface is nowhere better evidenced than in the streets around its university. There are, many will argue, several universities in the city, but the original on Gilmorehill is the only one founded in 1451, and the one that defines an aspirant, over-achieving Glasgow. It is marvellously Gothic and its corridors literally echo into the past.

The university is also home to the Hunterian Museum, a previously overlooked and under-used fixture that has restated its status with outreach and interpretation. It is home to the various artefacts collected by the 18th Century surgeon William Hunter and it is a museum whose time has come. This is partly because its peculiarly diverse exhibits speak directly to the way we now absorb information as a constant flow of parallel histories. For many of us, natural history, anatomy, art and music are not at all strange bedfellows and The Hunterian satisfies a public craving for an holistic sense of the past.

If the diversions of the gentleman collector eventually make you feel claustrophobic, then it might be an idea to head for The Lighthouse in Mitchell Lane. It's also known as The Mackintosh Tower, which was designed to hold an 8000-gallon water tank within the original premises of the Glasgow Herald newspaper. Once home to reporters, sub-editors, copy boys and printing presses, the building extended along Mitchell Street from the corner of Mitchell Lane, parallel to Buchanan Street.

Built in 1895, it was designed by Charles Rennie Mackintosh, an architect whose name is synonymous not only with Glasgow's architectural landscape, but the influential Arts and Crafts movement of the late nineteenth and early twentieth centuries. His wife was Margaret MacDonald who was also a highly regarded designer and draughtswoman working in what later became dubbed 'The Glasgow Style'. Their legacy is a highly distinctive and personal spin on architecture, interior design and the decorative art, which is comprehensively recorded in this refurbished exhibition space.

The Lighthouse epitomizes the persistent and highly visible remodelling of Glasgow as a centre of original thinking. As you ascend the helical staircase, you pass through a comprehensive story of the building. On the way up, you will be moved by the personal triumphs and tragedies of the Mackintoshes, and bear witness to their version of a modern Glasgow. At the top, there is an observation deck that affords an uninterrupted view across the cityscape. It is a very fine place to see what Glasgow used to be, what it has become, and what it might be in the future.

In many ways, Glasgow is too busy getting on with the business of living life to the full to stop and examine itself too closely, or take itself desperately seriously. Quite what our inspectors would make of it is anyone's guess. Frank Buckland would almost certainly delight in the passing parade of humanity from the top deck of a tourist bus, and come away with many a curious anecdote for publication.

Spencer Walpole would, perhaps, find safe harbour in the refinement a gentleman's club, but he'd have to be very careful when asking which of them was the most convenient and convivial. He might end up somewhere quite different from The Athenaeum.

As for Archibald Young, I see him stepping on board 'The Waverley', until very recently the last operational paddle steamer in the world, perhaps setting off from the angular Transport Museum's riverside landing with fishing tackle by his side.

The old vessel, presently under repair, may yet have just enough puff to carry the Edinburgh advocate, and other Glasgow day-trippers, to Millport where he might enjoy a day's fishing. He might even find a spot near the Field Studies Council buildings, which until 2013 housed the now defunct Millport Marine Biological Station, owned and operated by the University of London as an educational and research centre.

If this personal view of Glasgow seems utterly inadequate then that is because the comprehensive Glasgow narrative is yet to be told, and it would fill five volumes of thick, dense text. It is better, by miles, to go there and find your own version of a city that defies definition. One thing is for sure; you will have your own Glasgow story to tell.

Findings

"The Scotch fishermen are great readers of the bible, and by one of them I was referred to the passage of Scripture which gives presumable authority for the herrings leaving certain coasts of Scotland on account of the "wickedness of the people." We find in the book of the prophet Hosea (chapter iv, verse 3), the following passage :- 'Therefore shall the land mourn,.....yea, the fishes of the sea shall be taken away.'" - **Frank Buckland in Report on the Herring Fisheries of Scotland, 1878.**

We have heard in the preceding chapters the authentic voices of nineteenth-century fishermen throughout Scotland, speaking directly to the government of the day through Her Majesty's commissioners, Mr. Buckland, Mr. Walpole and Mr. Young.

The evidences placed before the 1877 commission conflicted and concurred over a number of issues, thought at the time to be potentially 'injurious' to the 'Scotch' herring fishery. In many instances, Buckland Walpole and Young heard compelling cases for firmer controls, further regulations, a number of prohibitions, and judicious enforcement of the law.

The principal concerns raised with them suggested that the following practices were harmful in both the long and short term to the continued success of the herring fishery in Scotland.

The commissioners broadly heard that:

• Nets with meshes smaller than those previously considered 'standard', and often used to catch sprats, were also catching very immature herring, which were either sold on among sprats, or discarded as a damaged fish having been injured in the nets.

- Daylight fishing for herring, universally understood to be a nocturnal species, resulted in the scaring of fish, their desertion of fishing grounds and, in the worst cases, contributed to over-fishing and local extirpation.

- Fishing for immature herring was harmful to future recruitment and perpetuation of fish stocks.

- Fishing on, or near, spawning banks was harmful to future recruitment and growth of herring stocks.

- Trawling was generally harmful as an aggressive, invasive and ultimately destructive method of fishing for herring, especially in narrow waters, on spawning banks and in competition with drift net fishermen.

- Trawling had the capacity to rapaciously harvest local herring stock and, more generally, selfishly over-fish a finite resource.

- Sea birds, principally gannets, took many more fish than the herring fishermen of Scotland. Were it not for natural predation, there would be no question of the perpetuity of the Scottish herring fishery.

The commissioners heard these reports time and time again, everywhere they went, but their findings come as a bit of a shock, even when their primary goal of maximising yield is considered. There is also much about the report that hints at conversation, discussion, and perhaps even argument among themselves in the course of their evidence gathering.

Naturally, it is Buckland's voice as the lead author that comes through most clearly, since the report was ostensibly written up by him and published the following year by Her Majesty's Stationery Office. Buckland also had a secretary in his employment, so it is safe to assume that he had help collating and organising the raw data, the notes, the records, the correspondence and written submissions. As a government document, though, it is not the singular view of the lead author and his colleagues. The various appendices suggest that several hands made the work of producing such a comprehensive and convincing document a little lighter.

For once, though, the devil is not in the detail. At some point, during or after the evidences were gathered, the commissioners came to a consensus view about all that they had heard in Scotland. They had listened to everything that the fishermen had to say, but in the end, they heeded only those voices that advocated free trade.

The momentum that gathers pace in any reading of the 1878 Report is fully behind the premise of governance, if not regulation and control. In all parts of Scotland, there was a clear, pent-up demand for greater oversight, better understanding and more prudent management of fish stocks, spawning grounds and access to fishing grounds. Yet, the trawling sector comes out the winner from the commissioners' conclusions.

It is true that the trawling lobby, even then, was rich, powerful and forceful, but no coherent argument springs from that quarter. The trawling rhetoric is shot through with self-interest, specious testimony and a confrontational, deaf-to-all reason pugnaciousness. By the same token, if we give in to our own, modern prejudices about wasteful practices, ruthless opportunism and belligerence personified in the age of industrialised fishing, then we do the discussion no favours.

It might appear on the oddly decimalized pages *xxxv* and *xxxvi* of the 1878 report that the commissioners have executed a jaw-dropping *volte-face*, having faithfully, fairly and painstakingly listened to every concern, from the most pedantic measurements of net meshes to tall tales of fishermen almost neck deep in spawn.

Their main conclusion was that the herring fishery in Scotland was on the increase, and *"Nothing that man has yet done or is likely to do...is likely to diminish the general stocks of herring in the sea."*

In their minds, the logical inference of that was plain as day, *"It is therefore inexpedient to either impose or continue any restriction on the free action of fishermen with the view of increasing stocks in the sea."*

When we come to read the rather brutal bullet points that do little to soften this view, we can only conclude that the sustainable conservation of natural resources only ever entered the commissioners' minds as an inconvenience. Not even the birds are spared.

"The Sea-Birds Preservation Act, protecting gannets and other predacious birds, which cause a vast annual destruction of herrings, should be repealed insofar as it applies to Scotland."

This particular recommendation undermines, rather uncomfortably for his fans, the notion that Frank Buckland fathered the public communication of nature conservation and natural science in Victorian England. To many, including myself, he has been a hero of natural history and a precursor of television popularizers who have created an enduring media strand from engagement with nature in the raw.

It is true that he frequently spoke up with great erudition against wasted natural resources and pollution of the environment. It's also the case that he consistently promoted the need to acquire more knowledge in order to have a better understanding of the natural world around us. But, that doesn't make him a nature conservationist, or even an authoritative commentator on the complexities of natural systems.

It is doubly surprising, therefore to discover that Frank Buckland had a role in the establishment of the very Act he and his fellow inspectors now sought to repeal. He was, in fact, a member of the expert committee convened to advise on the matter of a close season at seabird colonies around Britain.

This committee, provided the impetus for the Seabirds Act of 1869, which was proposed on behalf of the Association for the Protection of Sea-Birds by Christopher Sykes, MP for Brantingham Thorpe, near Hull. The Act is significant to this day as one of the first pieces of nature conservation legislation to be passed in the U.K. Yet, here is Buckland, in 1878, apparently backtracking on previously held views, if not principles.

In order to understand his actions, the modern mind must adjust its own moral antennae. Subsistence hunting of vulnerable birds at the nest had long been a feature of life for the human inhabitants of places like Flamborough Head and Bempton Cliffs. It had always been an unattractive enterprise, but nineteenth century fads such as egg collecting amongst the gentry and feathered hats for the ladies encouraged a wholesale and quite unseemly slaughter. The Seabirds Act was never about sustainable populations. It had much more to do with public revulsion at the cynicism of large shooting parties descending upon helpless prey, and the visible barbarism on display during these annual culls.

This kind of 'wanton killing' is something that Buckland found repellant and he is on record saying just that. It may not have been so difficult, however, to persuade him that the reintroduction of an open season on seabirds could be justified on the grounds of some greater good. Buckland never wavered in his view that the creatures of the Earth were placed here for the benefit of humanity to dispose of as we see fit.

In the end, the Seabirds Act wasn't so much repealed as absorbed into Protection of Wild Birds Act (1880), itself later repealed and replaced by the Bird Protection Act of 1954.

The Wildlife and Countryside Act of 1981, eventually succeeded these Acts, and it's worth noting here the grudging, piecemeal approach to nature protection in Britain, and the relative ease with which it can be altered, if not undone.

The Seabirds Act can be seen as a landmark, but it was designed to address behaviours and not attitudes. It generously provided protection for thirty-five species by introducing an annual close season between 1st April to 1st August, but egg-collecting at seabird colonies was inexplicably excluded from the legislation - a status quo that persisted until the 1954 Protection of Birds Act.

We also have to remember that Buckland's promotion to H.M Inspector of Fisheries was hard-won, and that it represented everything he sought to achieve in life. In his diary, he memorably wrote of his appointment, '*I have achieved the object of my life*'; something he surely wouldn't relinquish simply for the sake of squaring up against the man who gave him the job.

If Walpole is the dominant voice among these conclusions, then we will probably never know how far it went unchallenged by the others. Archibald Young may only have been there to provide guidance on matters of the law, and there is nothing to suggest in his subsequent writings that he offered any reservations, much less a dissenting voice.

Young may have been a weekend countryman who celebrated the virtues of nature, but it's clear that he valued his status as one of H.M. Fisheries Inspectors more. It's equally clear that he would seek to avoid argument with his peers in the interests of preserving his position on the periphery of greatness. He wrote frequently about his experiences as a fisheries inspector and never forgot to sign himself off in correspondence to the Scotsman as *'former Inspector of H.M. Fisheries.'*

From this distance, it looks as though the commissioners sought to wash their hands of controversy by falling back on the 'common sense' view, prevalent at the time, that each man had sole control and ownership of his own destiny. Even so, there is something unconvincing about the dismissive language of their conclusions. These men, historical biography tells us, were fond of nature and had a deep understanding of it.

Yet, they sound here like corporate executives seeking to sweep aside interfering legislators in pursuit of maximum yield and limitless exploitation, regardless of the potential consequences. It is harder still to believe that they gave no thought to consequences, for they could not function as professional men without a good grasp of cause and effect.

The answer may lie with the past decisions, or the lack of them, that led to catastrophic loss of life, displacement and economic migration. The ghost in the room throughout the final assembling of the report was famine, and its helpmates, poverty and want. No one was more animated on that topic than Spencer Walpole, and his views on the matter, spoken without fear, favour or apology, are a matter of record.

Although Buckland was the senior author, it is Walpole who was the senior civil servant. It was Walpole who hired Buckland, and although they became friends, it is hard to escape the conclusion that they occupied quite different strata in society. Young's influence in the final statements is much harder to divine, but as I've said, he had little cause to rock the herring boat.

I focus on Walpole with good reason, because Frank Buckland who died in 1880, could not be there to see one of his most cherished dreams come true, 'The Great International Fisheries Exhibition of 1883'. Walpole, by then elevated to the lofty position of Lieutenant-Governor of the Isle of Man, was a senior organiser and contributor, and he addressed the related conference on the subject of 'Fish and Fish Markets'.

I think it's interesting that he resorts to the first person when paraphrasing (of all things) the collective opinion contained in the 1877 herring report.

"I do not believe that the fisheries of the ocean can ever be exhausted by any operations which man is likely to undertake, and I am quite sure that the ocean is producing still as abundantly the moving creature that hath life, as it did when the first chapter of Genesis was written. I do, therefore, hope that whatever may be the outcome of this Exhibition, and of these Conferences, that no steps may be taken to impose unnecessary restrictions on fishermen, but that fishermen may be left, in Professor Huxley's words, to go on fishing where they like, when they like, and how they like."

Walpole's presentation then becomes somewhat prosaic, with lots of facts, figures and verbal flourishes. Yet, it is the foregoing remarks, and the pedantry that follows, which support the contention that Buckland and Young may have done the spadework in 1877, but it was Walpole who ensured that the conclusions in the subsequent 1878 report harmonized with establishment thinking.

"I see that an illustrious Duke (of Edinburgh), in a paper read at one of these Conferences, has estimated the gross take of fish in British waters at 615,000 tons a year....with respect to this 615,000 tons of fish, I find if we add to it the 45,000 tons which are imported from abroad, and if, on the other hand, we subtract from it the 110,000 tons which are exported from this country, we shall arrive at the consumption of fish in the United Kingdom, viz., 550,000 tons. That is the contribution which the British fishermen are making to the food of the United Kingdom.....in point of weight, 550,000 tons of fish are about equivalent to a drove of 1,500,000 oxen, and that they would supply every man, woman, and child in these islands with a dish of fish three-quarters of a pound in weight on one day in each week throughout the year."

The issue of famine in a time of plenty was raised during the post-lecture discussion by Huxley, who'd stepped up to offer a vote of thanks followed by questions. His remarks were provoked by an observation from the floor that free-market policies should not preclude humanitarian action. Huxley's response was later echoed by Walpole himself in his *Life of Lord John Russell* (1898), and it is all the more indicative of the attitudes of the day for being a public statement.

Huxley, who had previously visited the Isle of Skye with colleagues, observed:

"The worst part of Ireland, which was (at the time) in the most depressed state, could not show a population in greater misery than the people who were to be seen within a mile and a half of Portreath..... the total earnings of one of those peasants, his whole property and everything belonging to him would not come to more than £5.

Certain interested parties in Glasgow some years before, for no other purpose but a desire to clear their own markets, had got a law smuggled through the House of Commons, where nobody cared anything about it, by which it was made penal to catch a herring during the three summer months of the year, a time at which herrings were swarming in innumerable millions.

The Act was of so stringent a character that the mere fact of finding scales in the boat was sufficient to ensure a man's conviction, and he was fineable £20 or more. That meant that he would be totally ruined or might be put in prison for doing this; or even for the suspicion of having done it.

Now there was not the smallest imaginable reason why that enactment should have been passed. It was a stupid, mischievous and utterly useless thing. Yet because there was no one of sufficient intelligence to understand the interests of these unhappy people they were fined and imprisoned in this way at a time when their children were starving, when their potato crop had failed. There were thousands of herrings within a mile of the shore, and a man might not take his boat out and catch the herrings, simply because of this preposterous law."

This is an important passage and Walpole's remarks, following on, are revealing.

He should be very sorry, he said, *"...if in anything I had said to-day was thought to display any want of sympathy with Ireland or Irish fishermen'* He further ventured to say that, *"There was no person in the room, Irish or English, who felt more deeply for the woes of Ireland"* than he did.

"But....the Germans, like the Irish, were endeavouring to develop their fisheries, and....a society in Germany had built for German fishermen a fleet of twelve large vessels to fish in the North Sea.

One of those vessels had been lost. The other eleven vessels lay most of the year idle at Emden, whilst....the whole of the German markets were now supplied, not by the vessels which the Germans had built, but by the Scotch, Norwegian, and Dutch fishermen.

That was an instance to prove that industries which did not flourish of their own selves would not flourish because someone wished them to do so." He was he said, "One of those old-fashioned people who could not get out of his head that an industry which was worth having must be one that took its own root and grew by its own effort."

There is a fine line between tough love and hard-nosed cynicism, but it is almost impossible to fully understand the British attitude to starvation, whether it occurred in Ireland or on the Isle of Skye. We could do worse than look at modern reactions to climate change, crop failure, desertification, people going foodless, people without access to water, and people driven to migrate out of denuded landscapes. The collective response is just as contradictory, just as dysfunctional, and just as blind.

There is much in Frank Buckland's contrasting life and work that frames him as a humanitarian, although most of that has percolated down through broadly sympathetic biographies. It is generally accepted, however, that he had the ability to communicate effectively and sympathetically with every class of person.

His purpose may have been to glean the smallest fact of nature from anyone and everyone with such knowledge but, but he does seem to have had the common touch. One biographer, his brother-in-law conveniently enough, has him giving handouts to street urchins, and generously over-tipping bird-catchers, carters and conveyors of animal cadavers to his London home in Albany Street.

It was his stated aim to apply himself to the perpetual problem of providing food for the masses. In the post-famine world of the wider British Isles, the growth of concentrated living in cities, and the shift in agricultural activity from arable crops to livestock and grain, concentrated minds on demand and supply.

Buckland saw a niche and an opportunity for himself as an all-round animal man; one who could readily identify fecund, tractable, wild animals as species suitable for propagation and human consumption. He was utterly immersed in the function, form and physiology of animals, and he made introduction, acclimatization and the economic breeding of edible creatures a central plank of his philosophy.

His chance came to really show his mettle when Walpole brought him on board as an Inspector of Fisheries in 1867. This work interleaved perfectly with his particular focus on the abundance and variety of fish species, and fell neatly within his purview of the seafood diet as a means of effectively feeding healthier nation. It is for this he is credited as something of a visionary, but his motivations are somewhat clouded by personal ambition and a constant, nagging worry that his proper place in gentle society would forever elude him.

In 1867, he was given the chance to prove himself and he worked tirelessly for the next twelve years to justify the faith that others had placed in him. His rewards were greater financial security than he'd ever known; a place closer to the upper echelons of society than the middle; and his name forever etched in annals of antique natural history. His health faltered though, and his fame as a writer and leading personality in the Victorian milieu quickly faded following his death in 1880 at the age of fifty-four.

Buckland did not avoid personal conflicts or political controversy, but he only courted them when he felt his reputation or his beliefs were threatened. He was a creationist, a Conservative, and, by any standard, a casual racist who was typical of his class, background and experience. There is, in some quarters, an image of him as a jolly, avuncular, egalitarian eccentric, but he is much more a product of his imperial times and the ordering of the classes.

In every perverse instance of hierarchies built on fabulous wealth, privilege and discretion, it is curious that those near the top make familiar judgements about who is far below, and the degree, if any, of their importance. If Buckland had a view about widespread poverty, or a want of food, then it is expressed largely in his actions as a deeply God-fearing man, who constantly sought greater purpose in his life.

This is invariably achieved through dedication in the course of a life's work, and Buckland was unswerving in this overarching aim. It was the poet Dylan Thomas who later memorably wrote that he submitted his lines,

"...for the benefit of man and in praise of God". This is particularly true in Buckland's case, and it makes him more convincing as a genuinely caring personality.

Archibald Young was tactfully silent on the subject of unpleasant things such as the dispossessed poor. His brother, James Gerard Young, on the other hand, held much stronger views about the pastoral need to care for the members of your particular flock. If there was ever a frank exchange of views between the brothers on the matter of assistance to the needy, then it must be contained in private correspondence, presently unavailable to the author of this book.

James Gerard Young, as the indefatigable minister at Monifieth and champion of the ordinary folk, certainly believed in empowerment as a means of self-improvement. He made sure that his parishioners had a school, a church hall and, after his death, a cottage hospital at their disposal. He pro-actively encouraged philanthropy among the local rich, and he made sure that the transference of wealth from the wealthy to those less well-off was proportionate and transparent.

It has been a privilege to write about these events and the people who have passed through Scottish history. A great deal more waits to be written about Buckland, Walpole and Young with access to private papers. In all three cases, the patrilineal line ended with them, and it would seem that much of their respective private correspondences were either scattered, lost, destroyed or are now held in private hands. It's possible that their true voices may one day be fully heard. We might not like what we hear, but it is likely to be uncomfortably familiar, if the dominant narratives the 21st Century so far are anything to go by.

Whither Now?

It is always dangerous to write about the present day. Things have a habit of changing. People less so. The mindset, motives, attitudes and language of fishing folk, in particular, show an incredible capacity to carry forward unaltered through changed times and shifting seas. Today's industrial fishers may be more sophisticated, better equipped and market-aware, but their subsistence cousins are equally modern in their subscription to science-based, marine conservation. There is no need for them to be in conflict, but they often are.

Such conflicts begin, and will end, with an argument about what is finite and what is not. The definitions alone are far from clear-cut. A species can be effectively extirpated long before the projected endgame scenario of visible eradication. This happens when a species is effectively extinct (i.e., where it exists in numbers insufficient to perpetuate itself), and it's been a well-known phenomenon for a very long time.

Similarly, a super-abundance of individuals, especially a localized one, can give a false impression of infinite bounty. In both cases, the advice to step back and assess, (i.e. call a moratorium), is greeted with dissent and opprobrium. Reason departs the scene and bellicose noise beds in for the duration of a sterile debate.

Extinctions, local and global are a fact of life. Every biologist, environmentalist, natural historian, economist and fisherman knows this. They also know, all of them know, what is meant by accelerated extinction at human hands. It can be dressed up as the tacit acceptance of a craven new world in 'The Anthropocene', or tolerated as nature denigrated by the belittling term, 'Natural Capital'. But it's a collective inability to change the tone and tenor of the conversations about natural resources that will be the real undoing of the natural world we do not govern, but merely occupy.

In 2010, science demonstrated what common sense had told all present at Ballantrae in 1877; that resources are indeed finite. In their comprehensive analysis of 'a marine ecosystem nearing the endpoint of overfishing', Thurston and Roberts (2010) described an 'Ecological Meltdown in the Firth of Clyde, Scotland' coincidental with 'Change in a Coastal Marine Ecosystem' over two centuries of lasting change.

There are two points to take from their extensive haul of historical fishing data. The first is that Ballantrae Bank is now effectively a desert, and the second is that mechanization without concomitant controls leads firstly to diminishing returns, and ultimately the complete loss of the resource. We have seen it with coal, we have seen it with primary forests, and we have seen it with rivers, lakes, glaciers and entire sections of the Arctic ice shelf.

Not only that, resources can be finite in the very places where super-abundance is so great that it appears divinely endless. The vested interests who met with the commissioners in 1877 heard claims, complaints and counter-claims in an alternating series of dismissive, if not confrontational arguments amid sensationalist claims. Yet, there was consistency enough in the evidences to give them pause for thought. There are still real-live gannets nesting and flying around Ailsa Craig but the Firth of Clyde herring fishery, as it once was, now exists only in history books.

Buckland, Walpole and Young were *right and wrong* in their eventual conclusions. It was true that the herring fishery was entering a new phase of prosperity, and the Firth of Clyde fishery was recovering. Their wait-and-see philosophy was right for the times, but their suggestion that the resource was infinite, no matter what the *'ingenuity of man might conceive'*, simply doesn't stand up to the test of time.

The fisheries men could not have foreseen the catastrophe of the First World War, but international tensions were not born by immaculate conception in the early twentieth century. Walpole himself wrote about the history of his own age, much of it birthed in trivial political rivalries and steeped in the mud of war. They may not have envisaged the relentless offtake of herring either, but they did witness the explosive expansion of the rail network and had already seen just how rapidly mechanisation altered the economic landscape.

In recent years, there have been conflicts between oyster farmers and kelp dredgers, antipathy between creel fishers and scallop dredgers, and open hostility towards the broad scope and bedevilled details of a common approach to fishing for a shared natural resource. More disappointingly, the commentary is desperately familiar and replicates much of the rhetoric contained in the 1877 evidences.

There is no shortage of conversation, but much of it is informed by conflicting interests that are resistant to a harmonized approach. In the online age, the cyber seas are awash with subjective commentary and social media spats, pouring cold water on up to the minute technical reports based on sophisticated data collection techniques.

A frank exchange of views took place at the very time of writing of this book between The Clyde Fisheries Association (CFA), principally through its affiliate the Communities Inshore Fisheries Association (CIFA), and the Scottish Creel Fisheries Federation (SCFF). Their differences are similar to the ones that exercised minds in 1877, but in this case the primary disagreement is about the access of mobile scallop dredgers to inshore waters.

As I write, the SCFF have been lobbying for the reinstatement of the three-mile exclusion zone, with the essential goal of excluding mechanised fishing from inshore waters. The arguments and counter-arguments revolve around how disruptive (or not) dredging is to the sustainable living of crab and lobster fishermen, who are harvesting a low yield but valuable commodity from the coastal seas. Similarly, the CFA/CIFA position asserts the right to fish freely in the absence of such legislation, and bemoans the obstructive attitude of the creel fishermen.

This is more than just a territorial dispute. It revolves around the same contentious proposition from the nineteenth century that the sea belongs to everyone, and that free enterprise should not be shackled by new laws. In both cases, science is regarded as a 'useful idiot' that is sometimes convenient for propping up a partisan point of view.

Organisations will, naturally, cherry-pick the data to support their respective cases. Individual fishermen can be even less choosy. They don't always discern between a perfectly legitimate international fisheries science organisation such as ICES, and a meddling, 'non-expert' pressure group. Once again, those that do the fishing appoint themselves 'those who know best'.

The Scottish government has gone out of its way to arbitrate through frequent scientific and technical reporting and numerous consultation processes. They are, in the main, thorough, impartial and diligently executed. The government has also established marine conservation zones, which ought to placate conservationists, forward-thinking fisheries managers, and all but the most belligerent fishers too. Yet, the government seldom pleases all the people, all the time.

Once more, I can point to the recent conflict between the creelers and the dredgers for a direct comparison with the 1877 findings. Buckland, Walpole and Young heard repeated calls for the permanent presence of one or more fisheries protection vessels to enforce the law. In 2018, the SCFF, along with a small armada of environmental groups, attempted to lobby for more aggressive policing by Marine Scotland of scallop dredgers in marine parks.

There is no more appetite (much less resources) for that today than there was when Victoria sat on the throne. According to their website text, Marine Scotland is *'responsible for the integrated management of Scotland's seas.'* That is the broadest remit imaginable, and it includes ongoing research, monitoring marine environment, balancing recreational use, licensing, compliance, grants, aquaculture and renewable energy.

Marine Scotland is, however, neither the coastguard, nor is it a police force on the high seas. The compliance division has three surveillance vessels and two light aircraft at its disposal, and their results indicate a strategy of deterrence rather than clocking up a large number of prosecutions.

In the period between March 2017 and the time of writing, there had been only ten enforcements and prosecutions. The offences were mainly concerned with reporting failures, but they also included a couple of breaches of net regulations and two instances of electro-fishing. The range of fines began at £1000 with the most expensive lapse attracting a demand for £3,200.

Once more, the government cannot, will not, and probably should not commit disproportionate resources to the enforcement of regulations that are designed to perpetuate a healthy marine environment that is a benefit to all. The lessons of the past tell us over and over again that a free-for-all is damaging in the short term and catastrophic in the long run.

No one in fishing today can suggest there is a lack of information. They cannot claim either that the collection of data is not ongoing. Fisherfolk, by and large, are not only compliant with but actively involved in the gathering of electronic data; the development of new and more effective systems; and the creation of new research pathways. The flashpoints have more to do, perhaps, with the pinch-points, pressures, markets share and the squeezed margins of the modern fishing economy.

Buckland, Walpole and Young exercised their minds over harbour accommodation, quality control, and the train times to London. Walpole, in particular, was especially excited by the contribution to the economy as a whole. I am not sure that even he would see the sense of sending Scotch Herring to the Far East, or exporting fine seafood almost exclusively to overseas markets.

Buckland, thoroughly scunnered by the ubiquitous finan haddock, would no doubt be utterly fascinated by today's supermarket shelves populated with the pre-packed fish and king prawns imported from Thailand. He might equally be shocked and appalled at the price of cod, and the absence of ling, or jellied eels. Kippers are cheap as chips, but they are far from returning as the staple food of the Glasgow poor.

I think if Archibald Young were here today, his extensive investment portfolio would include a salmon farm or two. As a former fisheries inspector, he would also be well-qualified to oversee their day-to-day management. Archibald, in fact, organised a fisheries exhibition in Edinburgh ostensibly to honour Frank Buckland and his pioneering advocacy of fish propagation, but it didn't do his own reputation much harm either.

In Scotland, fish and seafood remain important, but Buckland's vision of a food for the people has largely evaporated. Can the nation's eating habits change? Are there really enough fish in the sea to feed us all? What will it cost to discard chicken nuggets and bring fish back into the mainstream diet? These questions pop up frequently, but they are rarely addressed with any great seriousness.

The answers may lie in steering our society towards a food strategy that values diversity over monoculture. The suppliers, the vendors and the people could achieve such a shift by building on the pre-existing appetites for fish and seafood. People the world over like a 'nice piece of fish', but the culture of 'ready meals' and 'long-life' packaging kills flavour, texture and consistency.

I would look forward to a world of fish, infinite in variety and prepared creatively, as many dishes are now from Goa to Japan, and onwards to the Pacific coast of the USA. I am not a great world traveller, but I've been around and seen a few things. It is one of those fascinating ironies that the most memorable fish dinners I ever had were at my parent's retirement flat in a fishing village on the east coast of Scotland. I think that there is nothing quite like fish 'fresh of the boat'. It reminds us that whenever good food is placed on our table, it is a gift and a treasure that must never be taken for granted.

Interesting Notes and Curious Observations

Neil Munro (Para Handy) at Inveraray in 1876 - Royal Circus - Archibald Young on Ben Nevis - The 'Cran' as a standard measurement of the herring catch - Buss fishing in the Firth of Clyde-Ultima Thule-The Fisheries Exhibitions of 1882 and 1883 in Edinburgh and London - Storm Lothar's Big Brother - Mr. Jamrach - Steamships on the Firth of Clyde.

I am extremely fond of the way that factual, antiquarian books are often structured intuitively with wordy chapter headings and loquacious paragraph sub-headings. The contents of each chapter are often non-sequential and extremely diversionary, but it can fun to flit amongst quite unrelated musings and suggestions.

Perhaps the writers feared their readers would suffer fatigue and distress when confronted by lengthy passages of intellectual discourse and minute historical detail. In the nineteenth century, non-fiction for popular consumption seemed designed to be picked up, browsed and laid down again without fear of losing one's place in the overall narrative.

I. Neil Munro (Para Handy) at Inveraray in 1876 - In an especially cosmic happenstance at Loch Fyne, Frank Buckland is recorded in a time and place concurrently with a significant personality who helped shape Scotland's image of itself.

At the same time that the Commissioners were taking evidences at Inveraray, a young lad named Neil Munro had just left school in the town, and begun work as a clerk under a local lawyer, called William Douglas. Munro moved to Glasgow when he was eighteen in order to pursue a career in journalism, and later became famous as the author of the Para Handy tales.

These humourous vignettes followed life aboard a puffer called 'The Vital Spark', 'the smertest boat in the coastal trade', and they were reprinted many times in anthologies, and retold on radio and television. The stories, uncredited even as an inspiration, were also telescoped into the script of the Ealing comedy 'The Maggie', directed by Alexander MacKendrick.

Munro, of course does not feature in the evidences, and his stories first surfaced in 1906 as light-hearted pieces in the Glasgow Evening News. They are, nevertheless, useful as an authentic reminiscence of life on the west coast of Scotland when the nineteenth century already had one foot in the twentieth. They are also evidence, albeit in a semi-fictional account, of lightly governed coastal communities, distant from the outside world and often at odds with the strange notion of regulations.

II. Royal Circus - Archibald Young lived for most of his adult life in Royal Circus, in what is known as the second phase of the New Town. It was, as it is now, frightfully exclusive and terribly expensive. In the nineteenth century, however, it was much more even than that. It was a town within a town where professional elites such as senior surgeons, lawyers, financiers, explores, high-ranking officers of the army and navy congregated and consolidated their status as the Scottish Establishment.

One of the architects involved in the design of the Eastern New Town (Third Phase), William Playfair, himself lived among the aristos on the nearby Moray Estate, established by the 12th Earl of that ilk. Other New Town notables of that area included explorer Mungo Park's well-off widow, Bouverie Francis Primrose, and Sir Robert Christison, toxicologist, physician and a pioneer of modern forensic pathology.

Christison first came to prominence during the 1826 trial of the unhappy Mrs Smith who poisoned her husband with arsenic, but he's more famous for his work on the notorious killings in 1829 involving the murderous body snatchers Burke and Hare.

His conclusions from post-mortem examination of one victim, Marjery Campbell (and some rather gruesome comparative experiments) resulted in charges that sent Burke to the gallows, and Hare first into protective custody, and thence into exile. Fans of crime scene dramas are invited to peruse Christison's article 'Murder by Suffocation' in *The Lancet, Volume Two*, if they really can't sleep without having all the prurient facts to hand.

III. Archibald Young on Ben Nevis - One of the major diversions that Young undertook on this particular holiday was his ascent of Ben Nevis, and his account in *'Summer Sailings'* flags up the promotion of the mountain from major topographic feature to national icon. People came from all over to attempt the climb, often wholly totally ill-prepared for the challenge that lay ahead of them.

Young's vignette memorably caricatures a *'Glasgowegian'* and *'Dutchman',* a pair of hapless dandies who have no understanding of the work they've taken on. Moreover, they suffer at the hands of a usurious 'mountain guide', who all but abandons them to their fate on the mountain. The two clowns make it to the top and return safely, but not before they chip a stone or two off the old block as keepsakes of their tribulations.

It's a tale we can tell today a dozen times over and it still speaks loudly of the need to constantly recalibrate the finely balanced cost/benefit ratio that is a salient feature of responsible access and eco-tourism.

The hijinks on Ben Nevis also help a little with sorting out dates. Young states, *'In those days there were was no royal road to the top of Ben Nevis, no (weather) observatory, and no hotel, and the climb was a very long and very steep one.'*

The escapade occurred long before the observatory was built in 1883, and very likely many years before the first feasibility assessment, which took place in 1877 whilst Young was accompanying Buckland and Walpole around Scotland.

There is more yet, that helps us bring Archibald Young into the light that he really ought to share equally with Buckland and Walpole. A major insight into what sort of man he was is revealed in the following lines.

' The writer has been at the top of forty-seven mountains in Scotland over 3000

feet high, but none of them were...steeper than Ben Nevis was.'

Young is describing himself, rather disarmingly, as a seasoned, experienced climber and a determined 'munro-bagger'. It is the kind of demanding physical exercise that in youth tends to ensure fitness, good health and a very sound mind later in life.

Archibald Young may not have been as politically connected as Walpole, or as well-known as Frank Buckland, but in 1877 at the age of fifty-seven he was, in every other respect, every bit the equal of his somewhat younger and more celebrated colleagues.

IV. Buss fishing in the Firth of Clyde - It's the purpose of every survey to generate raw data with the general aim of establishing patterns. The herring report does that admirably well, but it also contains another useful by-product of such an exercise; the unexpected anomaly.

Archibald Cook, a fisherman, reported that it was, *'the habit at Campeltown to go out with two skiffs. The men in the skiffs catch the fish on a Saturday night and place them on a large boat, which is lying at anchor, and in which the men live. These large boats are employed in the Irish fisheries. The fish are stored (presumably salted and cured in barrels) in the large boats till (sic) the buyers take them.'*

He is, in fact, describing the Dutch *'buss'* system of fishing, which had been in terminal decline for decades. The *buss* was essentially a large factory ship and the method described by Cook was responsible for the dominance of the Dutch herring fleet throughout the 15th and 18th centuries.

The last purpose-built ship of this kind was launched from Vlaardingen in the province of South Holland 1841, but the buss fishery in Ireland seems to have persisted. Certainly, the *buss* was never a salient feature of the herring fisheries around the Scottish coast, and the single instance from Campbeltown speaks to an even rarer confluence of Irish and Scottish fishing interests.

V. The 'Cran' as a standard measurement of the herring catch - Herring were customarily sold in Britain by the cran, a measurement that can be expressed in a number of ways. It is equivalent to thirty-seven gallons, or six cubic feet. It consists, on average, of about 1,200 herrings. That figure could vary widely according to season and ground from 700 to 2,500 herrings for different fisheries. A cran measure is roughly equivalent to 28 stones, or 177 kg of herring.

The newly-caught herring came ashore in baskets with four baskets equal to one cran, and one basket, naturally enough, holding up to seven stones (or 44.5 kg) of herring.

A Herring Barrel containing cured fish is also a measure of volume, although the statutory obligation to make barrels in Scotland to a prescribed size was removed in 1963.

In theory, herring barrels now can be of any size, but barrels that could hold around twenty-six gallons of fish and brine would have been commonplace in 1877. A full barrel of cured herring would, therefore, consist of about 700 to 1,100 fish depending on the size of the fish and the quality of the catch.

VI. Ultima Thule – Let me say this clearly, so that all may understand. This mythical, final destination, as mentioned by Frank Buckland in his account of HMS Jackal's voyage to Shetland, has nothing to do with Nazis. It may please the popular press to attempt artificial resuscitation upon the corpse of Himmler's baseless propaganda, but it is irrelevant here.

Buckland, in all his writings, liked to pass himself off as a Latin scholar by dropping lengthy references and quotations from classical literature. The 'Thule' he is referring to here is a partially invented place that appears in Latin and Greek literature and the earliest maps. The origins of the word 'Thule' are disputed and obscure, but the prefix *Ultima* is, of course, from the Latin for the furthermost or eventual destination.

Academics and charlatans alike have argued for and against the real geographical location of Ultima Thule with Norway, Iceland, Sareema (Estonia), Greenland, Orkney and Shetland all emerging as candidates.

Buckland, in his fifties and still indulging in undergraduate humour, was lampooning the northern isles as beyond the edge of civilisation. Yet, even for a garrulous Frank Buckland, the feeling of travelling into the mystic seemed an inescapable sensation.

Ultima Thule is one of those word combinations that never fails to stir the imagination. Perhaps it has inherent connotations of cosmic questions finally answered, and understood in any language because it is rooted in ancient tongues. It is still evocative today, and relateable as long as humanity remains lonely in the Universe

In January 2019, NASA sent the space probe New Horizons on a fly-by mission to investigate a curious object more than 100 million miles from Earth. This heavenly body, disappointingly named *2014 MU$_{69}$*, consists of two conjoined bodies nicknamed, Ultima and Thule, which are located in the far-distant Kuiper belt.

Following *New Horizons'* flyby at 05:33 on 1 January 2019 (UTC time), 2014 MU$_{69}$ became the farthest and most primitive object in the Solar System ever visited by a spacecraft. It therefore seemed natural and sensible to re-christen these twins 'Ultima Thule', and thus re-invent them as a strange and curious destination, almost beyond normal, everyday comprehension.

VII. The Fisheries Exhibitions of 1882 and 1883 in Edinburgh and London - Modern marketing professionals understand the importance of reaching a large and influential audience, but their Victorian counterparts were slow to build on the success of the Great Exhibition in 1851. The fisheries industries of the nineteenth century understood the potential of international expositions, but it required a mover and shaker with Archibald Young's energy to get things going.

Frank Buckland died in 1880, with many of his greatest ambitions unfulfilled. Above them all, he desperately wanted to translate his knowledge, experience and understanding of fish and fisheries for the public understanding of a scientific natural history. The primary means he envisaged for achieving this aim was to directly address public consciousness through his Museum of Economic Fish Culture. That dream would have died with him, had it not been for Archibald Young.

It was Young who was the galvanising force behind the International Fisheries Exhibition at Edinburgh, which he described in his circular to all the Vice Consuls in the Scottish capital.

'*Re: INTERNATIONAL FISHERIES EXHIBITION*

22 Royal Circus, July 7, 1881

"Sir, We have the honour to inform you that an international fisheries exhibition will be held in Edinburgh in the month of April next.

The exhibition will include, as far as is possible, objects illustrative of or connected with the fisheries of the world, such, for example, as models, drawings and photographs of boats used in fishing and of steam-engines adapted for fishing boats; models of fishing-boat harbours and of fishermen's houses; nets, lines and fishing tackle of all kinds for both sea and inland waters; piscicultural apparatus; live fish in tanks; collections of stuffed fish and aquatic birds; life-saving apparatus, fog-signals, and lights for fishing-boats; fresh fish, cured and tinned fish, and preparations for preserving fish; models of fish passes and ladders and other similar objects.

We shall esteem it a favour if you will bring under the notice of those engaged in, or connected with, the fisheries in your country the fact that such an exhibition will be held therein April next; and if you will also kindly inform us whether you are likely to send us many contributions. An answer to the above may be sent to Archibald Young, esq., Commissioner of Scotch Salmon Fisheries, 22 Royal Circus, Edinburgh.

We have the honour to be your obedient servants,

Sir I.R.S. Maitland, Barrister
  Wm Skinner, City Clerk
  F.N. Menzies, Secretary to the Highland Society
  Archibald Young, Commissioner of Scotch Salmon Fisheries.'

The Exhibition is interesting as a cross-institutional initiative, and Young's circular, *'approved by the joint committees of the town council, the Highland Society, and the Scottish Fisheries Improvement Society'* was an effective convincer.

The Edinburgh fisheries expo was successful, but it was nothing like the scale of the 1883 Fisheries Exhibition held in London. It does, however, deserve the distinction of being the first one in Britain and is creditable for its conception as a tribute to Frank Buckland.

The following year, The International Fisheries Exhibition took place between 12th May and 31st October 31, 1883. It was held on the twenty-acre site of the Royal Horticultural Society grounds in South Kensington and attracted in excess of two million visits, peaking on 15th May at over 25,000 attendees. In all, there were exhibits from thirty-one countries and colonies, with many of the materials on display coming from Buckland's Museum of Economic Fish Culture.

The proceedings from the exhibition, and specially commissioned hand-books, were published over the six months in fourteen volumes including forty-nine conference papers, thirty-one prize essays, the official catalogue, and the opening and closing ceremony addresses. There were also numerous private catalogues published by national delegations and several private exhibitors. It seems that even in 1883, a visit to such an exhibition meant carrying home any amount of 'bumf'.

The 65,000 gallon exhibition aquarium was something of an innovation, and the building formed the entire eastern boundary of the grounds with third saltwater tanks and nine freshwater tanks. In addition to fish there was also outdoor exhibits of live animals including flamingos, pelicans, cormorants, and herons; otters and seals; reptiles; and some of Bute's beavers in an enclosure near the West Gallery.

A quite different exhibit altogether seems to have generated a great deal of interest, because it was highlighted in press reports and deemed worthy of the photographic record. I'm not sure whether Grace Darling's boat was a reproduction, a fraud, or the genuine article, but it constituted a conspicuous centrepiece in an otherwise unremarkable gallery of prints.

The story of the twenty-two-year-old lighthouse keeper's daughter who, during a storm in the early hours of 7th September 1838, rowed out with her father to rescue nine survivors from shipwrecked paddle-steamer made national news. Her subsequent fame made her a celebrity, but it was her early death at the age of twenty-six that made her a folk heroine.

It shouldn't be any surprise that she was remembered at the exhibition more than forty years after her premature passing. Schoolchildren in the 1960's were still learning about her thoughtless courage in between morning milk and afternoon playpiece, such was the resilience of the story.

VIII. Storm Lothar's Big Brother - There is constant reference in the Herring Report to the summer 'storms of 1876', which were repeatedly put forward to account for the widespread and alarming reductions that year of the Scottish herring 'take'. There were also consistent reports from important fishing stations that boats didn't even go out to sea, much less catch fewer fish. So, why was the weather so bad that particular year?

There are extensive and detailed meteorological reports from much earlier than 1877, and they are all diligently recorded on a daily basis in neat, albeit tightly-squeezed, longhand. Very little that is worrying about the weather leaps from the pages of these log books. They are all online and laborious to trawl, but since they are records of observations from the coast, they tell us little about conditions at sea.

There is another indicative record to be found from a quite different source, and it could explain why fishermen in 1876 were extremely reluctant to take any unnecessary risks.

On the 12th of March 1876, a great storm did indeed make its fearsome presence felt as it swept up through central Europe. The re-insurance company SWISS RE, the world's second-largest re-insurer and one of the oldest, described it as, 'a 19th Century event with a footprint similar to Storm Lothar in 1999.'

The 1876 howl has passed into legend among insurers as 'Storm Lothar's Big Brother', and its status is based upon the havoc it wreaked as much as the considerable force it exerted.

Swiss RE reported a 'wealth of data' for 1876 that allowed them to credibly estimate that the scale and cost of property losses in France, Germany, Belgium, Luxembourg and the Netherlands. Aside from property, a whole forest comprising more than 100,000 trees was 'flattened in the space of a few hours.'

The path of Storm Lothar's Big Brother came nowhere near Scotland. It did, however, pass through the English Channel and it headed, significantly enough, straight for Hamburg, the herring capital Europe.

Bad news travels fast, but such a story would have gone viral in fishmarkets across Europe. In light of such an ill-omen from the continent, it's plausible that Scots fishermen, particularly boat and net owners, revised their assessments of likely catastrophe upwards.

As long as the benefits were uncertain, it made sense to fish only when the signs were completely favourable. If there is one thing that the figures and tables clearly show, it's that the herring catch slumped dramatically in 1876, despite being bracketed by bumper years before and after.

IX. Mr. Jamrach - Mr Charles Jamrach is one of the most potent names in the history of wild animal management. He was the principal animal dealer in London in the nineteenth century with premises on the Ratcliffe Highway, a large warehouse and a network of worldwide contacts. He was originally from Hamburg where his father, Johann Gottlieb Jamrach, was the chief of the river police, and an opportunist.

In Germany, the appetite for public and private aviaries and menageries had been firmly established in previous decades, and Jamrach's father had already begun trading in animals and birds. Before long, he was running a lucrative sideline in exotic wildlife with branches in Antwerp and London.

Charles Jamrach was seconded to the London outpost where the business grew exponentially. He supplied private collectors and circuses alike, orchestrating his affairs from *Jamrach's Animal Emporium* in east London. His name has been synonymous with the questionable motives and dubious spectacle of the trade in exotic animals ever since.

It will be no surprise that Jamrach's business flourished as a result of Britain's imperial reach into the world's most exotic places. New and exciting examples of wild animals from every occupied territory flowed in and out of his yards, sometimes in huge numbers.

Jamrach's relationship with the Zoological Society of London and other established 'Society' zoos in Europe consolidated his fundamentally commercial enterprise. His close association with Frank Buckland, who refers to Jamrach frequently in his writings, also helped to legitimize his activities as useful to science. That doesn't mean, however, that his business was conducted especially responsibly.

One famous incident in 1857 involving an escaped tiger is vividly described by Buckland in *Curiosities of Natural History* and it records a moment of high drama on the Ratcliffe Highway. Jamrach's tiger had escaped from confinement and immediately set about roaming the street before attacking a hapless young boy. The tiger had the lad in a jaw-lock and the youth appeared doomed, but for Jamrach's quick and selfless actions.

In Buckland's account of the incident, he first declares, '*I have made it my rule to get my information on such matters, if possible, first-hand, I therefore give the story as Mr. Jamrach told it me himself.*' There follows a detailed description of the escape from start to finish in which the newly arrived tiger was transported from the docks in a rather dodgy wooden crate to Jamrach's yard. According to Jamrach, as told to Buckland, the female tiger simply pushed her way out of the 'rotten' crate and walked through the yard gates, and out into the street.

'*A little boy, about nine years old, happened to be playing there. The little fellow, thinking that the tiger was a big dog, walked up to her and began patting her...the animal then turned her head and seized the boy with her tremendous fangs. Jamrach immediately ran up, and grasped the tiger by the loose skin of her neck...although a very strong man, he could not hold the beast, which immediately started off down the street at a gallop, carrying the boy in her mouth as a cat would a mouse.*'

The tale may have come from the horse's mouth, but it carries the faint odour of literary embellishment. In Buckland's version of events, Jamrach heroically wrestles the tiger to the ground while his 'man' fetches the beast '*three severe blows to the nose*' with a crowbar. The child is released, dazed but unharmed, while the tigress decides the best course of action is to seek safety by returning to Jamrach's yard and the sanctuary of her sodden crate.

'*Mr Jamrach got the worst of the affair; for having to fight the tiger, he then had to "fight the lawyers" and the whole business in damages and law expenses, cost him over £300*", wrote Buckland, ever the loyal friend, and only moderately sympathetic towards the innocent, young bystander. "*I really think, and doubtless my readers will agree with me, that Mr. Jamrach deserves very great credit for attacking his fierce...runaway tiger single-handed, and rescuing the poor little boy. I record the story as a testimony to his courage and pluck.'*

Today, Jamrach's profession as an international animal dealer is virtually the sole preserve of criminal gangs. In my time as an animal keeper, the last significant British dealer in existence was seen as efficient, professional and conscientious, but never viewed as heroic. In fact, the image, if not the whole 'zoo idea', struggles to overcome reservations about its purpose, relevance and effectiveness in the early twenty-first century.

The presumption that zoological gardens ought to focus on endangered species and propagate them from existing stock has been ingrained in the zoo psyche for over thirty years. That does not mean that animals are no longer bought and sold by zoos, far from it. There are still arrangements of convenience, and egotistical 'stamp-collector' curators who think it a virtue to be the sole collection exhibiting a rare species that only they can obtain.

The mass consumption of huge numbers of threatened animals, whether they creep, crawl, brachiate, prowl or gallop continues to feed the profit motive. If it has moved from the docks at Wapping, where Jamrach once ruled over his animal empire, then that hardly absolves us of individual and collective responsibility. The whole attitude of humanity towards other living things has to change, not just the business addresses of those who deal in the misery of animals.

X. Steamships on the Firth of Clyde - In chapter thirteen (Glasgow), I fudged the issue of timetables between the Broomielaw and destinations on the Firth of Clyde. It is true that the travelling times would vary from service and one boat to another. We can, however, be fairly sure that a svelte naval vessel such as HMS Jackal, compared to a cumbersome passenger craft, would cut through the waves at a consistent rate of knots. Neither would Captain Digby think of operating a hop-on-hop-off service, although he seems to have to be pretty much at the inspectors' beck and call.

There are many histories of the Clyde steamships and the maritime history of Glasgow, and some of them are as deep and dense as the Atlantic Ocean. I often prefer older references. They are more authentic for being contemporaneous and very well-written compared to the raft of coffee table memorabilia.

A quick compendium and easy-reader gazetteer is *'Clyde River Steamers of the Last Fifty Years'* written by Andrew McQueen and published, (with forty-eight illustrations) in 1923 by Cowans and Gray of Glasgow and London. Everything about this little book is a charm, and the author's technical descriptions of the various vessels are written with some diverting anecdote or another attached.

Happily for me, the period that the book covers is exactly synchronous with the decade in which Buckland, Walpole and Young were gadding about Scotland on fisheries business. I previously suggested that the inspectors may have had to take their foot off the Jackal's powerful throttle, and in order to ease up the pace and enjoy the scenery, but that doesn't mean steam packet vessels, by comparison, were incapable of impressive speeds.

In his chapter, 'Sailings from Broomielaw', McQueen sings the praises of the steamship Sultana, built by Robertson of Greenock in 1868 and put into routes from the Prince's Pier, when it opened in 1869.

'Her straight stem and knife-like entrance, with the rake of mast and funnel and the sweeping curve of her paddle-box, conveyed to the beholder and impression of speed which her performances did not fail to bear out.' He could be talking fondly about one of many girls he met in port in his sporting youth, rather than a wide-beamed, matronly passenger steamer. It actually begins to read more like a racy romantic novel as his enthusiasm gathers pace. *'Though her engine was not powerful, she had a very rapid stroke and travelled at great pace, her fine lines offering no resistance to the water.'*

If his ardour is earnest then so too his faithful recording of the Sultana's voyage from Rothesay on the Isle of Bute to Prince's Pier. *'She left Port Bannantyne (on Bute) each morning at 7.10, calling at Innellan and hence direct to Prince's Pier where she lay ill 10.50, connecting with the 10.05 train from St. Enoch.'*

If that sounds a little underwhelming, then consider the barely concealed pride in his closing remarks. *'About the end of the century she was sold to France, and has now disappeared from Lloyd's register. It is generally conceded that she holds the record from Prince's Pier to Rothesay by the usual route via*

Kirn, Dunoon, and Inellan, having covered the distance in fifty-seven minutes from pier to pier.'

McQueen's writing is companionable and authoritative, but it reads a little like he's cribbed his style form the wordy mannerisms of nineteenth-century journalism. He's not so affected, though, that he'd edit out the genuine voices of his contemporaries on the Clyde.

In a vignette worthy of Para Handy Tales, he relates how Captain McLean of the later vessel 'Marquis of Bute' often arranged evening trips around Bute. He also employed a local worthy, brass-buttoned and blue-coated, to officiously march up and down the quayside ringing his officious brass bell, calling out,

"Notice! *The fine steamer 'Marquis of Bute' will sail this even', weather permittin', on a pleeasure excursion to the Head of Loch Struvvin. Leaving Rothesay about five o'clock. Calling at Port Bannantyne, goin' and returnin'. Cabin, ninepence; steerage, sixpence."*

It somehow seems fitting, then, to leave that not-quite-lost world of steam and 'smeddum', with the actual words of the Rothesay bellman ringing in our ears. A personality such as he is a truthful representation of an actor frequently miscast as a figment of Neil Munro's imagination. All too often, the consequence of that is the belittlement of human ordinariness when it really ought to be celebrated from the rooftops.

I sense today that an urgent search is underway for a Scots argot that I fear is hiding in plain sight. I very much hope that Scotland maintains this spirit of inquiry in all things, not just 'Scots things', and will continue to reconnect with its characterful past. But I also hope that it may separate archetype from identity, and eventually recover its one, true voice.

Frank Buckland

Francis Trevelyan Buckland (1826-1880) was born at the 'venerable house in Thom Quad', Christ Church College, Oxford, on 17th December 1826. His father was William Buckland (1784–1856), and his mother was Mary Buckland *née* Morland (1797–1857).

Buckland's father was, at the time, the canon of Christ Church, and Frank was baptized accordingly by his father in the college on 28th June 1827. Frank Buckland was the eldest of the Bucklands that survived beyond adulthood. They included his brother Edward (1828-1873) who predeceased him, and the two sisters who survived him, Elizabeth (1837-1919) and Mary Ann (1829-1915).

Mary Morland Buckland had been adopted by Regius Professor of Anatomy at Oxford, Sir Christopher Pegge following the premature death of her birth own mother. She was privately educated in genteel circumstances and enjoyed some early successes as an illustrator of fossils. Some of her drawings can be seen in Georges Cuvier's *Animaux Fossiles*.

William Buckland later became the Dean of Westminster where he automatically became a prominent figure in Victorian society as the 'Queen's vicar'. He was also engaged in the popular sciences of palaeontology and natural history. Frank very much admired his mother and father and he grew up with his two younger sisters in an intellectually nurturing and deeply religious household.

Throughout boyhood, Buckland was fascinated by the animals he encountered in semi-rural Oxfordshire. His mother frequently took him on educational and instructive countryside rambles, while his father became an enormous influence as both a theologian and naturalist.

Frank was sent away to elementary school, first to Cotterstock in Northamptonshire (1835–7), and thence to Laleham in Hampshire (1837–9), where he was tutored by his uncle, the Reverend John Buckland. He later attended Winchester College (1839–44), and eventually went up to Christ Church College, Oxford, receiving his BA on 18th May 1848.

Buckland at university, more often than not, stayed in college during breaks and recesses. He famously kept a variety of exotic animals in his college rooms including an eagle, a monkey, a marmot and, infamously, a juvenile bear. Frank was apt to wander in the countryside, making observations and recording experiences of animals both wild and domestic. These experiences, along with childhood memories and later adventures with animals, formed the basis of the natural history writing that brought him widespread fame and a little bit of scientific notoriety.

There were more serious excursions during his university career, including trips beginning in 1845 to Giessen in Germany where he studied chemistry with the eminent Professor Liebig. After graduating, he trained in medicine at St George's Hospital in London between 1848 and 1851, and practiced as a house surgeon from 1852 until 1853.

Buckland apparently acquitted himself quite well at St. Georges, where the work was hard, varied and intense. It seems also to have equipped him with credible skills as an anatomist, which would subsequently feed into the legend that he was effectively London Zoo's first consultant pathologist. Nevertheless, he must have quickly concluded that it was not a career path that would lead him to fulfil the manifest destiny he'd begun to formulate - in his own mind at least.

The next thing he did owes more to the connections he'd made and used to his advantage as the son of the former Dean of Westminster. Letters from influential friends had helped him secure his place at Christ Church College, and his paid internship as a trainee surgeon at St. Georges Hospital. He was similarly recommended for the most unlikely military appointment in the history of the British Army.

On 14th August 1854, Buckland, who was portly and allegedly a little over five feet tall, was commissioned into the 2nd Life Guards as an Assistant Surgeon and he remained in that privileged post until 1863. It was a role that was apparently undemanding enough to allow him time to develop a parallel career as a writer, commentator and popular authority on natural history. He was doubly fortunate that Guards were not, at any time during his tenure, called into action.

His regiment moved between their barracks in Regents Park and Richmond, and this allowed Buckland to live and work in the best of all possible worlds. In London, he had the Zoological Society of London on his doorstep, while at pre-suburban Richmond he could once more become the country mouse.

He wrote ceaselessly about every aspect of animal life, sourcing as much from correspondence with like minds as he did from direct observation. There was nothing that was too trivial, odd or obscure to report. In fact, a general readership with a prurient interest in extremes of nature couldn't get enough of what he had to offer. He distilled his expansive, stream-of-consciousness musings into popular anthologies entitled *Curiosities of Natural History*, begun in 1858 and reprinted many times in four slim, eminently readable volumes.

In 1860, when the post became naturally vacant, Buckland was turned down for promotion to the position of Senior Surgeon with the Life Guards, and a capacity for reacting badly to rejection began to reveal itself. An elevated position in the Guards would have meant much greater financial security and further opportunities for advancement in society.

His application was unsuccessful, but the way he resigned his commission is indicative of a fit of pique. He decided to follow his literary nose and his scientific pursuits, and he was once more helped along the way with a word dropped in the right ear at the right time.

Buckland had already established himself as a *bona fide* contributor to 'The Field', a popular magazine with a reputation for producing informed and informative features. He began working for the magazine on a more formal basis from the time he left the Guards until 1865 when he felt financially fluid and personally ambitious enough to start a journal of his own.

The new, weekly paper was called '*Land and Water*' and, in circumstances weirdly prescient of the present-day blogger/publisher phenomenon, he authored and edited much of it himself. *Land and Water* was described as an '*independent channel for diffusing knowledge of practical natural history, and fish and oyster culture*', but Buckland soon found that even he couldn't cast the net quite that widely.

The magazine was an admirable, if quixotic exercise, but Frank Buckland had the wit to realize that he had to narrow down his focus and specialize. He turned primarily, and quite naturally, to all things concerning fish and fishing. Buckland undertook many diverse projects and initiatives and the questions he addressed included the artificial propagation of salmon, effective management of salmon rivers, and, importantly, the condition of salmon rivers that had been adversely affected by industrial pollution.

In May 1865 Buckland was appointed scientific referee on fish culture to the South Kensington Museum (now the V&A), although its hard to deduce if this was not a piece of tokenism on the part of the scientific establishment. He gave a course of lectures and demonstrations, and illustrated them with examples from his large collection of hatching apparatus, models of fish passes, casts of fish, and variety of fishing tackle and equipment.

Buckland, like most natural historians and erstwhile polymaths of his time, was an inveterate, but intuitive collector. His private fish and fishing-related paraphernalia soon outgrew the space and importance that the museum authorities had in mind. Instead of expanding the concept, they further marginalized it to the point where, after his death, it was first shifted from place to place and then finally broken up.

He'd been manoeuvering for years for a Museum of Economic Fish Culture but, in the absence of institutional support for his vast collection, this great ambition was never properly realised. Vindication only really came after his passing with the International Fisheries Exhibition of 1883, where his ideas and his artefacts were central to expositions and discussions on every aspect of fishing from every corner of the Empire. Although his collection was ultimately dispersed, some of his relics have since found a suitable home, somewhat ironically, at the Scottish Fisheries Museum in Anstruther.

In February 1867, following the resignation of a previous incumbent, he was appointed H.M. Inspector of Salmon Fisheries. Buckland, still only forty-one, had finally arrived. It was a role that fitted his experience, his ambitions, his passions and his vision like a second skin. It was also proof that the things he'd done, said and written mattered in the world. All he needed to do in order to secure his reputation as a man of science was to carry out the work as directed by the Home Office.

His job, with other colleagues, was to study everything about the salmon, and apply it to the economic management of productive fish stocks and healthy rivers. This included much travel to the rivers and coasts of the country, and the necessary inter-actions with every echelon only enhanced his pre-existing skills as a communicator. In all, Buckland authored or co-authored several comprehensive reports, in addition to the continuance of his natural history writing and contributions to a large variety of magazines and newspapers.

The private life of Frank Buckland was far less public than one might suppose, and it underscores the way in which privacy and discretion, necessary as they are, undermine the fullest understanding of a public figure and the times in which they lived.

Buckland met his future wife sometime in the late 1840's, when he was either an intern or a practicing surgeon at St. Georges. She was the daughter of a coachman and belonged to a family that lived in Pimlico, only streets away from St. Georges. How they met and courted is not recorded, although Buckland, like many other young folk, is known to have frequented Cremore Gardens, barely a ten minute walk from the Papps family home, and almost as close to St. Georges.

Hannah fell pregnant and on 23rd August 1851 and, at 18 Pulford Street, Pimlico, she bore the couple's one and only child, a boy they named Francis John. The baby, for reasons that are obscure, was nicknamed 'Physie', and there is but circumstantial evidence to suggest that Buckland actively inter-acted or supported his unexpected family with money. There isn't much evidence of a scandal either, not even when Hannah was following him between the Life Guards quarters at Regents Park and Richmond, presumably with the little Francis toddling at her heel.

There is plenty of speculation among his biographers about Buckland's attitude, much less his intentions, but precious little evidence from private correspondence that might have been useful survives. There is on record the advice of a brother officer to "end this relationship once and for all", but Hannah is not named, and the remarks are open to circular interpretation.

Sadly, Francis John did not survive beyond the age of six, succumbing in 1856 to 'pulmonary meningitis'. If Buckland was free of any perceived obligation, then his subsequent actions suggest that he either felt honour, or perhaps a solemn promise, had to be kept. As a single man of independent means with two married sisters, he also had to be 'kept'. So, on 11th August 1863, he finally married Hannah Papps.

It is worth consulting a pocket calculator when speculating about Frank and Hannah. She was born in 1829, and when she first met Frank she was either in her late teens or had just turned twenty. She was hardly likely to be entirely unworldly, and long past the age of *ingénue* when she had Francis John at the age of twenty-two. Buckland, even though he was twenty-five, and three years her senior, might have been naive about women, but not about human biology.

There may have been quiet pressure not to get more involved with Hannah and Francis John in certain quarters, but there may also have been equal determination from elsewhere that Frank should 'do the right thing'. The fact that Frank and Hannah married much later on, comparatively late in life, and stayed married until his death, meant that they had a relationship. Quite what the nature of their association might actually have been is frankly anyone's guess. She was, by this time thirty-four and he was thirty-seven.

We don't (yet) know what Mrs. Buckland really thought of Frank, but she features in his writings very much as the mistress of the household, and one who understand that free-roaming, exotic animals come with the package. He creates a fairly affectionate, almost comic vignette of her as the woman who runs the house, and to whom the servants defer. She more than tolerates Buckland's challenging pets and exotic tenants, but she has her limits, and isn't afraid to let Frank know about it.

Yet their lives are not quite the caricature that appearances might suggest, for there is evidence to suggest that Mrs Buckland was actively involved in Frank's working relationship with Abraham Bartlett, the long-serving superintendent of London Zoo. Apart from receiving Frank's personal consignments from Bartlett, she appears to have taken personal delivery of sick or infant animals sent to their home in Albany Street, essentially "around the corner" from the zoo.

In one revealing sketch about a particular pet, he writes about his adult female monkey, an African Spot-nosed Guenon *Cercopithecus nictitans* that he has uncharitably named 'Old Hag'.

"The Hag was the greatest possible friend with Mrs. Buckland. I don't know who likes The Hag best – the Missis (sic) or myself. The Missis used to frequently take her out and nurse her of an evening."

I do suspect Buckland of considerable artistic license in the telling of his anecdotes, but here, for once, I think his guard is completely down. It is an astonishing image of a bachelor couple, brought together by circumstance and fate, who inhabit their own world and completely understand the compact they have made.

None of the characters in this scene think their strange version of a nuclear family the slightest bit odd. Least of all 'Old Hag'. Perhaps, they might *both* be considered eccentric because they were 'animal people', but to other 'animal people' (and there are many) they will seem normal enough. This isn't the slightest bit conjectural when you understand that the Bucklands and the Bartletts were family friends as much as Frank and Abraham were cronies.

Hannah outlived Frank well into the twentieth century and died in London in 1920 at the age of eighty-nine. Buckland had bequeathed £10,000 to establish The Buckland Foundation, which would come into force upon her death. Her own inheritance from Frank's estate and the sale of 37 Albany Street enabled her, eventually, to buy her own house. She chose a charming little semi-detached villa, newly built in West Hampstead, a long way from Pimlico and a safe, suburban distance from the wilds of London Zoo.

Prior to that, in 1879, an illness with which Buckland been struggling for some time began to take a serious hold on him. His friends were alarmed at the distressing and apparently rapid deterioration in his condition, and remarked upon it in their reminisces of him. His medical records are now a matter of guesswork, a situation not at all remedied by the multiplicity of causes lazily inserted in an amount of unhelpful potted, pseudo-biographical accounts online.

Buckland worked almost until the day of his death. His last report was presented on 31 March 1880, by which time his health had all but failed and he knew he was dying. He spent his last remaining months working intermittently on new specimens for his fish museum and organising his affairs. In June, he underwent an 'experimental' procedure at home, probably to remove fluid from his lungs, but little could be done to halt the progress of his disease. He died at his London home in Albany Street on 19th December 1880, and was buried alongside his infant son at Brompton cemetery.

Buckland gave is name and a bequest to the establishment of The Buckland Foundation whose mission it is to support fisheries research in the UK. It is responsible for organising the annual Buckland Lecture, which began in 1930. Subjects covered by guest lecturers have included such appropriately diverse topics as Salmon Hatching, River Pollution, the Herring Fisheries, Stocks of Whales, the Norway Lobster, North Sea Cod and has even posed the leading question, "How Smart Are Fish and Does it Really Matter?"

There is no doubt in my mind that, if such a thing were possible, Buckland would be in the front row for each and every one of these absorbing talks. He is, at the very least, there in spirit, and that is no small thing.

Spencer Walpole

Sir Spencer Walpole (1839-1907) was a senior civil servant who entered the service as a young clerk in the War Office, working periodically in the office of the Home Secretary. He then became a fisheries inspector at the Home Office, and later Lieutenant-Governor of the Isle of Man, rounding off a solid administrative career as Postmaster-General.

Walpole was also an historian, biographer, political commentator and writer who was well-respected in his time. He is remembered primarily for his five-volume history of nineteenth-century England, his biography of Lord John Russell, and his authorship of government reports. Modern reassessments of his legacy, however, have been the stuff of mixed reviews.

Spencer Walpole was born in Serle Street, Lincoln's Inn Fields, London, on 6th February 1839. He was the eldest son of Spencer Horatio Walpole (1806–1898) and Isabella Perceval (1801–1886). Walpole Sr. was a lawyer, a politician, and, latterly, Home Secretary under Lord Derby. Isabella was the fourth daughter of Spencer Perceval, the prime minister who was infamously assassinated in the lobby of the House of Commons in May 1812.

Walpole may have been born into a political dynasty but his own career path partially reflected the mixed fortunes of his famous family. He was descended from Sir Horatio Walpole, 1st Baronet of Wolverton, a prominent government minister, diplomat and land-owner. The baronet was the younger brother of Robert Walpole, remembered as the first Prime Minister of Great Britain. Both of these men enjoyed long tenure and influence, but eventually fell foul of tensions between Crown and Parliament over the use of force to protect colonial trade and expansion.

Spencer Walpole rose to no such dizzy heights in Parliament, due primarily to the adverse effects of his father's involvement in failed government. The family is said to have suffered a financial penalty as a result, and the knock-on effect for his son was the barring of the gate to university and subsequent success and fame at the very highest levels of public life.

As a boy, Walpole's health was considered 'delicate', and it's the principal reason given for the family's move from congested central London to the leafy, and presumably healthier garden suburb of Ealing. In the autumn of 1852, Spencer Walpole was sent to Eton College, where he was a diligent scholar and a keen rower. His general health had evidently improved enough for him to become captain of a boat, and acquire a robust constitution.

Unfortunately, Walpole's promising academic career was cut short when his father entered office as Home Secretary in Derby's disastrous administration of 1852. Walpole Sr. had to give up his practice at the bar, and we're told he had insufficient funds to allow his son to acquire a university education.

Instead, Spencer Walpole left Eton in 1857 at the age of nineteen to become a clerk in the War Office. Walpole repeatedly rued missing out on a university career, but the paradox of Pitzhanger Manor, the family home in Ealing, might well have figured in his resentment. He eventually inherited the entire property, and did not hesitate to sell it on in 1900, when the last of the Perceval sisters died there at the age of ninety-five. It was bought by Ealing District Council and the house and grounds where it still stands were renamed Walpole Park.

A little further investigation of the Walpole milieu reveals that the impoverished paterfamilias, Spencer Horatio Walpole, acquired Pitzhanger Manor in 1843. It was a substantial mansion set in its own grounds, and the cost of its upkeep would not have been trivial. Pitzhanger Manor was the former home of the renowned Georgian architect Sir John Soane, and Walpole Sr. must have had access to sufficient funds to ensconce not only his own family there, but *four* sisters-in-law from the Perceval side of the family.

If Spencer Walpole begrudged his father's decisions then he'd gotten over them by the time his father once more became Home Secretary. In 1858, Spencer Walpole was appointed private secretary to his father, alternating between this function and his duties at the War Office until March 1867. He was, with his father's assistance, appointed as one of the two inspectors of fisheries in England and Wales, and his next step was to hire Frank Buckland, who came highly recommended.

Walpole also felt able to marry and, on 12th November 1867, Marion Jane Murray became his wife. They had one son, who died at the age of two, and a daughter, Maud, who later married the Francis C. Holland, another career mandarin, who was Clerk to the House of Commons for thirty-eight years between 1888 and 1926.

Spencer's writing bifurcated into political history and the management of fisheries, perhaps because the raw resources were so close to hand. His major work on England's rise as an imperial power and publications such as his *Manual of the Law of Salmon Fisheries* (1877) seem oddly contrasting, but there was plenty of socio-economic overlap to exploit in these respective narratives. They were also an extension of his knowledge, experience and insights as a meticulous government administrator.

At some point, Spencer Walpole 'lost money in a bad investment' and his income was compromised to the extent that he began to supplement it by writing. This turn of events seems odd for a man with a head for figures, and perhaps even more so while he produced financial articles for the *Pall Mall Gazette*. He also set to work on a biography of his grandfather Spencer Perceval, which was published in two volumes in 1874. He produced an authoritative work based on exclusive access to family papers, and it remained a credible resource until well into the twentieth century.

The head of the Perceval family, the sixth Earl of Egmont, certainly welcomed Walpole's contribution to his namesake's legend. The earl bequeathed £10,000 to Walpole, and conveniently died shortly afterwards. The inheritance gave Walpole financial independence, and the means to work on his *History of England from the Conclusion of the Great War in 1815*; presumably when not roaming the countryside inspecting fisheries with Frank Buckland.

The first two volumes were published in 1878 but, if it was conceived as a history of the century pretty much as a whole, then work proceeded more slowly than expected. Perhaps, his fisheries work impeded his writing. The year 1890 had come and gone, but Walpole had still only reached the early 1860's. Posterity has judged his 'History' as a largely unoriginal, if useful account of the Victorian flirtation with 'progressive' thinking. In 1904, he condensed the story with *A History of Twenty-Five Years, 1856–1880* and continued working on further volumes until his death.

Other works included two volumes in the English Citizen series—*The Electorate and the Legislature* (1881) and *Foreign Relations* (1882), which to some extent reflected his disaffection with prevailing Tory doctrines. In 1882, he began his tenure as Lieutentant-Governor of the Isle of Man.

He held the post for nearly twelve years and was, by all accounts a popular figure on the island. It was during this period that he wrote another significant, official biography, *The Life of Lord John Russell*, published in 1899 in two volumes, and based largely on privileged access to the Russell family papers.

Spencer Walpole also wrote *The Land of Home Rule: an Essay on the History and Constitution of the Isle of Man* (1893) and articles for the *Edinburgh Review*. In another little quirk of personal history, Walpole's treatise on Manx politics coincided with his departure from the island.

In 1893, he became secretary to the Post Office, where he earned a reputation as a reformer or, at least, someone capable of embracing alternative thinking. In 1897, he was sufficiently engaged with all matters postal to attend to the postal congress in Washington as the official British delegate.

A knighthood followed in 1898 and Walpole retired from the Post Office the following year to live in the Sussex countryside at Hartfield Grove, on the edge of the Ashdown Forest. There, as president of the Literary Society, he lived the life of the gentleman scholar and accepted a chairmanship from the Pacific cable board and a directorship from of the London, Brighton, and South Coast Railway.

In 1904, he was finally accepted into academia with an honorary DLitt, awarded to him on his installation as chancellor of Oxford University, an honour consolidated by his subsequent election as a Fellow of the British Academy. At home in Sussex, he participated in public life as a magistrate and took up golf, perhaps to stretch his legs between writing and researching his histories.

Sir Spencer Walpole died suddenly, the result of a cerebral haemorrhage, on 7th July 1907, aged sixty-eight, at his home in Hartfield Grove. Sir Alfred Lyall kindly completed on his behalf the two remaining volumes of the *History of Twenty-Five Years* (1908). Walpole's *Essays Political and Biographical*, were also published posthumously in 1908, and they stand as a collective postscript to his painstaking, and largely reliable, accounts of the patrician view of empire.

In the course of writing this book, I have found Spencer Walpole to be an elusive figure for someone who led such a public life. As an historian, he may well have felt the need to maintain a degree of detachment, but was he just as aloof in private? Certainly, he seemed happiest when withdrawing into the writer's room to work on a succession of essays and book projects.

Yet, the subject matter was, from a researcher's point of view, hardly ever more than an arm's length away. His diligence and oversight may have kept him at his desk for long periods at a time, but he had privileged access to most, if not all of his subjects.

I feel that I can detect him every now and then in the Herring Report, but there are times when he seems invisible, or even absent. His presence is most keenly felt around discussions of figures and data, and it's frustrating that the commissioners are not identified alongside passages of questioning and discussion.

I also find it significant that Walpole continued to work on his very demanding writing and publishing projects at the same time that he is supposed to have taken almost three months out of his year to gather evidences in Scotland with Buckland and Young.

This is not to say that Walpole merely put his name to these reports. His obituary of Buckland contains references to memories of life on the road with an unconventional, but endearing colleague. So, I think Walpole in 1877 was around, but not necessarily in attendance at each and every session in every single backwater village on the seablown coasts of Northern Scotland.

One reason for this line of thinking is that outside of his personal contribution to the fisheries literature, Walpole has left us no substantial memoir of an utterly memorable period in his professional life. His position may not have been as elevated as he would have liked, but the adventures of the fisheries men ought to have been grist to any biographical writer.

Buckland had already proved that the material sold books, but perhaps Walpole was saving it all to add colour to the biography in which someone might one day write kindly of him. I think that Walpole liked the outdoor life well enough, perhaps as much as any cultivated English gentleman. All the same, and given the choice, I think he'd have been happiest with his books.

Archibald Young

Archibald Young (1820 - 1900) was born to practice the law, but his private passions often seemed to take precedence over the career that had been chosen for him.

He was born in Edinburgh on the 3rd of December 1820 to William S. Young (1794-1855), an advocate and Writer to the Signet (WS), and Agnes Gerard Young (1800-1889). Archibald was the eldest of four children each of whom benefited from a privileged and eminently genteel upbringing in Edinburgh's New Town. He was educated at the Edinburgh Academy and Glasgow University, graduating in law in 1841.

Archibald's father, William S. Young, was born in Glasgow and was the second son of the successful surgeon and surgical instrument maker, also Archibald Young. William married Agnes Gerard, the only daughter of James Gerard of Whitehaugh, in Edinburgh on 21st January 1820. It was a good match and one that assured a middle-class lifestyle for both partners.

Their children, Archibald, his brothers James Gerard Young (1822-1899) and John William Young (WS) (1836-1897), along with their sister, Agnes Wilson Young (1823-1900), were all successful or prominent in their respective fields of the church, the law and Christian charity.

James Gerard Young became a minister at Monifieth Parish Church where he was an extremely popular and influential figure. There is more about him elsewhere in this book because he epitomizes a highly assertive and interventionist brand of pastoral care.

Agnes Wilson Young was, with her mother, highly visible and clearly committed to Victorian values of patronage and benefaction. They clearly had leading roles in charities formed to address destitution and worklessness in the city, for they are listed as such in the Edinburgh Post Office directory of 1877.

The youngest son, John, also became an advocate and Writer to the Signet (WS), perhaps restoring a little professional honour to the family in memory of the William whose early death at sixty-one must have dented their collective prosperity.

It's worth digressing here to explain the significance of the initials (WS) in Scotland. The Signet, as a symbol and gold standard, has a long history, essentially as the private seal of medieval Scottish Kings. Today it is personified as an incorporated body of top lawyers subscribing to the equally historic *Writers to the Signet Society.*

Originally, the Writers to the Signet, who are to this day identified by the suffix WS, were those authorised to supervise its use, and function as clerks to the Courts. As far as is known, the Signet was first used in 1369, and Writers to the Signet were also members of the College of Justice, established in 1532.

Most Writers to the Signet today are solicitors working in both the public or private sectors. They still take a special oath before an officer of state, the Keeper of the Signet, 'committing themselves to exceptional standards of competence and integrity'.

In the nineteenth century, there were many high status WS advocates living and working in Edinburgh, but there was no shortage of work either. The legal interests, great and small, of the landed gentry, the minor aristocracy, and the monarch herself had to be served, and such work was complex, fussy, demanding and lucrative.

The Youngs lived *en famille* at 22 Royal Circus, a well-appointed, terraced town house at a desirable address. In the years following William Young's death, James Gerard Young took up the ministry in Monifieth and John became an independent advocate. In later years, the household consisted solely of Archibald, John, his mother, and sister Agnes. Archibald Young was, therefore, a bachelor for most of his adult life, able to come and go as he pleased with no obligations to family save for the upkeep of the property.

That may have been burden enough, but he certainly had enough income to enjoy long climbing and walking holidays, frequent fishing, and by his own account, several chartered sailing expeditions.

His books, *The Angler and Sketcher's Guide to Sutherland* (1880) *and Summer Sailings* (1898), are collections of picturesque travelogues and reminiscences, that are both readable and sought-after today. He corresponded frequently to the newspapers on a wide variety of subjects, not least the outdoor pursuits that split his time between chambers and the salmon rivers of Scotland.

None of this means that Archibald Young had little scholarly ambition. He was known as the author of long essays and detailed arguments in a variety of publications and books where he was the sole author. These included the 'prize-winning essay' on the harbour accommodation debate he wrote for the proceedings of Edinburgh Fisheries Exhibition, which was also published separately by William Blackwood.

Young also produced a biography of the 'poet and orator' Ulrich von Hutten, 'The Great Knightly Reformer of the 16th Century'. It was not an original work, for it was based on Young's translation from the French of Chauffour-Kestner's 'Etudes Sur Les Reformerateurs du 16me Siècle'. It was published in 1863 by T. and T. Clark in Edinburgh, but whether it might have been an ill-considered vanity project is open to conjecture. Ulrich Von Hutten (1488-1523) might well have been pretty obscure to his readership, but Young makes a fairly persuasive case for him in his preface.

"Hutten's works amount to fifty separate publications, in prose and verse, many of which deeply stirred the German mind and materially contributed to the triumph of the Reformation....and polite learning over the old scholastic teaching." Young thought it *"somewhat remarkable that there should be no life of such a man in the English language"* despite the existence of *"several biographies of him in French...and German".*

In many respects, von Hutten is a romantic figure. He was a poet, a soldier, a satirist, an activist, and a revolutionary who openly criticized the Catholic Church. He was an outspoken champion of Martin Luther's teachings and agitated for the secularization of church property. It's possible that Young saw him as a significant, yet overlooked historical figure, but von Hutten seems like a hard sell in any age.

In 1869, the Edinburgh publishing firm of Edmonton and Douglas published Young's *Historical Sketch of the French Bar, from its Origin to the Present Day; with Biographical Notices of some of the Principal Advocates of the Nineteenth Century.*

It is every bit as long-winded as it sounds, and the critics said so at the time. They could not, however, fault Young's good intentions and his skill as a translator of French legal procedures. Young had plenty of recognition elsewhere and a by-line on several fisheries reports sealed his reputation as a man of note. His interests were nothing, if not diverse, and his writing features in the *Wesleyan Index of Victorian Periodicals* covering miscellany such as, Cuba, Fish Culture, France and Scotland, and The House of Savoy.

Young's contribution to the fisheries reports where he is credited as co-author with Buckland and Walpole is, I think, understated. When we consider the difficulties that contemporary neighbours have with even a generic version of Scots, the need for a Lowland, much less a Highland interpreter would have been necessary for the evidences to have any worth.

Language, dialect, vernacular, accent and vocabulary are all highly differentiated in the various constituent parts of Great Britain. These differences consolidate identity and preserve linguistic richness, texture and intuitive communication. It is, however, an obstacle to understanding where there is a need to gather accurately recorded, unambiguous oral evidences.

Archibald Young gives every impression of being very much at home travelling around Scotland immersing himself in its landscape. His penchant for escaping to all parts of the country would inevitably have attuned his ear to local speech and nuances of expression. This is not to say that Buckland and Walpole were strangers in a strange land, but Young must have been invaluable when it came to translating localized language.

There are a couple of episodes towards the end of Young's life that are rather curious, and they make the lives of the Young family worthy of further investigation. Firstly, the younger brother, John, inherited 22 Royal Circus ahead of his elder siblings, but, in an extraordinary quirk of fate, he predeceased his older brothers by three years. Perhaps the family wrongly thought that he would easily outlive his brothers Archibald and James Gerard Young.

Secondly, Archibald left it late to marry. In fact, he was 74 when he and Alice Cuthbertson tied the knot on 17th January 1895. Alice was fourteen years younger than Archibald and her given home address was 27, Collingham Gardens, South Kensington. If this was a marriage of convenience on either part, then the motives of both parties are obscure.

At sixty, Alice was the youngest daughter of Andrew Gray Cuthbertson, identified on Archibald and Alice's marriage certificate as a 'Fundholder'. Alice died in November 1895, a mere eleven months after marrying Archibald. It looks, on the face of it, like a rather an unseemly outcome. Certainly, Archibald's final years appear to be mired in pedantic concerns about money and inheritance.

It might appear fortuitous for Archibald to have been predeceased by his sister, Agnes Wilson Young. She died on the 29th of January 1900, but any benefit he derived was unsatisfactory and short-lived. Archibald was now the sole occupant of 22 Royal Circus, but he was aggravated by the terms of his sister's will. He thought her directive to dispose a significant portion of her estate 'for charitable purposes' too vague to be useful, and therefore contestable.

Archibald was very sure of his ground, and did not hesitate to act. He immediately sued her executor for these funds, and won convincingly. It turned out, however, to be something of a pyrrhic victory. Archibald died a little over three months later on 8th May 1900 while the action was still being heard in the Court of Session.

In the end, he left everything to *"my brother James Gerard Young, Doctor of Divinity at Monifieth, Forfarshire, James Barker Duncan WS Edinburgh, (and) William Percival Lindsay WS Edinburgh."* He goes on to explain that other potential beneficiaries were to include any other persons, "hereafter named" by him, or assumed to have a reasonable claim on the Trust he created at the time he drew up his will.

That complication may well have arisen because James Gerard Young, confusingly and inconveniently, had already died on 4th October 1899. Archibald's will was apparently left unchanged, so, pending any further detective work, it must be assumed that Archibald's estate passed into the hands of named executors and potential beneficiaries James Duncan and William Lindsay, and/or the Young Family Trust.

One thing that we can say with certainty about Archibald Young is that he was a wealthy man. He had invested in an astonishing variety of stocks and shares, almost all of which were itemized in his will and were, in one way or another, profitable for him. His estate, before duty, totalled an enviable £21,579 and 12 shillings, which would equate to around two million pounds today.

A Brief Natural History of the Atlantic Herring

The Atlantic Herring *Clupea harengus*, hereafter described simply as 'the herring', is an abundant, shoaling fish with a large range in the North Atlantic Ocean. It is migratory and appears annually in the spring and summer months at its inshore and offshore spawning banks and nursery grounds in the North Sea.

The herring is a carnivorous, nocturnal, surface feeder and its prey includes a wide variety of planktonic animals including small copepods and the fry of congeners such as sardines *Sardina pilchardus* and sprats *Sprattus sprattus*. It is, in turn, taken by a similarly enormous number of marine predators including larger pelagic fish, cetaceans, seabirds and human beings.

Its ubiquity belies its vulnerability as a species that aggregates in huge numbers at predictable locations. They shoal in their millions in the open sea and spawn in their thousands around Europe's shores. Yet local populations are susceptible to periodic crashes, if not extinctions. This is especially evident in areas associated with spawning and nursery shoals where excessive disturbance and exhaustion of reproductive stocks by commercial fisheries have caused desertion of these sites.

Herring become reproductive in their third or fourth year and may enjoy a lifespan of approximately twelve to eighteen years. Their preferred spawning grounds are characterized by gravel beds on offshore sandbanks, or complex rocky shorelines that offer extra protection from would-be predators of the emergent fry.

A mature female will release anything between 20,000 and 40,000 eggs, which the males fertilize by simultaneously releasing a steady stream of sperm (or, more accurately, 'milt') over the eggs. Each fertilized egg is encased in a sticky substance that fixes on gravel, rocks or marine vegetation. Egg maturation is temperature dependent and occurs between one and three weeks, depending on environmental conditions.

If the temperature of the water lies between 14-19 °C then the hatching of the egg will take place six to eight days after laying. If the water temperature falls to 7.5 °C then the egg will take up to 17 days to hatch. The eggs will, however, *only* mature if the water temperature remains *below* 19 °C. The hatched larvae are about 3 to 4 mm long and transparent. The fry, at this stage, are amorphous, and conspicuous only by the presence of their dark, nascent eyes.

The dorsal fin begins to form when the herring is about 15 to 17 mm long. The ventral fins emerge and the tail is visibly forked when the fish attains 30 to 35 mm in length. The fry starts to look like a proper herring as it reaches 100 mm in length, by which time the developing fish is about six months old.

The immature 'matties' referred to in the 1878 Herring Report are non-reproductive fish that are too large to be confused with sprats, and so must be fully in their second year. 'Full fish' are clearly more than three years old, and the loss of both reproductive females and immature 'replacement' individuals would be immediately harmful to any living creature. The herring, however, at least has the capacity to desert those areas where it is persecuted excessively, persistently and disproportionately.

The massed 'armies' of shoaling herring appear off Scotland's western shores as early as late March and the beginning of April. They aggregate, then disperse and migrate from west to east, seeking out suitable spawning grounds around the coastline from the waters of The Minch, following the Atlantic inflows between Orkney and Shetland, into the eastern seaboard. They gather throughout the summer at coastal spawning sites, notably Buchan, Shetland and Dogger Bank in August and September, but also as far south as the English Channel for a winter spawning between November and January.

The breeding season is over by early October, but the developing larvae that do not settle in Scottish nursery grounds drift towards suitable habitat further eastwards along Scandinavian shores. Dispersal of herring back into their native feeding grounds in the Atlantic is poorly understood at the present time. So too is the nature of the pelagic population, which may consist of several sub-populations, if not differentiated races.

The Atlantic Herring is widespread in the North Sea although different age classes tend to show zonal fidelity to specific areas. The Atlantic Herring in European waters may, for all intents and purposes, may be considered a contiguous population still hunted by the northern fleets with as much vigour as ever. The offshore herring fishery, which modally forages more than fifty miles from land, exploits herring shoals that breed on the outer banks, or else meets the migrating shoals heading for inshore spawning and nursery grounds.

It remains difficult, however, to predict the reasons for the super-abundance of stocks in particular seasons, nor is it easy to completely understand the factors that provoke sudden desertion and the periodic collapse of stocks in certain areas. For all its commonplace familiarity, the much-studied herring is still an enigmatic fish of great interest to natural historians and scientists alike.

Epilogue

Time stands still for no one. We have travelled with the fisheries men from their past into our present, only to learn what we already knew in our hearts and in our minds; that we can change our world quite readily, but find it far harder to change our own nature. There is, however, something else in the air. We are used to discord and disruption in our efforts to preserve natural systems, but there is now a growing, and deeply unsettling, appetite for complete destruction of the natural order of things. It is the 'wanton destruction' that Frank Buckland, for all his subscription to the utilization of natural resources, disliked so intensely.

It is easy to understand the inflamed passions of 'rewilders' and 'extinction rebels', but it is consensus around a set of recalibrated values that is more urgently needed than direct action. The latter is the *modus operandi* of the self-righteous, which may great for grabbing headlines, but it has signally failed to have any lasting effect on the destructive impulses of the human mind. The values that I have in mind are not new, but they must be prioritized in order to avert the radical transformation of natural Earth.

I touched upon a number of flashpoints in the conflict between those who would ring-fence nature for its own protection and others who would corral it for profit. One of them was about the European beaver reintroduction in Tayside. The ink dry was barely dry on the last chapter of this book, when a sorry postscript emerged confirming a risk that was self-evident from the start.

The BBC reported that a heavily pregnant beaver had been illegally shot in somewhere in Tayside; in direct contravention of the regulations governing licensed culling. Now, apart from the questionable morality of allowing beavers to breed freely and then killing them under licence as a 'management tool', it is clear that, in this case, someone was out to make a point. The same goes for the 'dozens of dead crows' irresponsibly dumped in a loch near Dunkeld, presumably as a message to those who would like to see government controls on culling of 'pest species'.

As far as the fisheries are concerned, the issues and arguments ping back and forth like a table-tennis ball. The kelp dredgers did not accept defeat gracefully, and have been seeking a second bite at the seaweed through the very current 'Kelp Harvesting Review'. This gives rise to the familiar sight of an incumbent government bending over backwards to please everyone all the time, when they know perfectly well that any such thing is a physical impossibility.

It does not follow that environmental laws should be weaker than others, and 'winked at' as they so often are. Neither does it help the discussion that both fishermen and scientists both feel deeply wounded when stung by criticisms. They ought not to feel that way, for they alone are not to blame for our dysfunctional relationship with wild nature. In truth, no one is blameless.

This polarization and hardening of positions on all sides of an environmental question is not new, but it in this century it has gone global. Some might say that entrenched opposites are impervious to change, but we cannot allow that kind of sophistry to prevail. A much more deferential relationship with the natural world is essential if we are to avoid the prospect of living on an artificial earth where all the 'useless' sand dunes have been replaced by something 'productive'; where the diversity of garden birds can be counted on the fingers of one hand; and where wild animals are free-roaming only within the confines of closely managed and shrunken home ranges, where they are controlled and contained just as much as any creature pitied for its confinement in a zoo.

A lot of store is set by what we as individuals can do. I have never believed this to be effective in the long term, and there is little evidence to prove me wrong, for I do not see any evidence of empathetic, creative and responsible pole-to-pole management of the earth's resources. The response, for me, has to be institutional, organisational and governmental, underpinned by respect for the rule of law.

Closer to home, Marine Scotland has recently sought consultation with everyone involved in the exploitation, management and conservation of the marine environment around our shores. The organisation is, I think, attempting to secure support for an holistic set of pre-existing core values rather than introducing new ones.

They should be pushing at an open door, but the lack of engagement on social media, a chosen platform among the fishing community for communicating frank visceral responses, is concerning. The 'likes' and 're-tweets' for Marine Scotland's call out could be counted in single figures and are reminiscent of the absence of fishermen at various locations during the commissioners' enquiries in 1877.

If fishermen distrust not only Marine Scotland, but also rubbish the validity of other stakeholders, then they do the process an injustice. Admittedly, Marine Scotland is not necessarily empowered to deliver on perceived imperatives, but that only returns us to the conundrum of 'pleasing all the people all the time'.

The responsibility actually lies with individuals, communities and influencers not only to agree core values but also to uphold them. This must mean placing marine protection topmost in our considerations. Environmental imperatives have for too long been characterized merely as 'concerns', bolted on to the backside of the body politic.

I feel the same way about communities that strive to stay organic in the sense that strong identities grow from firm roots. Those identities are preserved in rituals, customs, practices, and even passions that are peculiar to people and places. Is it possible that traditions from Eyemouth to Burghead may be authentically preserved within the fabric of communities? They can be, and they should be, but it will require more than just a handful of dedicated devotees. If they are not supported as a strand that is integral to Scotland's cultural DNA, then communities will inevitably suffer 'cultural drift' and ultimately 'cultural extinction'.

This has been the fate of Wick's Herring Queen tradition, which was once a vibrant part of the town's summer season. It is ironic that the Queen's realm should extend only to the interior of a few glass cases in Wick Museum, given the runaway success of the North Coast 500 circuit that circumscribes northern Scotland. The tourists are driving in droves but they have little time to stop and stare, much less connect with local life, as they tick list their way from Inverness to Applecross, Ullapool, Thurso, John O Groats, Wick, Dornoch and back to Inverness via Dingwall.

The visitors, assuredly welcome though they are, have already created a local problem by leaving a breadcrumb trail of litter along a route ill-prepared for success. We cannot snap our fingers and expect local people to re-instate or even re-invent reasons for tourists to stop and stay longer in communities which would benefit from the resultant per capita spend. Too much of tourism is already about performance, and folk have their own lives to lead. Yet, the overnight success of the North Coast 500 trail does demonstrate the predictable pitfalls of allowing once lively villages and hamlets to go to sleep in front of the television in the dormitory habitat of a dormitory town.

Aside from local skirmishes and my lamentations about cultural fragmentation, my main bone of contention is that 21st Century Scotland is re-living the environmental paradigms of the late Victorian period. The principal similarity may be the binary nature of the arguments, namely exploitation vs. protection, but the sense that all sides seek 'a once and for all outcome' to an environmental endgame constitutes an important difference. The Victorian conceit was that 'Nature's Bounty was infinite'; the prevailing conceit of our age is that it doesn't matter one way or the other.

The Scottish government and its agencies understand that the nation's greatest, visible asset is its natural face. It has moved to preserve it with assertive measures, but it is wrong to frame them as victories for the environmental lobby. Each new law, as Huxley observed, creates a new offence. They are not an impediment to exploitation, they are a further incentive to challenge and overcome the law.

Scotland is in a position to create an environmental Charter that sets out inviolate core values, and it really doesn't have time to dwell upon such an obvious need. These values must presume against gross, alteration, extraction, and appropriation of natural resources. Scotland is a small country and, in reality, it has far less left to sacrifice than many of us would care to imagine. More importantly, such a charter and such values can only establish terms of reference for responsible use, protection and restoration of natural resources with consensus, respect and, dare I say it, honour. A charter without an oath is, after all, only a piece of paper.

Glossary

Barrel – A cured barrel of salted, preserved herring contained anything between 700 and 1,000 individual herrings. This would depend on the size and condition of the fish caught, which varied from one locality to another, and the season in which they were caught.

Cooper – A cooper was skilled craftsman employed to construct wooden barrels. The coopers were also part of the migratory workforce that followed the fishing around the coastline. They were employed to build barrels to a specific size for the curing of and transportation of herring.

Crans – A cran is a measure of landed herring that is equivalent to 28 stones. That translates into 177 kilos of fish. The herring were transported in baskets from the boats to shore. Each basket contained about 7 stones, or approximately 44 kilos of fish.

Crown Brand Herring – A cured barrel of herring was assessed for quality and issued with a crown brand to indicate the quality assurance, relative value and the source of its contents.

Curing – In the nineteenth century, the process of curing in the herring industry was monitored by the Fisheries Board. The curing of herring dictated the preservation of fish in salt and water to specified proportions.

Farlings – The women who were employed as gutters and cleaners in the herring industry were part of a migratory labour force that followed the boats around the coast of Scotland. They processed freshly landed herring "at the farlings", large open-air stations on the quaysides, sorting and gutting the fish at enormous sunken tables constructed of heavy timber.

Forage Fish - Forage fish are, by and large, small, pelagic fish that are preyed upon extensively by larger fish, seabirds and marine mammals. Forage fish species are pivotal to the complex food webs in our oceans as a predator of crustaceans and the fry of other forage fish such as sardines and sprats. Naturally, predators take a keen interest in their movements, either by following in their wake or gathering at known sites of super-abundance.

The herring is just such a shoaling, forage fish, known for migrating in large numbers between feeding grounds in the open ocean, spawning grounds inshore, and spawning banks offshore. It has been depredated mercilessly by man and beast alike, yet it remains as abundant and eminently edible. As Buckland pithily observed in his monograph of *Clupea harengus*, 'The herring has no friends'.

Garvie – A Scottish word for the common sprat *Sprattus sprattus*. In Buckland's time, it was purportedly confused with and, at times, mistaken for the immature herring. It was a bone of contention throughout the commissioners' investigations in 1877, albeit clouded by misinformation and (perhaps deliberate) obfuscation.

Herring – The herring, which is the subject of this book, is the Atlantic Herring *Clupea harengus*. It is a shoaling, migratory, forage fish closely associated with schooling behaviour in coastal zones and offshore fisheries. There are two other species in the genus, which are: The Pacific Herring *Clupea pallasii and* the Araucanian Herring *Clupea bentincki* (See also, 'A Brief Natural History of the Atlantic Herring' in this book).

Herring 'Matties' – A 'mattie' is an immature fish of either sex that is not yet of breeding age, but presumably large enough to warrant curing. They were considered a delicacy among some curers, particularly those selling into the continental markets.

Herring 'Full Fish' – A 'full' herring principally describes a female fish that is literally full of ova, but may also refer to mature males capable of reproducing and whose sexual organs (milt) are full of spermatozoa. Such herring were invariably considered high value, 'Full Crown' fish.

Herring 'Spent Fish' – A 'spent' herring is a male herring whose milt organs have been all but fully evacuated, or (more commonly) a female herring that has already spawned. They are the least valuable fish in the herring catch, although they still had value in the fresh fish markets as a 'food of the poor', wherever proximity and effective transportation allowed.

Meshes – The nets traditionally used in the herring industry before the rise of cotton in the mid-nineteenth-century were made of hemp. The mesh of these nets varied in size from one location to another, and there was no regulated mesh size, although there was much debate about what was optimal, effective or 'injurious'. Hemp nets were prone to shrinkage while cotton nets were not. Cotton was also more durable and less likely to snap. The shift from hemp to cotton was inevitable, but mesh sizes were no more standardized in factories where nets were made to order for curers and fleet owners.

Small-meshed nets were said to catch a disproportionate amount of very immature herring. It is never made clear anywhere in the industry literature, however, what constitutes a legitimately catchable young 'mattie' or, conversely, an immature herring that is too small to go to market.

Shoaling – A shoal of fish are describes the habitual aggregation in large numbers of a fish species for the purposes of mass reproduction, the optimal exploitation of small-sized, widely dispersed prey, and protection from predation.

Schooling – A school of fish describes a group of fish that is swimming in the same direction in a coordinated manner.

References

Anonymous (1869-1905) Post Office Directories, Scotland. National Library of Scotland.

Anonymous (2017) Shetland in Statistics 2015 &2016. No. 42. (PDF). Shetland Islands Council.

Bompas, George Cox (1885) Life of Frank Buckland. Smith Elder and Co, London.

Brown, C.; Green, T & Mair, J. (2016) Religion in Scots Law Chapter 16, pp 331. The Humane Society.

Buckland, Francis T. (1858) Curiosities of Natural History, Vols 1-4. R. Bentley, London.

Buckland, Francis T. (1886) Notes and Jottings from Animal Life Smith, Elder and Co, London.

Buckland, Francis T.; Walpole, S; and Young, A. (1877) Report on the crab and lobster fisheries of England and Wales. H.M. Stationery Office.

Buckland, Francis T.; Walpole, S; and Young, A. (1878) Report on the Herring fisheries of Scotland. H.M. Stationery Office.

Burgess, G.H.O (1967) The Curious World of Frank Buckland. John Baker, London.

Coull, K.A., Johnstone, R., and S.I. Rogers. 1998. Fisheries Sensitivity Maps in British Waters. Published and distributed by UKOOA Ltd.

Girling, Richard (2016) The Man Who Ate The Zoo: Frank Buckland Forgotten Hero of Natural History. Vintage 2017.

Jones, P., Cathcart, A., and Speirs, D. C. (2015) Early evidence of the impact of preindustrial fishing on fish stocks from the mid-west and southeast coastal fisheries of Scotland in the 19th century. ICES Journal of Marine Science, 73 (5): 1404–1414.

Martin, A. (1998) Fishing and Whaling. National Museums of Scotland.

McQueen, A. (1923) Clyde River Steamers of the Last Fifty Years. Gowans and Gray.

Pugh, Michael George (2011) Once proud burghs: community and the politics of autonomy, annexation and assimilation - Govan and Partick, c.1850-1925. PhD thesis.

Smith, R. (2003). The Making Of Scotland: A Comprehensive Guide To The Growth Of Its Cities, Towns And Villages. Canongate.

Young, Archibald (1898) Summer Sailings: By An Old Yachtsman. David Douglas, Edinburgh.

Young, Archibald (translator). (1863) Ulrich von Hutten: Imperial Poet and Orator; The Great Knightly Reformer of the 16th Century by Chauffour-Kestner, V. T. & T. Clark, Edinburgh.

About the Author

Michael Stephen Clark is a freelance writer and author. He has written about a wide variety of subjects including Natural History, Music, Travel, Culture and Heritage. He has also co-authored a number of scientific papers describing the conservation of wild animals in captivity and in nature. His full and extensive biography, including information about past present and future works, can be found on his comprehensive website at 1320Elements (www.1320elements.com).

Printed in Poland
by Amazon Fulfillment
Poland Sp. z o.o., Wrocław

54851289R00150